Praise for the first edition of

Camping Made Easy

"Whether you are planning a weekend trip to a local forest campground, or a month-long wilderness backpacking trip, this book will answer all your questions—and then some!"
—*Journey* magazine

"With this guide as a learning tool, you'll soon be pitching tents, making mouth-watering meals, and enjoying nature up close."
—*Genesee Valley Parent* magazine

"Loaded with tips to help you on the way to good camping adventures."
—*Record-Eagle* (Traverse City, Mich.)

Help Us Keep This Guide Up to Date

Every effort has been made by the authors and editors to make this guide as accurate and useful as possible. However, many things can change after a guide is published—trails are rerouted, regulations change, techniques evolve, facilities come under new management, etc.

We would love to hear from you concerning your experiences with this guide and how you feel it could be improved and kept up to date. While we may not be able to respond to all comments and suggestions, we'll take them to heart and we'll also make certain to share them with the authors. Please send your comments and suggestions to the following address:

The Globe Pequot Press
Reader Response/Editorial Department
P.O. Box 480
Guilford, CT 06437

Or you may e-mail us at:

editorial@GlobePequot.com

Thanks for your input, and happy travels!

CAMPING
MADE EASY

A Manual for Beginners with Tips for the Experienced

Michael Rutter

Second Edition

Guilford, Connecticut

Also by Michael Rutter

Basic Essentials Fly Fishing, 2nd edition

Fly Fishing Made Easy, 4th edition

Fun with the Family in Utah, 3rd edition

Myths and Mysteries of the Old West

Outlaw Tales of Utah

Utah Off the Beaten Path, 5th edition

Wild Bunch Women

To buy books in quantity for corporate use
or incentives, call **(800) 962–0973**
or e-mail **premiums@GlobePequot.com.**

Cover photo © Index Stock
Text design by Lisa Reneson
Text illustrations by Mary Ballachino
Top photo, p. 173, ©2001 www.arttoday.com

Library of Congress Cataloging-in-Publication Data
Rutter, Michael,1953–
    Camping made easy / by Michael Rutter.—2nd ed.
       p. cm. — (Made easy series)
Includes index.
ISBN 978-0-7627-0749-2
    1. Camping. 2. Outdoor recreation. I. Title. II. Made easy series
GV191.7.R88 2001
796.54—dc21   00-069617

Printed in the United States of America
10 9 8 7 6 5 4

ACKNOWLEDGMENTS

Thanks to Jim Ried at Coleman.

Thanks to my parents, Josie and Paul,
for introducing me to the outdoors,
for taking us camping again and again and again,
for instilling a love of wild places.

Thanks to my wife, Shari,
my camping mate for the past twenty-three years,
and for our children,
Jon-Michael and Abbey.

Special thanks go
to Jon-Michael for all the nights
we've spent under the stars.

Contents

Introduction

So why camp, anyway?

Why leave the comforts of home and head off to wilder parts to live outdoors? Why eat with your fingers, smell camp fire, and sleep on the ground?

For most campers the answer is easy. There's nothing like the immediacy of nature at her finest. And by the way, can those stars really be that bright? Yes, they can, and they can be all yours for an evening or two.

Camping brings you closer to the natural world and puts you in touch with things you may have lost or forgotten: things civilization leaches from human beings. Maybe it's something that isn't far from the surface. You'll discover and cultivate a harmony with and a respect for wilderness and a reverence no nature show on public television can generate.

It doesn't get any better than this! Being out in nature is better than therapy.

What four-star hotel can parallel waking up in Wyoming's Grand Tetons with a layer of frost on your sleeping bag, the sun's rays probing the tops of the jagged peaks, still dark and mysterious, and a couple of love-starved bull elk calling across the meadow? You break the skim of ice in your coffee pot and start the water boiling while watching a glorious autumn sunrise while you're snuggled in your sleeping bag.

It just doesn't get any better.

What bleached-pool resort with perfect tennis courts, cleverly manicured lawns, and trendy restaurants can top the smell of bacon frying angrily in the pan or equal a small stream fumbling around in bubbling eddies, tumbling about a rocky mountainside over mossy rocks and fallen logs? What could be more refreshing than ice-cold, gin-clear water on your trail-hot feet?

Camping is a time of solace, a time of dawning, a time of renewal. It's also a lot of fun.

In the days of yore, mankind camped by necessity. Being outdoors, however, might not have been as much fun as it is nowadays. You had to deal with ice-age weather, savage-tempered saber-toothed tigers, prowling cave bears looking for a tasty bit of *homo sapiens*, and rat-sized mosquitoes. Things have changed.

Modern technology has allowed us to enjoy the comforts of civilization while we blend with nature on her own terms. There has been a Renaissance in camping equipment in the past few years. Now a camper can be comfortable in almost any situation nature provides and have a minimum impact on the environment.

So let's go camping!

Camping brings you closer to the natural world.

Section One

Getting Set Up—Camping Gear

Chapter 1

Let's Camp!
Camping Should Be Easy

I started camping with my folks when I was knee-high to a black bear cub. I can't remember when Rutters haven't camped. My dad used to say he "loved camping because it put you *right there* in nature."

At age four I was lost for half a day in a large logged-over track in the Green Springs Mountains of Southern Oregon. The fact that no one bothered to look for me during the first six hours of my youthful adventure indicated either what a hardy camper I was or, as my mother suggests, what a pain I must have been.

In the late 1950s my parents would pack up the family station wagon, and we'd head off. Every holiday, every vacation, and a lot of weekends were family camping trips. As kids, we thought everyone camped on vacations and motels were where you stayed if you had no imagination. Camping was what you did when you wanted to have fun!

When you camped you were out in nature firsthand. You were there when the sun broke over the mountain for the first time in the crisp dawn. You were there scrambling to pitch your tent while the sky's bottom started to drop out. You were there sipping a cup of hot chocolate as the sun drifted over ice-capped peaks. You were there to smell a hint of aspen and spruce in the light wind. You were there to see Canada geese fly across the rough surface of a mountain lake while gray clouds hung low.

My sister, brother, and I started camping when we were very young. We saw a lot of life from the door of a canvas tent my folks still use. It was our outdoor home away from home.

So what if your fingers got a little dirty and you swallowed a little sand with dinner? The fringe benefits were great. There's nothing like a moose in the meadow, the howl of a mated pair of timber wolves at midnight, or the dance of a loon when it takes off from a river marsh.

When you camp, you call the shots: You can make your camping adventure as rustic or as sophisticated as you desire.

Let's get you camping. This book will show you how.

If you've never camped a day in your life, I'll show you where to start. I'll discuss everything you need to know to camp like a pro. If you've camped before, I'll show you a few things to make your life outdoors a little easier. You can make your camping experience as rustic or as high-tech as you desire.

You might want to bushwhack across the Appalachians on a ten-day-long adventure, wearing the same clothes; eating Top Ramen, trail mix, and oatmeal; rolling out your sleeping bag on your rain poncho under the stars; and giving up luxuries like toilet paper, the tops of tea bags, and deodorant.

Or you might use your global positioning system to locate your favorite campground; pitch a palatial, three-room tent with a bug porch; stretch out in an adjustable–temperature, breathable-but-waterproof sleeping bag on a wide, 2½-inch luxury model Therm-a-Rest; bathe in the shower/Port-a-Potty tent; cook on a Coleman Camp Kitchen with generous counter space; electronically light your gas stove and serve up a seven-course dinner that would make the Frugal Gourmet jealous; then follow it all up with a few cups of espresso and some reading under your bright-as-day lantern.

The most difficult part about learning a new skill is figuring out where you want to start, then deciding the level you want to achieve. Most of us are somewhere between rustic and high-tech. *Camping Made Easy* will take the guesswork out of the process. I'll specifically look at how to car camp and backpack. You'll be an expert before long.

In Section I I'll talk about camping equipment, including gear you may not need now but that might be useful later. In Section II I'll talk about "camp craft." I'll discuss how to plan your trip and set up camp—including

Camping and hiking are a lot of fun for the entire family. Jon-Michael climbs the last part of a steep trail. The view is worth the effort.

how to start a fire and collect safe drinking water. Section III will cover other forms of camping and outdoor fun, including canoeing and canoe camping, biking and bike camping, and RV trailer camping. In Section IV I'll look at having fun in the great outdoors, specifically at several of the most popular camping activities: hiking, fishing (including fishing with your kids), and wildlife watching.

So grab your kids, and let's go!

My children, Jon-Michael and Abbey, are veteran campers who are always ready to go. Children can make better campers than adults.

Chapter 2

Introduction to Camping Equipment: Getting the Gear You Need

Where do you start?

It's a jungle out there, and I don't mean the outdoors. I'm talking about the retail jungle, cleverly disguised as camping and sporting-goods stores. There's a lot of "craft" to being a good camper; nevertheless, good equipment can make it easier.

Getting the gear you need can be stressful, but having the proper equipment also makes campers and camping trips environmentally friendly. Except for emergencies, the days of cutting fresh boughs for bed liners, sawing branches for tent poles, or trenching around tents—which were once fundamentals of traditional camp craft—are over. (If every one of the 45 million American campers cut boughs and branches and trenched, just once a year, we'd have an ecological mess. After a few years every tree within 100 yards of the road would be wasted, and every camping area would look as though someone with a trenching machine had gone berserk.) You can accomplish the same purposes more effectively with proper equipment selection. And, of course, the impact on the land is greatly reduced.

It's a jungle out there, but you can set up a comfortable camp in no time. Pack up your car and go camping. When I was growing up, every holiday was a camping holiday.

Don't sweat the equipment tangle, though. I'm going to give you a crash course in camping equipment, so you can make the best decision for yourself and your camping situation. You'll be up to speed on everything from sleeping bags to hiking socks in no time.

Those who've been camping since they were kids have learned the hard way what is and isn't needed. They've been through the basic list of emergencies: a bear in the stew pot; an unexpected rain drenching all the bedding; and leaving the brand-new Coleman stove at home.

This is *Camping Made Easy*, however, so making camping easy is what we're going to do. You get to learn from someone else and skip all the trial and error. Basic equipment selection is the first hurdle. After reading this section, you'll have an idea about what you already have and what you need to set up a comfortable camp. You'll know what's essential and what you can live without.

No question about it, camping can be a gear-oriented sport. Don't forget, however, that you're the one in control. You can get by with a minimum of equipment, or you can stack up on all the camping luxuries. Either way you won't have to take a second mortgage on the house. In this chapter, I'll introduce you to the equipment you realistically need for the camping you want to do, which is not the same as what a store clerk on commission might suggest.

I'll also cover the gear you might want to add later but don't need now. Also discussed are a few odds and ends that will help make the sport more sublime. You won't be able to get everything at once, but you can acquire items as your budget allows. Camping is like furnishing a house or apartment: Few of us can buy everything at once. There are some items you can do without and some you can't.

An overview of the "stuff" will help you determine the best choices for your current circumstances and your budget (so you won't end up in the poorhouse). After

So what if your fingers get a little dirty while you're in the great outdoors? The fringe benefits are fresh air, good camp food, and family fun. Abbey has just picked a few wildflowers for the picnic table.

Pitching a tent is easier than you think. Half the battle of camping is setting up, but you can do it in no time.

all, camping is a nearly $2 billion industry. You don't need to contribute any more than is necessary.

In this section we'll take a close look at:

- sleeping bags;
- sleeping pads;
- tents;
- day packs and backpacks;
- camp cooking gear (stoves);
- knives, hatchets, saws, flashlights, and lanterns; and
- outdoor clothing, including rain gear.

Chapter 3

Taking a Close Look at Sleeping Bags: Comfort in the Great Outdoors

I take sleeping seriously.

I've made snoozing an art form. I can get up at the crack of dawn to fish, hunt, watch wildlife, or view a sunrise. Otherwise I sleep late.

At one time or another, I've slept in almost every bag on the market. In other words I know sleeping bags from the ground up. Over the years I've slept in the best, and I've slept in the worst. No matter how you look at it, a good night's rest makes a difference. Sleeping in the wild may not be the same as snoozing on your California king-size mattress, but there's no reason why you can't sleep well.

I'm not too old to remember my early packing days. I had a heavy car camping bag, but I needed something that didn't weigh eighteen pounds, something that would fit on my homemade wooden backpack frame. In the ninth grade I bought a light $19 army-surplus down bag with money I had earned cleaning stalls on a horse ranch. It was a good investment. I used that bag through my sophomore year at Southern Oregon State College. I made it do. I really didn't know any better until I was nineteen and borrowed my father's brand–new $125 goose-down bag. I bought one just like it a year later.

As I look back now, I smile at my enthusiasm. At best my army-surplus special was an April-through-October model. It was a light bag, never really intended for four seasons. To beef it up, I sewed in a generous draft tube along the snaps (there was no zipper). Later I sewed in a fleece draft collar to keep my shoulders warm. (I use the term sew advisedly.) It worked. I learned that if you have bucks to spend on all the nifty gear, it's swell; if not, you can

Sleeping well runs in the family. My son, Jon-Michael, is sleeping well into the morning. You can get a good night's sleep outdoors, if you have a good bag.

make do comfortably, if you really want to get out and camp.

In the winter I slept in heavy long johns, two pairs of wool socks, and a stocking cap. I covered my bag with my parka. If the weather got colder, I slid on another pair of long johns and a down vest and fired up a hand warmer. Sometimes I slipped a blanket inside the bag if I could afford the extra weight when ski camping. Some nights I was cold no matter what I did. I kept telling myself it was better than backpacking with a blanket or two and some oversized safety pins to hold it together.

Since I started camping with my parents as a boy in the late 1950s, there have been several sleeping bag renaissances. I'll spare you the details, except to tell you that sleeping bag technology has come a long way. When I was young, you didn't have many sleeping bag choices.

Despite the many improvements, the essentials have remained the same: You need to stay dry and warm (and the lighter the bag the better if you plan to carry it on your back).

A sleeping bag is the most important element of your sleeping system, which includes your sleeping bag, a sleeping pad, and protection from the elements, such as a tent, ground cloth, or lean-to.

A thick pair of pajamas is a good way to keep children (and adults) warm. My daughter, Abbey, couldn't wait until morning to run out and find the doll she'd left at our Coleman cooking station.

Bag Basics

First we need to assess your sleeping bag needs, because the type of camping in which you engage will greatly determine your selection. Sleeping bags have become somewhat specialized to meet a variety of outdoor needs. Making sleeping bags has become quite a science. So although the selection can be a little complicated, the good news is, today you'll pay a lot less and get a lot more.

Let's take a look at some bag basics: temperature/comfort ratings, fills, and styles. In addition to these considerations, know how much you can afford before you walk in the door. Be informed. Otherwise an eager-beaver clerk will sharpen up his or her pencil and tell you what you need.

A sleeping bag is the most important part of your sleeping system (bag, pad, and optional shelter, such as a tent).

During What Time of Year Will You Camp?

Let's take a close look at the camping you plan to do, as well as the time of year you plan to go.

What are the temperature extremes? How cold or warm will it get? There's overlap, but when you look for bags, you'll find they fall into three general categories:

- four-season bags: heavy-duty winter bags, great for cold, probably too hot for comfort in warm weather;
- three-season bags: all-purpose bags, will take a fair amount of cold, but will also be more comfortable in warm weather;
- summer bags: lightweight bags that won't be too hot for summer camping.

Get the right bag for your kind of camping. That means you don't need a state-of-the-art four-season bag at a four-season price if you'll be summer camping or camping in warmer regions. Not only will a winter bag be pricey, but you'll be too warm on summer nights to sleep comfortably. You'll be better served by a lighter—and less-expensive—bag.

Whether you head down the trailhead or pull into the campground, you need to keep warm and dry. Even in the summer, mountains can be chilly at night.

If you plan to do spring or fall camping, you might want to look at a three-season bag. Spring or fall storms can be nasty, so it's nice to have a good bag in which to curl up. And if you plan to visit the Rockies, where temperatures can drop even in the summer, a three-season bag might be a good way to go. Most folks don't do much of their camping when a blizzard is likely to occur. If you want to camp comfortably during January in Montana and August in Georgia, you may need two bags.

Many campers, myself included, have found a three-season bag—good to ten to twenty degrees Fahrenheit—a fine general-purpose choice. If I had to guess on bag choice, I'd go warmer rather than cooler. Maybe the reason is where I live; it can get cool even in the summer. For me it's easy to unzip a bag or sleep on top of it if it gets warm. If a storm blows in, as it can in the mountains, I want something warm.

What Sort of Camping?

If you want to carry your bag on your shoulders, you need a lightweight, compressible bag. If you plan to car camp, larger size or weight won't be a problem. Maybe your mode of transportation will be a float plane, a canoe, a horse, a mule, a mountain bike, a motorcycle, or a four-wheeler. Depending on the circumstances, weight or compressibility may or may not be a factor. For example, I've been on bush planes with a forty-pound limit on personal gear for a ten-day-long trip. I've been on canoe trips where we carried a Dutch oven and ice chests, and on other trips where space was at a premium.

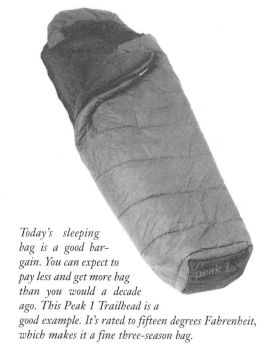

Today's sleeping bag is a good bargain. You can expect to pay less and get more bag than you would a decade ago. This Peak 1 Trailhead is a good example. It's rated to fifteen degrees Fahrenheit, which makes it a fine three-season bag.

To select the best bag for yourself or a family member, you need to consider what sorts of outdoor adventures you'll be going on and how often. If you camp a lot, a higher-quality bag is a good investment. If you camp every now and then, such a bag may not be the best choice because you won't use it enough to get your money's worth.

Many of us can't have a bag for every specific need, but we still like to do different types of camping. One bag has to do for all. Maybe in a year you'll plan several three-day-long backpack trips, a youth camp trip with your church, a canoe camping trip, a cross-country car camping trip to visit relatives, and a fall elk hunt in Colorado. Once again a good three-season bag that can be compressed will probably be your best buy. It won't be perfect, but it will meet most of your needs.

Temperature/Comfort Rating

While shopping, you'll notice that most bags have a temperature or comfort rating. This can be helpful in your selection, but it's only a guide. It's about as accurate

A good bag is comfortable. After a snowstorm, the sky cleared, and we were too tired to worry about setting up the tent. We threw down a ground cloth, a pad, and our bags. The night got cold, but we slept warm even without a tent.

Choosing a bag is an important decision. The kind of camping you're going to do will help you determine your sleeping bag selection. If you're going to backpack, you need a warm, compressible bag. Size isn't as critical when you're car camping.

as a weather forecast or a traffic report.

Some manufacturers are more careful than others about how they establish their comfort ratings. I always figure about a ten-degree fudge factor. I have one sleeping bag with a fifteen-degree Fahrenheit rating that's warmer than another bag with a zero-degree rating. It's been my experience that higher-end manufacturers are more careful with their numbers. Also remember that manufacturers factor in a tent and a good sleeping pad when they calculate sleeping bag ratings.

If you tend to "sleep cold" (an industry term meaning you get chilly in your bag), you need a bag with a lower rating. My wife, Shari, sleeps very cold, so a bag rated for zero or minus five degrees is just right for her on a twenty-degree night. Conversely my friends Gary and Alan sleep hot. A bag rated at twenty-five or thirty degrees is just right for them on frosty ten-degree nights.

Metabolisms were not created equal, so assess how you sleep. As a rule of thumb, women sleep colder than men. In the latest sleeping bag renaissance, manufacturers such as Kelty and Sierra Design have taken this into account. The first thing they did was make a shorter bag, because the average woman is about 5 feet 4 inches tall. Not only does this cut weight, but more important, the bag warms up faster. These bags have as much as 20 percent more insulation to compensate for lower metabolisms. Some bags are cut with wider hips and narrower shoulders, whereas others have more insulation added to the "footbox" (the bottom of the bag).

Draft and Collar Tubes

One major reason a camper gets cold is a poorly-made or nonexistent draft tube. A draft tube covers the sleeping bag's zipper to keep out cold air. Unless you want a cool summer bag, make sure your purchase has a draft tube that covers the zipper for its entire length.

A draft tube is critical in a cold-weather bag and very handy otherwise. A collar tube is a flap that fits around your shoulders to keep out the cold air.

Bag Fills

Bags are filled with either down or a synthetic material. Let's look at the pros and cons of both.

Down Bags

Some of the best waterfowl in the world have given their all so that you can have down, the softest sleeping bag fill known to man or woman. Down comes from the plumes under the bird's larger feathers. When you see the word "down-fill" on a label, it refers to how much loft the down has: 550 down-fill is good loft; 650 down-fill is pretty good loft; 750 is great, very lofty and fluffy. While we're talking down, goose down is the best down because it's a little longer and thus a better insulator. (The North Face, for instance, makes several excellent sleeping bags from 750-fill Hungarian goose down, which I recommend very highly. These bags have chevron buffers to keep the down from shifting, excellent draft tubes, and first-rate zippers.) Geese that have lived in colder areas obviously make the best down. If the manufacturer lists "waterfowl," the down is probably a mix of duck and goose plumes.

Down bags are light, warm, compressible, and expensive. Don't think about getting into a down bag for less than $200. However, they will last twenty to thirty years if you take care of them. My father has several down bags that are at least thirty years old and very functional. It's very likely that the outside shell on your bag will go before the inside fibers. Down feels good around you, too. It's soft, light, and breathable, and no synthetic is quite like it.

Down is the standard, the fill with which other bags are compared. It's hard to beat down—except when it's wet. The major drawback is that wet down has no insulating power. All you have is a bunch of wet feathers. You'd better have a big fire, because you'll get mighty cold otherwise. Down does dry out quickly, but that won't do you any good if your bag is sopping wet and it's nineteen degrees Fahrenheit with a north wind blowing.

Synthetic Bags

If you're on a budget, take a good look at synthetic-fill bags. Synthetic bags have become quite attractive of late. The price is right for one thing. Equally important, if you get your synthetic bag wet, you can still use it because it will retain about 70 percent of your body warmth. If you're around water, especially canoe camping, or in a wet, rainy climate, and on a budget, this might be the bag for you.

The disadvantage to most synthetic-fill bags is that they're heavier and don't compress like down. Put in more practical terms, you can have an excellent down bag that weighs three pounds. To get the same insulating value with a synthetic, you'll have a bag that weighs five or six pounds. Compressed down is also about 25 percent smaller than a synthetic fiber. To campers concerned with space, especially backpackers, this is important. If you're carrying your bag in a canoe, the few extra pounds and extra bulk might be meaningless. The major synthetic fills are discussed below.

This would be a fine four-season bag because it's rated to minus fifteen degrees Fahrenheit.

Polarguard/Polarguard HV: Polarguard is a durable, continuous-length polyester fiber, a fiber that's been around a long while. It doesn't compress very well. A newer version, Polarguard HV, is hollow, somewhat softer, and a little more compressible. It's supposed to be 20 percent warmer. It's still not super–compressible, though, and after a while the fibers will break down and some of the loft will be lost.

Polarguard 3D: This is the new, improved Polarguard HV. The filaments are 40 percent finer, which gives the bag a greater warmth-to-weight ratio. It also makes it more downlike—softer, more compressible, and more durable. One study from Kansas showed that 3D outperformed all other synthetics in durability. This shows great promise. I have a Cascade Design bag with this fiber. It's light, warm, and compressible.

Quallofil: This fiber by DuPont is made from short polyester fibers containing seven chambers. The ends are slickened to retain loft and drape about you. This reduces the weight and makes it compressible. Once commonly used, this fiber is being replaced by other synthetics that retain their loft longer.

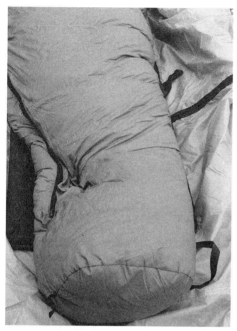

Check the zipper before you buy a bag. Is it a quality zipper? Is the foot, or box section, of the bag reinforced? Look for quality in the store before you buy.

Hollofil: This inexpensive large-diameter fiber has a four-chamber core with slickened ends to help it drape about you and compress. Many summer or entry-level bags are filled with this fiber.

Thinsulate Lite Loft: Fiber for fiber, pound for pound, Lite Loft is one of the warmest synthetics available. You may have a shirt, jacket, or boots with Thinsulate. 3M has bonded polyester and/or olefin fibers to create Lite Loft, which gives it great loft. Don't put Lite Loft in your dryer, however.

Primaloft: A blend of different-diameter polyester fibers gives Primaloft a downlike effect. It's water resistant, too. Unlike down, however, this fiber insulates well when wet. I'm impressed with this stuff.

Micro-loft: A downlike synthetic fiber, Micro-loft has lightweight warmth and suppleness. Boasting the loft and insulating power of down, it will keep you warm even when it's wet. I have a jacket made out of this fiber, and I'm quite impressed with its loft.

You can purchase a fair synthetic bag for a little more than $60. For around $100, you can get a good all-around bag. For about $150, you can get an excellent synthetic that will serve you for years. I've had years of use from my Peak 1 bags.

If you keep it stored in a small stuff sack, your synthetic bag will start to lose some

 Polarguard is a solid-core, continuous fiber.

 Hollofil is a continuous poly fiber with four hollow channels running lengthwise. This helps lighten the bag.

 Polarguard HV is a hollow-core, continuous fiber. It's 25 percent lighter and more compressible.

 Quallofil has seven holes running the length of the fiber. This helps improve warmth—also giving the bag a soft, downlike feel.

Tips on Sleeping Warm

❑ Wear a hat. (Remember your mother's nagging.) A lot of body heat escapes through your noggin. In cold weather use a bag with a hood. Stuff a stocking or a polar-fleece cap in the bag.

❑ Remember that wind and moisture rob your bag of heat. If you sleep in wind, there's convective heat loss. A tent or a lean-to protects you from the zephyrs and helps your bag do its job.

❑ What you eat fuels warmth. Have a meal or snack before you snooze. Have a hot drink (unless it makes you get up and go potty). Drink water, because dehydration brings on hypothermia. Indulge yourself and eat a candy bar. No alcohol, though; booze gives you an artificially warm buzz because it actually robs you of heat.

❑ A sleeping pad is critical. There's not much loft under you; your body weight has crunched the fill, so the insulating value is greatly reduced. Cold ground saps heat. A good pad keeps your warmth in and the cold out.

❑ The better shape you're in, the warmer you'll sleep. Remember, your body does the heating. Your bag just holds it in.

❑ Avoid going to bed cold. Do a little physical activity. Take a walk or do twenty-five jumping jacks.

❑ Make your twenty-degree bag good to zero or lower. Depending on your metabolism, wear expedition-weight long underwear, fleece pants and top (sweats will work), a sweater, a down vest, or a neck gator (a very handy article that weighs almost nothing). And don't forget a hat!

of its loft after a few years. If you store your bag in a loose fashion, it will keep its loft quite a bit longer. The problem is, synthetic fibers break down if they're stored compacted. Your bag will still be usable, but it won't be as warm as it once was because some of the loft is gone. If your bag was originally rated at zero five or six years ago when it was new, it might now be comfortable at fifteen, twenty, or twenty-five degrees. I have several synthetic bags at least fifteen years old that still serve me well because I've taken care of them. There's a lot of life in them, but they aren't as warm as they used to be.

Bag Sizes and Shapes

Bags come in different sizes and shapes. Remember, your body heat does the heating and your bag holds it in. You want a bag with enough room that you can stretch out comfortably and still have a little left at the bottom. You don't want too much left over, because your body heat has to keep the space warm.

Some bags come in regular (to about 5 feet 8 inches), large (to about 6 feet 2 inches), and extra large (to about 6 feet 6 inches) lengths. Others are in total inches—for example, 75 inches (6 feet 3 inches), 80 inches, and 78 inches. You'll want a bag a little bit longer than you're tall but not too much.

Before you buy a bag, crawl into it. You wouldn't buy a car without driving it, so try a bag on for size. Spend five minutes in it. I know it looks stupid and it might be hot, but see how it feels. Roll around on the floor, turn in it, zip it up, sit up in it, move around. How does it feel to you? Now roll it up and see how small you can compress it.

Mummy bags were named by someone with a sense of humor. Like mummy wrappings in early Egypt, the mummy bag is a close-fitting bag. This saves on weight, but, more important, it keeps the sleeper warm by retaining heat more efficiently. With the hood over your head and your nose popping out, you sleep as warm as toast.

It's a good idea to air out your sleeping bag in the morning. Unzipping the bag and letting it air, even for a few minutes, will ensure that you have a dry bag the next evening.

This bag is a favorite of backpackers, who love to shave ounces. (They even cut the tags off tea bags and cut back on food to save on toilet paper weight.) When you sleep in a mummy, the bag turns with you when you turn; you don't turn in the bag. This is very important to remember.

If you haven't slept in a mummy bag, climb into one at your favorite store and see if it's comfortable. My wife gets claustrophobic. She'd rather freeze than feel confined. If the confined shape doesn't bother you, it's a great way to go. It's no problem for me. In very cold conditions, this is the bag to have.

Semi-mummy bags are loose mummy bags. This bag is cut a little

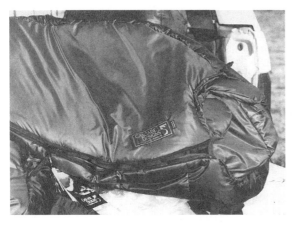

A good night's rest means getting a bag that fits you. Before you buy a bag, try it on for size. Perhaps the most exciting new bag shape is made by Cascade Design. It has a trapezoidal box-shape for the feet. If you don't like the way your feet feel in most mummy bags, take a look at Cascade Design's sleeping bags. This is fast becoming my favorite bag.

A mummy design traps your body warmth and retains heat quite well.

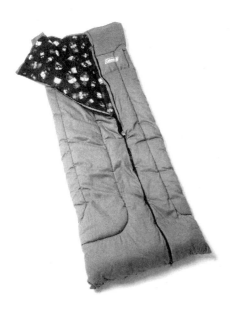

You can increase the warmth of your bag by inserting a bag liner. A liner made of polar fleece is especially warm.

larger than a rectangular mummy, but it's still lighter than a traditional bag. It's still snug, though, so it retains much of the warmth. This bag weighs a little more. For those who don't like the tight fit of a traditional mummy, this bag is a nice compromise.

Rectangular bags are great for camping during summer or in warm-weather conditions. They're open at the top, so a lot of heat escapes around the sleeper's head and shoulders. They have a lot of room and are comfortable as sin. These bags weigh a lot more than other styles, but it's a great way to go for the summer car camper or the couple on a honeymoon.

Several manufacturers make excellent cold-weather rectangular bags. I have an extra-large bag from Coleman that I use during the spring in northern Alberta. It's very comfortable, but a lot of air escapes at the shoulders (the price you pay for roominess). On nights of less than twenty degrees Fahrenheit, I wear a hooded sweatshirt or a long T-shirt, stocking cap, and neck gator. I also have a pillow to block out some of the draft.

Checking Your Zipper

Before you buy a bag, crawl into it and work the zipper a few times. Then consider the following factors:

- ❏ Look for a zipper stiffener. It should be as long as the zipper.

- ❏ A two-way zipper might cost a little more, but it's a nice addition if you buy a warmer bag. You can open the bag from the bottom to stick out a foot or let in some cool air.

- ❏ Nylon zippers don't get as cold as those made of metal. You also aren't as likely to tear a hole in your bag if it gets caught.

- ❏ Heavy-duty oversized zippers are best. They cost a little more, but they work nicely and don't seem to get hung up as much. The North Face bags have wonderful zippers. Cascade Designs bags have very good zippers.

- ❏ A bag should have a draft tube.

- ❏ If you want to join two bags together, try mating them in the store before you buy them.

Other Bag Features

There are several other bag attributes with which you need to be familiar. I've talked about one, the *hood*. A hood is part of a mummy bag and usually part of a semi-mummy bag. It keeps the toasty air in and the nasty cold air out. A hood is a must for packers and cold-weather campers.

A *collar*, sometimes called an inside or shoulder collar, helps keep your body warmth in the bag. This is an important element for cold-weather camping. A *tube*, sometimes called a draft tube, lines the zippers and keeps your warmth in and the cold air out. A tube is a must for cold-weather campers or backpackers.

Carrying and Storing Your Bag

When you buy your sleeping bag, it will come with a stuff sack (unless it's a heavy-duty rectangular bag you roll). If space is critical, you need to get a *compression sack*. A compression sack lets you compress your bag and reduce the volume by 25 to 40 percent. This is very handy if you're backpacking or cramped for space. Higher-end makers sometimes include a compression sack with the bag. Usually, however, you

Washing Your Bag

Some people are far fussier about washing their bags than I. I air my bag out every day, if I can, and always after a camping trip. Unless I've spilled something, however, I'm not one to wash a sleeping bag any more than necessary. Washing it once a year is as often as I'd do it (if that).

No matter how careful you are, if you wash your bag too often, it will wear out faster. One of my sisters washes her bag after every trip; she replaces her sleeping bags often.

Don't wash your bag at home. Head to your favorite Laundromat so you can use a large-capacity washing machine. Check the cleaning instructions on your bag. They're on one of those tags most of us cut off under penalty of law.

1. Use a liquid detergent (unless directed otherwise by the manufacturer).

2. Don't overdo the detergent; use a little less than you think you need.

3. *Use cold water!*

4. Unless you're sure the dryer setting is warm—not hot—don't dry your bag. Take it home and hang it up in the garage.

5. I don't dry-clean my down bags; I've heard too many horror stories about the toxic fumes that don't get aired out and thus have killed sleepers. I also don't like the smell of dry cleaning much; it makes me sneeze. Instead I wash my down bags gently in Ivory or a special down soap.

6. Don't send Gore-Tex-shell bags to the dry cleaner.

have to purchase one.

To get maximum life out of your bag, whether it's synthetic or down, store it loose. After you've used your bag, unzip it and let it hang overnight in a protected area, such as the garage or basement, so it can air. After airing the bag, make sure the bag is good and dry. Then put it in a pillowcase, or something larger, and hang it in a closet or storeroom. (You can also fold it loosely and store it on a shelf.) You don't want to compress the fibers.

Some sleeping bags come with a generously sized cotton storage sack. If yours didn't, some camping stores sell them. Although a pillowcase will do, the bag should be cotton and offer a loose fit so that the fibers won't compress.

The hood of this bag can be cinched down to keep the heat in and the cold out.

Chapter 4

Sleeping Pads:
Sweet Dreams and Outdoor Comfort

As an older and wiser camper, I wouldn't consider sleeping on the cold hard ground without a soft pad. It wasn't always that way, though. When I was a kid, I'd throw out a ground cloth and unroll my less-than-state-of-the-art bag. I don't remember noticing the ground at all.

I didn't know any better, and apparently my nerve endings weren't developed yet. It was a treat if there were pine needles to soften the ground, but it didn't matter. In the winter, I'd make a thick and somewhat lumpy bed of pine boughs to insulate my body from the snow.

For years campers have used many "natural" things to cushion and insulate their beds. The mountain men of the Rockies (as well as the Indians) would often spend an hour or two getting their beds ready. Traditionally, pine needles and boughs, grasses, straw, and dried leaves were favored. Nowadays, using such materials has rightly fallen out of favor because they aren't ecologically sound (and should be employed only in an emergency). There simply aren't enough trees and boughs to go around.

Furthermore, technology has since supplied us with sleeping pads that provide more comfort and insulation and have no impact on our fragile land.

While a sleeping bag is essential to a good night's rest, a pad makes the night more comfortable because it will help keep you warm and dry. Using a pad is also environmentally friendly because you won't have to cut boughs or pull up grasses to provide comfort and insulation.

A Sleeping Pad Means Comfort

About the time I turned twenty-one, I tried a foam pad for the first time. I've never looked back. Overnight I got sensitive or something. I've since avoided bare ground as if it was the IRS or the plague. In fact, unless I'm on a survival exercise, I can't face the bare ground. I've become like the girl in "The Princess and the Pea." I like my creature comforts. I can give up a lot, but I need to have a cozy sleeping system.

A good pad will soften roots, rocks, or lumpy sections of ground. Lee uses a thin foam pad; his back is young and tough. Even this pad, while not as comfortable as a thick one, will insulate the sleeper from the ground.

A good sleeping pad, such as this Therm-a-Rest LE, will keep you warm and comfortable. It makes a fine rest for reading, sitting, or, in this case, kneeling. It makes damp hard ground comfortable.

Camping doesn't mean austerity.

I won't stretch the truth (I saved that for *Fly Fishing Made Easy*). I don't sleep as comfortably outdoors as I did when I was a kid. I need help, so I've gone to a very thick pad and don't regret it. My friends laughed at me last summer in the Wind Rivers of Wyoming until one of them tried out my pad. I was offered $100 above what I paid for it.

Somehow, I always manage to end up in the lumpiest part of the tent, so I like something that will flatten it out. I'm getting either more sensitive in my old age or unlucky. There always seems to be a stubborn rock or root that picks that evening to break through the surface. Maybe the ground is harder than usual these days or maybe I've become a side sleeper. Who knows? My shoulders and hips get some discomfort unless the pad is thick. A good pad gives me a lot of comfort even if the earth isn't quite as cooperative.

A Sleeping Pad Will Keep You Warm

Beyond the comfort issue, there's something else: Without a good pad or mattress, even in a really great sleeping bag, you're likely to sleep cold even in mild weather.

A pad checks conductive heat loss! Conductive heat loss occurs when the cold ground sucks your body warmth away from you so you feel like an Eskimo Pie by 2:00 A.M. It doesn't matter if you're sleeping on the ground, in a cot, or on a reclining lounge, you need insulation; you need a sleeping pad.

There are basically four types of pads: extra blankets or an old sleeping bag, self-inflating mattresses, foam pads, and air mattresses.

Types of Sleeping Pads

Your sleeping bag alone isn't enough to keep you warm, because there's not much loft on the bottom of your bag when you're sleeping on it. Most campers won't spend more than one night outdoors without a good sleeping pad. So don't try (unless you're very young and your nerve endings haven't matured). You'll be at the nearest Holiday Inn before the second night. Sleeping under the stars or tent side may never be as luxurious as your Serta, but sleeping outdoors can and should be comfortable.

Ensure your comfort by selecting a good sleeping pad.

Extra Blankets/Sleeping Bags

If you're car camping and have the space, a couple of blankets folded together or an old sleeping bag will make a nice sleeping pad.

The problem is blankets are bulky, heavy, and take up a lot of space. They can wick up moisture and take a long time to dry. We've often used several quilts as pads for our children. We're able to get four bags on one stack of blankets. I used to use an old rectangular Eddie Bauer sleeping bag with a few blankets tucked inside as a pad, too. Such a system gives the sleeper about three or four inches of softness in which to melt.

Self-inflating Mattresses

A self-inflating mattress is great for any type of camping. It's been my experience that once someone uses one, it's all he or she will ever use. Yes, they're a little more expensive, but for most of us, they're worth it. They are that comfortable and durable. I saw my first self-inflating mattress, a first edition Therm-a-Rest, years ago in a sporting-goods store. I asked the clerk, one of my freshman English students at Brigham Young University, if these newfangled things were any good. "Try it," she said.

It felt great but I was in *the store*. Having worked for advertising agencies, I was used to a lot of product hype and poor performance, so I was skeptical. "Yeah, but will it work on the trail?" I asked caustically. "Will it flatten out them roots and rocks!"

"Stick your hand under that mattress," she said and smiled.

A self-inflating mattress has many uses. My son Jon-Michael uses his Therma-a-Rest to spend the afternoon reading a good book. Even on sharp rocks, he is comfortable on the edge of the canyon. We have a self-inflating mattress for each member of the family.

An open-cell foam pad, such as the one in the back of the Blazer, is comfortable but will absorb water like a sponge if wet.

I did. Under it were a few hobby hammers. I bought two Therm-a-Rests on the spot. I was in graduate school at the time and could ill afford such luxuries, but I decided I'd have them anyway. So what if Shari and I ate macaroni and cheese three times a week. I've owned nothing but Therma-a-Rests since.

A self-inflating pad is basically a high-tech air mattress and is heaven-sent to outdoor sorts. The pad is made of open-cell foam that self-inflates when you open the air valve. You can adjust your mattress either by letting air out or blowing more in to inflate it. Self-inflating mattresses also have an excellent R value. (An R value measures insulation. The average R value on a foam pad, for example, is about R–2; however, a self-inflating mattress has an average R value of R–4.5. Some of the deluxe Therm-a-Rest mattresses, such as the LE models, have values as high as R–6.)

The major drawback with self-inflating air mattresses is price. A good one costs from $40 to $120. The fact that you'll have it a long time should be factored into the cost. Punctures are another problem: What do you do when you've lost your puffy loft? The upside is you can quickly mend your mattress. You shouldn't camp without a simple repair kit. I've owned four mattresses over the years without an incident. Therm-a-Rest has an excellent guarantee: No matter how you wreck it, they'll fix it for $10!

I bought my first two mattresses in 1980. They're now twenty-one years old and have been used heavily every year since. Nineteen years ago, I bought a thinner mattress, one of the lightweight backpacking models of its day; this pad has been used yearly as well. These mattresses have seen hundred of nights of hard use. I've never punctured one and I can't say I'm really easy on gear. The nylon taffeta skin is tough and puncture-resistant, but I still faithfully carry the repair kit.

I recently purchased Therm-a-Rest LE Camp Rest Long, the two-inch-thick, nonslip surface, luxury model. Wow! It weighs a bit more than my other pads, but it's the most comfortable camping mattress I've ever owned.

Hints for Your Self-inflating Mattress

❏ To get maximum life out of your mattress, store it open on a shelf. This will keep the fibers from breaking down. Keep the valve open. This will also help the fibers dry out.

❏ If the weather is cold, don't speed up the inflation process by blowing into the mattress. Particles of moisture will collect and freeze on the fibers inside the mattress and you will sleep colder.

❏ Always carry a patch kit. If you get a rip, clean the surface with stove gas. Cut the patch about one-third larger than the rip and apply.

❏ If you get a rip—and don't have a patch kit—you can make a temporary patch with duct tape. As soon as you get home, take the tape off, clean the surface, and patch it properly.

Foam Pads

Foam pads come in two types: open cell and closed cell.

For the most part, I avoid open-cell pads unless they have a good waterproof/resistant cover to keep out the water. Otherwise you have a giant sponge waiting to happen. Open cells suck up moisture and, before you know it, your good night's rest is only a dream. My advice is to leave the open-cell stuff inside the living room furniture.

Closed-cell pads are a mainstay among back-packers. Closed-cell pads won't absorb water, which makes them a good choice for outdoor use. Even more attractive is the cost; closed-cell pads are inexpensive. And these pads are light weight and very warm. The cush per pound is also very good.

These pads are tough and indestructible. You can set one on very sharp rocks, burn a hole in it, or pick up a wicked snag on a sharp object with little structural damage. A major drawback is the bulk. A rolled-up pad is big and cumbersome. You have to tie it to the outside of your pack, and it's always

The foam pad on the back of my son Jon-Michael's pack is covered by a waterproof fabric. If you use open-cell foam, it should be in a protective cover.

catching on something. Still, you can't beat it for the price.

If you have to choose, go for a thicker pad. I don't like ⅜-inch pads; save this stuff for Boy Scouts on a budget or kids with strong backs. I'd rather fight the bulk and have a thick pad.

Cascade Designs has a couple of pads I think are worth considering. The full-length Ridge Rest Deluxe is very impressive with a very good R–3 rating; packed, it's $8\frac{1}{2}$ by 20 inches (this is also very good). The company also offers the Z-Rest pad that folds up into a handy 5-by-3.8-by-20-inch pack square that eliminates bulk. For a lighter pad, the Z-Rest is very comfortable. It has an egg-carton pattern that helps trap the dead air so you'll sleep warm. When folded the egg pockets nest to form a compact unit. This is probably the most compact closed-cell pad on the market. The hinges are very strong. As a point of interest, this pad received the *Backpacker Magazine* editor's choice for innovation in design, materials,

As Alan loads his kayak, he's not worried about getting and performance.
his sleeping pad wet. It's made of closed-cell foam.

Air Mattresses

The old-fashioned air mattress is okay for car camping, but it is tough to inflate and it's heavy. If I had an air mattress, which I don't, I'd carry a heavy-duty tire pump or an electronic pump that plugged into the cigarette lighter on my vehicle. If you've ever tried to blow up a mattress, you know you need a lot of hot air. Imagine blowing up a mattress for each member of your family by mouth!

For the price of a "good" air mattress, you can buy a self-inflating mattress that will last you a lot longer and be quite a bit warmer. Be aware that air mattresses are somewhat fragile

A Mattress Tip for Staying Warm

One pad may not be enough when camping on snow or in cold weather. Double the pad. A favorite combination is a closed-cell pad on the ground with a self-inflating mattress on top.

and subject to rips, tears, and slow leaks. Most problems occur in the middle of the night, during a rain storm, when your last flashlight batteries have died.

Too many campers overinflate their air mattresses. You need only enough air to keep your butt and shoulders off the ground. If you overinflate, you risk a puncture and you probably won't sleep as well.

Utah's mountains are wonderful to see at any time of year. In a comfortable sleeping bag, camping doesn't get much better.

Chapter 5

All You Need to Know about Tents:
Your Canvas House Outdoors

Consider a few pages of my journal. Some pages are a little smudged because they got wet:

May 15, 1996. Northern Alberta, Searching for bears.

3rd day, 4th night of rain.

Rained this morning. Still raining, but harder if that's possible. Can it rain this much without Noah's ark?

After sloshing about the bush, my toes are like white California prunes before molding. I wrung water from everything: don't need a shower. Gave up trying to start a fire two days ago.

Glad I waterproofed the tent seams during spring break.

Every flat place is a bog, every bog is a swamp, every swamp is a lake! The river's over its banks. I'm staying in my tent until it quits because it's the only place left on earth that's dry.

Waterlogged tundra holds puddles under my tent; they squish when I roll over. No leaks yet. I'm sitting naked, my wet clothes are "drying" in the vestibule. Actually it's not bad in here at all. I'm reading Edward Abbey.

May 18, 1996. Finally found bears.

No more rain. It's hot and muggy. Mosquitoes the size of flying, blood-sucking sewer rats! Plagues of blackflies and other biting things! Kasey got twenty-seven mosquito bites in a few minutes after the breeze quit blowing. I'm afraid to look at my own calves. Better not wear shorts.

I smell like sweat and bug dope (Cutter's Deet and Skin So Soft by Avon). When the wind dies, the plagues come in to suck my sweet blood!

My tent is a castle, a castle hotter than Dante's Inferno, but I get some breeze through the screens. This is the only place in the North Woods where I can hide from bugs. It's kind of pleasant. I'm now reading King Lear *and* MacBeth.

Hope the Cutters holds out.

A Tent Is Your Material Home

I've spent many happy outdoor moments in a tent. It's a refuge, a home away from home.

While the rain was discouraging and the bugs were awful on the Canadian trip I just described, my tent provided a nice escape. I had room to move about, so I felt human. A good tent can save your physical and emotional bacon when the elements aren't cooperating.

Another trip comes to mind, however; a trip from hell. We were enjoying Wyoming's Wind River Range several leg-straining days out of Elk Heart Pass. Without much warning, the menacing clouds dropped low about dusk. About midnight it started to pour. The rain scarcely quit, hardly letting up enough so we could sneak out to potty every couple of hours. Then the wind started to blow, rain turned to sleet, then snow, and back to rain. We stayed put.

We were on the first leg of a hellish, forty-four-hour stay-in-the-tent-athon. Three of us all more than 6 feet tall (okay, I'm just 6 feet), along with most of our gear, were cramped into a very very small tent. The tent was built for two but cleverly marketed as a three-man tent; three small Boy Scouts would be cramped.

To cook we opened the flap just a little, thanks to a handy vestibule, and boiled water on our trusty camp stoves. After a day there wasn't much left to say. We drank too many cups of hot chocolate and Lipton onion soup, ate handfuls of trail mix, and tried to sleep so one of us wouldn't punch another one out. The key word is *tried*, because space was so tight we had to turn on cue.

A tent is your home away from home. My daughter Abbey is peering from the door of our tent on a recent backpacking trip into Utah's Wasatch Mountains.

I read 816 pages of *War and Peace*, which I've started a dozen times before. Guess I'm not much for Russian realism. I can't tell you how happy I was to see blue sky. I pledged never to finish *War and Peace*. As a point of interest, pages of this fine novel were used subsequently to start the fire for the next five days, and for something else

A comfortable tent is a refreshing sight after a hard day enjoying the outdoors. This light packing tent from Coleman is just perfect for two persons.

This comfortable canvas tent is often used by outfitters. It takes a fair amount of time to pitch and the floor is usually dirt. Deadfall was used for tent poles in this instance.

when the toilet paper ran out. A bigger tent, a nicer tent, would have been worth its weight in gold. At least it didn't leak much. Another tent might not have made the experience memorable, but it would have helped. A tiny tent isn't always a bargain.

Tents have always been aesthetically pleasing to my eye, pretty if you will, reminding me of colorful mushrooms in a psychedelic forest. Maybe one of the reasons I love a fine tent is that I haven't always owned one. From the time I was in high school until the end of graduate school, I wondered if I'd ever have anything nice. I had a vintage "pup" tent, however. When I was in college at

Brigham Young University, it was my backpacking tent. (The truth is it was my everything tent). Later I bought a bigger tent for $19.50 at a garage sale after Shari and I were married.

A tent such as Coleman's Guide Series is a great family tent. You can expect it to last nearly a lifetime if you take good care of it. Packing your tent wet will take years off it. Dry your tent carefully before you pack it away.

For five years we camped over a good part of this country in what would have to be described as a brace of humble, nylon homes. The sleeping arrangements didn't look stylish, but they worked. The tents took longer to pitch and strike and weighed a little more than we liked. Sometimes we got a little testy with the lack of room on back-packing trips when we were holed up during rain, but our humble lodgings did a good job with a bit of tuning. We kept warm and dry.

After my first real job, I upgraded and retired both models as soon as I was able. I look back with nostalgia, but I'd never go back even if I had a choice.

Still, I learned a valuable lesson during those lean college years. You don't have to own state-of-the-art gear to have a great time outdoors. In temperate weather a less-expensive tent can be made to work. While I wouldn't recommend it, I've even used my old, humble standbys when I was backpacking (leaving the poles at home to save weight). I also used them during Rocky Mountain winters when it gets down right cold.

So if you want to use your old modest tent for a while, it will do. But when you're ready to move on, you'll need to learn a few things.

In this chapter I'll cover the least you should know about tents, and what you should know before you purchase a new tent. I'll also tell you how to beef up your old tent if a new model isn't in this year's budget. Then I'll discuss a few alternatives such as the lean-to.

The Least You Should Know about Tents

A tent is like a marriage. It can last a lifetime.

It can be a wonderful companion and a good friend on adventures. My parents bought a large tent when we were young (there were five Rutter rug rats). It's now more than forty years old but, apart from pancake syrup, peanut-butter-and-jam spills, a few rips in the mosquito netting, and a slightly bent pole, it's ready for another thirty years.

The Life of the Tent

My dad still has a pup tent he bought in the early 1950s. Yes, you've guessed it. It's the humble tent I used. I gave it back to him after years of abusing it when I upgraded. It was a little out of style even when I used it, wood poles and all. We rigged a new pole system, losing those heavy wood things. It's currently being used by his grandkids on scouting trips in southern Oregon.

In 1979 I found a green pack in the middle of a rutted dirt road in the Manti LaSal Mountains of central Utah. We ran an ad and checked with the local police, but no one claimed it. It would turn out to be one of my best finds. It was about midnight and we were coming home from an elk hunt. There it was in the dust, an almost-brand-new four-man Eureka Timber-line A-frame tent. This kelly-green jewel has been in hard use for almost twenty years now. It's a bit dirty nowadays, but every seam is strong and the fabric is good. I replaced one zipper and have mended the mosquito netting in several places where my son Jon-Michael speared it with a marshmallow stick. This tent has seen dew, dust, sun, snow, rain, and sleet in half the states and most of the Canadian provinces.

After you get the hang of it, pitching your tent is easy. Here my wife, Shari, sets up our A-frame Timberline (a tent I found years ago). We've spent hundreds of nights in this tent.

There's more, though. This tent has a lot of good memories connected with it: Among other things, an Alaskan brown bear has poked his furry head in the flap, several moose have tripped over the stakes, and in southeast Alaska a weasel crawled in to investigate. Once I saw a wolf through the back mosquito screen.

I'm being conservative when I say I've slept several hundred nights within its green walls. That doesn't count the times my good buddies Alan Baumgarten, Gary Frazier, and Lee Hipwell have borrowed it with, or without, my permission. This tent would have cost $85 in 1979 (it costs between $140 and $160 today). That works out to a lodging fee of about twenty-three cents a night. I could easily use this tent for another ten or twenty years if one of my friends doesn't steal it first.

If you take care of your gear and are careful in your selection, you can expect your tent to wear well and long.

Besides this Timberline, I'm very fond of Coleman, Coleman's Peak 1 line, The North Face, and Sierra Design products. I don't think you can go wrong with any of these manufacturers. They all stand behind their work and make very respectable products. Over the years, I've logged (along with my family) many nights in just about every tent these folks make. There's also a tent here for every price range.

This summer tent is light and easy to assemble. It's not a three-season tent; it doesn't have a full rain fly and the pole isn't solid enough to withstand a heavy fall or spring storm. The tent would probably collapse under the weight.

If you want a large, family camping tent, no one beats Coleman. The company has been in the business for decades and its reputation is solid. The tents are good values and affordable. If you want to get a higher-end tent or one made for a more specialized use, The North Face make very good tents.

What Type of Tent Do You Need?

Before making any tent decisions, you must first assess your camping needs. In the chapter on sleeping bags, I suggested you know something about the camping you plan to do, such as car camping, backpacking, canoe camping, or horse camping. I also suggested you have an idea how cold or warm it might get. Like sleeping bags, tents are specialized to meet a variety of outdoor needs, so there are a lot of models; it's a maze you have to navigate. The good news is these days—as with sleeping bags—you can expect to pay less and get more. Let's take a look at several things you need to know about tents so you can make an informed decision.

Types of Tents

It might seem that tents aren't just tents these days. There are models designed for different camping purposes, environmental conditions, and seasons of the year. It's important, therefore, that you have at least a rough idea about how and when you are going to use your tent.

Why Some Tents Cost More

❑ Why is one three-season tent a bargain at $123 while another is a bargain at $423? The answer is materials and labor costs, and you pay for those differences.

❑ While there may be subtle design differences, a more expensive tent is constructed of better-quality materials.

❑ How a tent is sewn tells a lot. Sewing is labor-intensive and, thus, costly. A more expensive tent is at least double stitched (or triple stitched on stress points). The stitches will also be small. A less expensive tent isn't as carefully sewn.

❑ A good zipper system versus a fair zipper system is always a factor. Such tent manufacturers as Sierra Design or The North Face use a superior zipper system, a No. 8 to No. 10 zipper. Coleman or Peak 1 tents have good zippers but you're not paying as much for the product. The zippers won't last as long nor work as well.

❑ A higher-end tent usually has a better pole system, and the poles are more carefully designed and manufactured. For instance, look at shock-cord poles and see how well they are finished. The inside of the poles are rounded and smooth and less likely to wear on the cord. A major element of North Face tents is the superior pole system.

❑ The seam sealing on a high-end tent is more carefully applied.

❑ The floor is usually waterproof, not just "highly water–resistant." The North Face tents have waterproof floors that have been coated five times and are waterproof for life.

Let's examine the five types of tents you'll run across. Consider your options and take a look at the tent that best fits your camping needs.

Summer Tent: A summer tent, sometimes called a *family tent*, is breezy and offers lots of ventilation. The fabric is light, and there will be a good bit of mesh to let the air circulate (including large doors, windows, and mesh moon roof). There will be some sort of a rain fly (less expensive tents have smaller flies).

Shielding from extreme elements isn't a consideration. This tent will allow you to survive a hearty rainstorm or two and separate you from blood-sucking, people-loving bugs that prey upon campers. The fabric on a summer tent should be lightly colored, so it will reflect, rather than absorb, heat.

Notice the heft of this tent's zipper system and the quality seam construction. This tent is fifteen years old and is ready for another fifteen years of service. You'll pay a lot for a North Face tent but expect a lifetime's use if you take good care of it.

Tent poles are important. The more expensive the tent, the better the poles. High-end manufacturers such as The North Face have superior pole design. Indeed, 25 to 35 percent of the cost of a good tent is the poles.

Even though it's not specifically made for tough weather, if necessary you can beef up a summer tent so it will do battle with harsher elements. I know families who've logged a lot of camping miles in a summer tent. When the weather turns they take a few extra precautions.

Three-Season Tent: This is a good all-around tent recommended for those persons who plan to do a lot of camping. It will cover most of the bases and is the best bang for your camping buck. It may not take extreme winds or piles of heavy snow like a mountaineering tent, but it will weather most of the elements. It will certainly handle the worst rainstorms. In short, it's a tent that will work in most situations.

Your three-season tent should have a waterproof fly and a breathable canopy. Avoid a single-wall waterproof tent unless it is a canvas model. If possible, find a tent with a waterproof floor. I prefer three-season tents to be a neutral, lighter color. A darker color can be warm in the summer.

For most car campers a summer or three-season tent will be more than adequate. You can start camping adventures in early spring and trickle into late fall. A three-season tent will work well in mild weather, but make sure it has plenty of ventilation. Such a tent will be a little heavier, a little better made. If you are car camping only, get a tent you can stand up in; if you're backpacking, get a compact model.

A three-season tent is a little heavier than a summer tent, and it should have a full rain fly and heavier zippers. I've been in a number of three-season tents when it snowed 6 inches and there was no problem. In other tents, however, with weaker ceiling structures, it would be necessary to brush away the white stuff after an inch or so.

This Peak Orion is a medium-range three-season tent. It has a tighter pole design as well as a full rain fly. A full fly is an important consideration when you buy a tent; the fly makes it more weatherproof and warmer.

Here we're having a slumber party. This tough North Face is a four-season tent capable of withstanding any sort of weather or a group of wild nine-year-olds. Notice the pole structure on this tent? There are no weak spots; every section is supported. Once the rain fly is on, this North Face will hold up to a heavy snow-storm.

Four-Season Tent: A four-season tent means you have a shelter that can face the elements any time of the year. It will work nicely in June (although it might be a little warm on a hot night) and very well in January, too. A tent for all seasons will be pretty tough. It also weighs more—about two to four pounds more—than other models. This tent should be constructed of a heavy material with hardy seams; it should have stronger poles (and more of them), two doors, and a generous vestibule (for extra cold-weather gear and cooking).

An all-season tent should be aerodynamic to thwart knife-edged winds and made of a darker material to absorb heat. It should have an excellent floor, sometimes called a "tub floor" to foil dampness and troublesome wet-ness. Even a lower-end four-season tent is on the expensive side; this is state-of-the-art stuff. It will frequently be freestanding. If it snows a foot, you aren't going to worry.

Canvas Wall Tent: It's hard to put this style of tent into a category. It can be a summer or a three- or four-season tent. At the least it's usu-ally big, roomy, and has canvas walls. It's very heavy and, even folded, it takes up a lot of space. Sometimes there's a floor. This is the tent traditionally used by outfitters, and you'll often find a woodstove inside. It takes a long time to pitch and is usually up for weeks or months. The tent is quite comfortable. I've spent many happy weeks in just such a tent. It's sometimes called a canvas cabin tent, too. In the far north, many miners and trappers have spent long cold winters in such an arrange-ment.

Climber's/Mountaineering Tent: Like the four-season tent, the climber's/moun-taineering tent has to withstand all the elements. In high alpine conditions, you never know what weather you'll find. This tent is designed to take snow, sleet, rain, and extreme winds.

As you'd expect, the tent is always quite small and compact. It's designed to be pitched on a glacier, an alpine meadow, or the edge of a steep cliff. It's a practical tent, but it's not a tent with the comforts of home. It's rather specialized and not the best choice for general campers. It's also expensive.

Remember, not all tents can be all things to all people.

If you camp a lot, or have specialized camping hobbies, you'll have two or three tents sooner or later. For most people a larger three-season tent for car camping and a smaller tent for backpacking takes care of all their camping needs.

If you plan to camp in more extreme conditions, you're going to need a better tent, and it won't come cheap. Yes, I know that I made do, but I was really poor and not as smart as I am now. Any good four-season tent comes with a fine price tag and isn't something you're going to run across at a suburban garage sale.

If I were to make a generic choice, not knowing your exact situation, I'd like to see you in a good three-season tent. You can purchase such a tent on sale for about what you'd spend for several nights in a moderate motel.

What Sort of Camping Will You Do?

Now let's look at the types of camping demands you'll put on your tent. This will help you narrow your camping needs. If you are backpacking or plan to do some backpacking later, your needs will be a little

This traditional wall tent can withstand about any temper tantrum Mother Nature can throw. I've spent many happy weeks in this tent with good friends Kasey Kox and Chuck Graves of Magic Wilderness Outfitters. Between chasing bears and casting for trophy-size pike, I've written a number of chapters for this book in this tent.

I've spent hours huddling about this fire-breathing stove. It is a handy addition to a big wall tent.

For most campers a three-season tent will provide the best value for the dollar. A smaller tent will be easier to pack and set up, but it doesn't offer enough interior headroom for you to stand up.

A large tent is great for car camping or if there are many campers in your family. You can stand up and there's plenty of room.

different from the car-camping family who likes a little elbow room.

When you backpack, weight is critical. You need a tent, whether it be a summer or three- or four-season or four-season tent, that's light and compact. As you'd expect, extra room will be a luxury. Remember, you are sacrificing space and a little bit of comfort for weight. For example, you won't be able to stand up in a backpacking tent; you'll probably get dressed on your knees and your sleeping area will be more restrictive.

The Coleman Dakota is a combination dome/hoop tent. My family enjoys this tent because there are three rooms so each of our kids has a room of his or her own. It's fairly weather-worthy, and it's also cool during the summer. This has become one of our favorite tents! My daughter calls it our apartment tent. There's a lot of room.

Tent Shapes

Just as tents have different functions, they also have different shapes. Let's take a look at the five main configurations.

Hoop Tent: A hoop, or tunnel, tent is a great choice for backpackers and bike campers. Several half-circle hoops create a fabric tunnel. A tent of this nature is light and quick to pitch and strike, and there is a lot of floor space. A hoop tent isn't the best tent for heavy winds or snowstorms, but it works well as a summer or a temperate three-season tent.

Dome Tent: This is a great tent for summer and temperate three-season use. The side walls are nearly straight up, so there's little wasted space and plenty of room. Be aware that this tent can be a little heavy. You can stand up and get dressed in comfort. Its Achilles' heel is its roof support. Sections of the wall or roof are unsupported and can collapse in snow storms and, sometimes, during heavy rainstorms.

Modified-dome Tent: To fix the dome support problem, some manufacturers have squared the floor and added extra poles for additional support. The unsupported sections are beefed up so this tent is more weather worthy. Many four-season tents are modified domes.

A-frame Tent: As the name implies, this tent looks like the letter A. The sides are sloping, so it will discard rain quite well and is okay in the wind. The major drawbacks of this design are the cramped insides (because of the sloping sides) and the number of stakes it takes to keep the tent secure in a wind.

Pyramid/Cabin Tent: A pyramid tent is a simple, tepee-like affair. There is a single stake in the center, while stakes on the sides keep it secure. This tent is light and easy to set up. There's rarely a built-in floor, so you must careful where you set it up or you'll get wet. This design also offers little security from bugs that suck blood. Car campers often use this design for the shower or potty tent. A cabin tent has a lot of poles. While it's very comfortable in summer, it takes a long time to put up.

The Cobra is my favorite tent for summer outings. It sets up quickly, weighs in at three pounds and a few ounces—and costs less than $100. It's compact and will repel a thunderstorm. I've spent nearly 50 nights in this baby. It's perfect for solo trips or for a parent and child. Two adults will fit, but it's cozy.

A rain fly will keep you dry from the inside out. It lets your tent breathe because it expedites the escape of your body moisture.

Tents are either freestanding or stake supported. Freestanding tents, as the name implies, stand on their own without corner stakes. A free-standing tent makes getting the perfect site easy. If you find a rock or a nasty root, all you have to do is pick up your outdoor home and move. Be sure to stake your freestanding tent, though, or a gust of wind will turn it into an expensive kite or a canvas tumbleweed. You may have to chase your home into the next county.

How Big Is Big Enough?

Most tents are rated by how many people they'll hold and the number of square feet they cover. As a rule of thumb, backpackers should have about 2½–by–6½–feet per person. General campers need at least 3-by-7-feet per person. You may need more room if you're camping in the same place for a long time.

If you must spend the day in your tent, it's nice to have a little room in which to turn around. If you have to keep all your gear with you in the tent, it might be cramped. I've always found that a two-person tent is perfect for one (but will fit two folks if necessary); a three-person tent is perfect for two (but can fit three); a four-person perfect for three; and so on.

Ins and Outs of Staying Dry

Consider Your Fly

A good rain fly is your key to staying dry and comfortable in rainy—and dry—weather. Unless you're exclusively summer camping in temperate conditions and don't expect a lot of rain or cooler temperatures, try to *find a tent with a full rain fly*. Many tents, especially those priced to move, have bikini tops that barely cover the top. Bikini tops work in warm weather, but they have drawbacks that you need to consider.

The more the rain fly covers, the more weatherproof your tent will be from both the outside in and the inside out.

Let me explain this outside in, inside out stuff. Some tents, in fact, almost all summer tents, have a see-through sky roof. It's great in warm weather because you can see the stars and it's cool on warm nights. But when the wind whips up the clouds and a summer thunder bumper blows in, a skimpy fly over the mesh screen will let in cold air and possibly rain. A fly protects you from outside moisture, which is why a full fly is better than a partial one.

A vestibule gives you a lot of extra space and provides a place to store your pack, boots, or wet clothes. This generous vestibule on the Peak 1 Apollo is a very beneficial extra.

Just as important, however, a rain fly lets your tent breathe. A full fly keeps your tent drier from the inside out. The moisture from your breathing and body can escape more easily because the fly allows the fabric of your canopy (your tent roof) to stay warmer (above the dew point) than the fly exposed to the outside air. During one night's sleep everybody in your tent will give off seven to nine ounces of moisture through perspiration and breathing. Unless your tent breathes too, you'll be snoozing in a sea of dampness by morning.

Obviously, the inside out stuff gets more critical as the weather gets colder or as more people are packed inside a tent. During good weather I don't bother with a fly. I usually have the tent windows, skylight, and door screen open. I'm really fond of star-gazing mesh because I like to watch the stars move across the sky. If it gets cold or rainy, I get up and put on the fly. I don't get damp since the mesh breathes.

"Waterproof" Tents Can Mean Trouble

Waterproof tents can spell trouble: *wet*. Waterproof tent bottoms and flies are desired elements in a good tent, but I'd avoid a completely waterproof model. A tent needs to breathe if you're to stay dry and comfortable. Don't confuse a "waterproof" tent with a tent that's waterproof and breathable (like Gor-tex). This fabric is entirely different—it breathes.

A "waterproof" tent won't let moisture from the inside of the tent escape. You might just as well sleep in a large Baggie with ineffective breathing holes.

Several years ago, I was photographing grizzly bears with my photographer friend, Bret Hicken, and I relearned this lesson. We were in a hurry to get to Montana and we grabbed the wrong tent out of his garage. We snagged a waterproof affair some misanthrope had given to him when he was a Boy Scout. It was pretty cold that first night, as I remember, but it got worse. Before dawn we were in a frigid sweat bath with sopped bags. The tent was small and little air circulated. We ditched that muggy tent, paying several worthy-looking drunks ten bucks if they'd take it off our hands and burn it.

It was late spring but the weather was still freezing. There was rain with batches of sleet and snow. We ended up camping in the back of my pickup with a reinforced blue plastic tarp spread over the bed in such a way that air could circulate. That was my first and last experience in a tent that couldn't breathe.

A waterproof tent won't seem like much of a bargain the first time you wake up wet at 3:00 A.M. This is why you want a tent with a fly that lets the moisture escape. If you have a waterproof tent, and have to use it before you can find some worthy-looking drunks, make sure you

An awning such as this is one way to keep your tent dry during very rainy weather.

vent the doors and windows with a Swiss Army knife, then throw it away later.

Other Tent Considerations

Now that you know a few of the basics about tents, let's check out some other tenting tidbits that could make future camping experinces more comfortable and enjoyable.

Seam Sealing

To ensure that your tent is waterproof, you must seal the seams unless the manufacturer has already done so (and even if they have done it, you might need to do it again).

Seam sealing, as the name implies, means that you treat the seams so that no moisture can seep through the stitching. It's great insurance. Sealers are available from a wide variety of sources.

It's a good idea to seam seal your new tent before you take it out. Set your tent up in the yard as tautly as you can. Let it sit for a few hours to stretch the seams. Before you start sealing, adjust it again to keep it taut. Make sure you go over all the seams carefully as you seal.

A Vestibule

If you can afford it, buy a tent with a vestibule. Not only is it a safe, dry spot to cook during a storm but, it's also a great place to store your pack, boots, and wet clothes—which means more room for you inside.

If you're buying a four-season tent or plan to camp in rain or snow, a vestibule is a necessity.

Check Your Zipper(s)

Check the zippers in a tent before you part with your cash. The zippers should work easily and not hang up. Make sure the windows zip open and shut without any problem. Also, check the zippers on the mosquito netting to ensure that they too open and shut easily. With insects of every stripe ready to eat you alive, you simply can't afford problems with your mosquito netting!

Know How to Set It Up

Take a few moments and practice setting up your tent in the backyard. Some unfamiliar tents have a way of being stubborn the first time you pitch them. There's an unwritten law among campers: It's likely to be raining when you pitch your tent for the first time, and if it's not raining, it will be dark.

Some tents are more difficult than others to set up. Make sure you know the finer points before you head off for wilder parts. Setting up your tent in the back yard first will let you know if all the pieces are there. Once in a while a pole is missing or a zipper doesn't work. It's not hard to correct the problem at home, but once you're camping you can't return to the store for help.

Most tents come with awful stakes. Look at the stakes. If they look flimsy, run to your camping store and buy a few more. Or better still, do

Have your kids help you set up the tent. Take a few minutes to practice setting up before you take off camping.

yourself a favor by replacing them entirely with high-quality stakes. They'll last a lot longer.

Staying Dry from the Ground Up

Let's look at keeping dry from the floor up. This is especially critical if you have an old tent or you're trying to make do with a tent that doesn't have a waterproof floor.

If your older tent has a waterproof floor, the first thing you need to do is seam seal it very carefully. Wait a couple of hours, then seal it again.

A few years ago, my good friend Cliff suggested we take a thirty- to forty-day camping trip through the Yukon and Northwest territories and Alaska. I found another graduate student to teach my summer classes at Brigham Young University and within four days I was off.

I learned a few things about keeping dry, because it rained all but two of the days we were in the north. Overall it was a gorgeous trip. I photographed lots of moose and bears, I caught tons of salmon. But it was wet: sometimes it was a mist; sometimes it was in buckets. Several times we were so tired, we were careless about setting up camp. As a result, we spent a very uncomfortable night in a four-wheel-drive vehicle trying to sleep. We were wet and cold and learning fast!

I'd never experienced anything like it. I'd weathered wet in Oregon, but never had I encountered anything like this. It seemed that most of the level ground we camped on was disguised wet tundra. We got smart fast. Except for marauding grizzly bears or a myopic moose stumbling into the tent, we slept the sleep of the just in a soggy climate.

Staying Dry without Trenching

In the old days it was customary to dig a trench around your tent to keep water from pooling under the floor. Many of the errors a camper made selecting a tent site could be compensated by a trench about the tent. When it rained, which it often did in southern Oregon, the water would run into the trench and not under the floor of our tent (which wasn't very waterproof). Even then, my family practiced minimum impact, always replacing the sod or dirt we had cut out.

Things have changed, however. In many places, especially high-use areas such as national parks and some national forests, trenching is no longer an acceptable tenting practice. With so many people camping nowadays, extensive trenching would turn most campgrounds into dirt piles in short fashion.

A good waterproof tent bottom is a better alternative to trenching. Many tents, though, don't have waterproof bottoms, while others, as they get older, lose what waterproofing they had.

Where you pitch your tent has a lot to do with your camping comfort. Look for ground that will drain, rather than collect, water.

So if the ground is damp or it looks like wet weather is on its way, you'd better do something to ensure your stay dry. Nothing is more pleasant than hearing the beat of rain on your tent, while you're dry and warm. Nothing is more troublesome, however, than realizing it's 2:00 A.M., it's pouring, and your bedding is soaking up pools of water.

The handiest insurance you can carry is a piece of lightweight blue plastic tarp several inches wider and longer than the floor of your tent. Keep your tarp in the same pouch as your tent, so you won't forget it.

Look at how this tarp hangs out from beneath the tent. These campers will probably get wet if it rains. Water will roll off the tent wall and collect and pool up under the tent. When you put a tarp under your tent to protect the bottom from getting muddy and wet, it must be slightly smaller than the tent floor. No part should hang out.

Some campers put their tarps under their tents: Don't follow suit. Instead, *place the tarp inside your tent.* Your tarp is longer and wider than the floor of your tent, so the edges will curl up and prevent a wet midnight interruption if it rains. This will also keep your tent clean inside. If you track in a bit of dirt or mud, all you do is carefully fold up the plastic, take it outside and shake it. Carry a whisk broom when you're car camping.

If you have the space, consider carrying another tarp slightly smaller than the bottom of your tent. It makes a great ground cloth. It will protect the bottom of your tent from mud, rocks, muck, mud, roots, and sticks. Make sure, however, that the bottom tarp is smaller than the bottom of your tent. If the edges hang out, they'll collect moisture and suck it under your tent.

Making a Tarp Tent

We used tarps all the time when I was a scout, even in rainy Oregon. We used the old heavy waxed-cloth coated tarps, but soon switched to the reinforced plastic tarps. For next to nothing you have a shelter, but it's neither bugproof nor protection from wind-driven rain. I spent many nights in a 12-by-12-foot tarp when I was young. Even now it's plenty for my family and our gear. Usually these sheets come with grommets, but you can make your own if necessary.

If you really want to stay dry, put your tarp inside your tent as you see here. This will keep the inside dry.

To successfully tarp camp, you need a lot of good rope (nylon parachute cord works very well), a roll of duct tape (for tears and ember burns), and some pegs (rocks will do in a pinch).

Find a couple of trees (the reason you carry a lot of rope is trees aren't always as close together as you'd like). Look for ground that has drainage and is flat so you can

A **double hitch** is a great knot for rigging up a clothes line or a lean-to. This is also a great knot for tying a rope to a tree.

A **clove hitch** is a great way to fasten a rope to a pole, tree, or post.

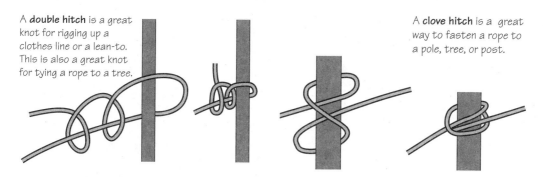

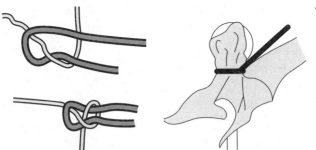

A **sheepshank** is a great knot for joining two ropes of unequal diameter.

- To secure a corner of a space blanket or sheet of plastic that doesn't have grommets, make your own.
- Use a small piece of cloth or a bit of wood.

sleep comfortably. Remember tarp tents and lean-tos aren't very windproof.

In Utah's Uintas Mountains my son Jon-Michael and I frequently camp with just a tarp. We make a lean-to and tuck the long end under for a ground cloth. The winds in these high mountains can be severe. We make camp in a secluded area, as sheltered from the wind as we can find. Whenever possible, I buy tarps that have grommets. Grommets are very practical when securing the ends because you can cinch your shelter. One night we had a howling wind, and I had set up the shelter carelessly. We had bits of blue plastic scattered all over Eden. It took us half the morning to pick them all up (it would never do to litter in paradise).

Lean-To

In good weather, tie the top rope (ridge line) about 6 or 7 feet up. If the weather is wet, tie the top rope about 4 or 5 feet above the ground to give more protection.

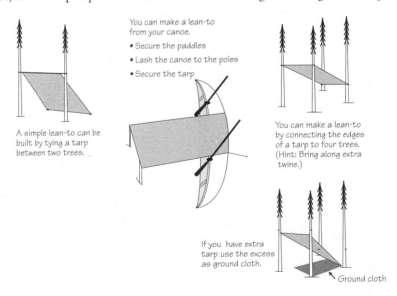

You can make a lean-to from your canoe.
- Secure the paddles
- Lash the canoe to the poles
- Secure the tarp

A simple lean-to can be built by tying a tarp between two trees.

You can make a lean-to by connecting the edges of a tarp to four trees. (Hint: Bring along extra twine.)

If you have extra tarp use the excess as ground cloth.

Ground cloth

You can tie the two ends or string the rope through the grommets.

If you have a long tarp, you can also use it as the ground cloth. Secure the bottom ends with a ground line rope, pegs, small log or rocks. If there's much wind, secure it carefully.

Tarp Tent

You can make a tarp tent quite easily. Tie a taut line between two trees. Adjust the height to the size of the cloth and the space that you need. Drape the tarp over the rope and secure the hanging ends with rocks or pegs.

Making Your Tent Stormproof

At some time you may have to stormproof your tent. This is particularly important if you have an older tent, if you're pushing that summer tent into three seasons, or if your three-season tent is being used as a winter tent.

- ❑ Seam seal your tent every year.

- ❑ Watch for "widow makers," trees that might blow down on your tent in a storm. (They aren't called widow makers for nothing.)

- ❑ Don't camp too close to cliffs or steep hills where wind or moisture could dislodge a boulder or cause a slide.

- ❑ Don't camp in a wash or gully where a flash flood could take out you and your tent. By the same consideration, set your tent above high water when you're camping near a stream, lake, or ocean beach.

- ❑ Have a plastic ground cloth inside your tent. This will protect you from a leaking floor.

- ❑ If you have an old tent, sew on additional stake loops so you can have better footing. You can also sew on more loops to attach additional guy lines.

- ❑ In severe winds run extra guy lines off the front and back of your tent. You may need three or four guy lines on the front and back and several on the sides. For this to work, however, you need loops. If you don't have extra sewn-on loops, tie a loop around a long, smooth stone.

Chapter 6

A Close Look at Day Packs and Backpacks: A Necessary Place to Carry Your Gear

It doesn't matter if you're hiking for the day or for a week, strapping on a pack gives you a feeling of freedom and independence. A pack is your luggage and your safety net. It carries the gear you need to meet nature on its own terms.

You need to carry a pack if you want to enjoy a camping or a hiking trip into the backcountry to see such areas as this alpine meadow 6 miles from the trailhead.

A comfortable, well-fitting pack is a great friend and a source of pride. An ill-fitting pack, or one that's poorly designed, is a nightmare. A bad pack can ruin a great day in the woods or make a backpacking adventure a seven-day torture from hell.

When you walk into a sporting-goods store, you'll notice scores of packs, in a plethora of sizes and a myriad of colors. To say that the pack section is a labyrinth would be no lie. Let's look at packs, their uses, and how to find one that fits your needs.

Selecting a Day Pack

A day pack or knapsack is a pack designed for day hikes. Some day packs are large enough to see use on short backpacking adventures.

Day packs have come a long way in the past few years. In the not-too-recent past, most day packs were tear-shaped with a pair of thin shoulder-abusing straps. To say they were uncomfortable after 1 or 2 miles on the trail would be a faint understatement. Now though, day packs are designed for comfort and practicality. You can carry a moderately packed day pack without feeling like Atlas at the end of the trail. Much of the innovation and research that has gone into backpacks has benefited their smaller cousins.

If you plan to do some hiking with a fair amount to transport, it makes sense to have a well-made day pack. A less-expensive pack will work nicely for children or if you are carrying only a few pounds. Beyond that, though, such a pack is nothing more than a pouch with a few straps. For $30 to $100, you can buy an excellent heavy-duty product that will fit you well, provide ample pockets, and last you twenty years.

If you hike very far, you'll need to carry your lunch, snacks, canteen, water purifier, jacket, rain gear, emergency kit, first-aid kit, and last but not least, toilet paper. Perhaps you'll want to carry a book, camera, fishing gear, or a guidebook, too. If you're hiking with kids, there'll also be parenthood odds and ends you can't be without.

Over the years I've discovered a few things about buying packs I'll share with you. I've used my last day pack for ten years and it has plenty more years to go. I've carried it on scores of trails with my kids. I've used it while hunting, fishing, and taking photographs. I've also used it as a briefcase, carrying my books and papers between classes.

Day Packs for Children

Children love to carry packs, so let them. It makes them feel grown up—and it helps ease *your* load. If your kids are fairly young, there's no point in giving them an expensive pack. Something for ten dollars or under will do just fine. It's not a good idea to have them carry too much, anyway. We let our kids carry their own jackets, rain ponchos, small water bottles, and maybe a few snacks. Don't overtax your kids; make sure they have fun.

Selecting a Backpack

A backpack allows you to be a self-contained camper, whether it be for an overnight or a two-week trip into rugged wilderness. The type of pack you select probably will be determined by the type of backpacking you want to do and how

This pack has carried a lot of important gear, but no gear more important than my Sage rod, waders, and fishing tackle. To reach very good fishing, you need to get away from other anglers. Hiking 1 or 2 miles from the crowds is a great way to find hungry fish.

When kids get a little older, they can carry quite a bit more gear. We hiked up to a mountain lake from our base camp. Jon-Michael was easily able to carry his fishing gear, rain poncho, extra socks, fleece jacket, water, and lunch.

Gear the weight of the pack to the child's ability. Jon-Michael, 13 years old, is easily carrying a 15- to 20-pound daypack. Abbey, 6 years old, can carry a 5- to 8-pound pack without complaint all day.

The Ram-FLX frame is molded nylon and tough as nails. A big advantage to this solid frame is that it floats with your body movements, which makes it a very comfortable frame.

much "innovation" you want to pay for. Let's take a look at backpacks, specifically the two major types: external frame and internal frame. And, also important, how to buy a pack that fits.

External-Frame Backpacks

An external-frame pack has an outside frame, or skeleton, to which the pack and gear are attached. An external-frame pack is a great choice for packers on a budget. You can buy a very good external-frame pack for quite a bit less than an internal-frame backpack with similar features. You can expect to pay somewhere from $100 to $200 for a good entry-level external-frame pack that will last twenty years or longer.

External-frame packs are well-suited to general backpacking but not for technical outdoor sports where balance is critical, such as snowshoeing, rock climbing, or cross-country skiing. A large backpack tends to throw off your center of gravity.

This pack is a great choice for the packer who carries a heavy load because an external frame distributes the weight over the hips. While a large pack (which extends above your head) can hang up in bushy or thick country, it has one major advantage: An external frame pack is cool! If you're hiking in the summer heat or in the desert, staying cool can mean a lot. The nature of the external pack allows air to circulate about your back and the frame.

External frames allow you to tie on all sorts of equipment or gear to the frame that won't fit elsewhere. The bag's construction also offers a number of external pockets that allow you to reach your stuff more easily when you're on the trail. There are a number of fine external packs

Fitting Your Day Pack

- ❏ Select a pack with a carrying capacity larger than you think you'll need. There will be times you'll need to stuff more in that pouch than you expect. A larger pack will weigh only a little more.

- ❏ Make sure the shoulder straps are well-padded. You'll thank yourself every time you set off down the trail with a full knapsack.

- ❏ Look for sternum straps; they help distribute the weight.

- ❏ Make sure the day pack has a wide, well-padded hip belt. A hip belt will distribute the weight of the pack evenly.

- ❏ Make sure the pack has good zippers that don't hang up. Bad zippers spell trouble. (A good zipper will, of course, add to the price.)

- ❏ Find a pack with side pockets.

- ❏ Put ten pounds in the pack and walk around the store for five or ten minutes. Try adjusting your pack. Are there any sore spots? A pack needs to be comfortable.

A good day pack is worth the price. Look at how well it's sewn and how the zippers work. I personally like a day pack with a lot of interior room. This pack, the Gunnison, also works nicely for overnight packing trips.

on the market. Most have aluminum frames, but some are made of nylon. If you get an aluminum frame, make sure it has been heli-arc welded and not soldered. A cheaply designed frame (sold in discount stores for $39.99 to $69.99) will come apart if you have a heavy load. Several excellent manufacturers of external-frame packs are Kelty, REI, and JanSport. Expect to pay between $100 and $200 for a pack that will last about twenty to thirty years before you give it to a poor, but deserving Boy Scout).

Another favorite pack of mine is the Peak 1 with a molded nylon frame called Ram-FLX. If you're on a budget, and want your money's worth, take a close look at this pack. I have a number of good external-frame packs, but I've logged many, many miles with an early edition Ram-FLX. I have no complaints. It's a well-designed outfit, and the one I usually take.

The Peak 1 has a number of lash points, or slots, for tying on extra gear, and you don't need any special fittings. This is something I like because I'm always attaching tripods, camera bags, fishing gear, and so on. Another plus is the pack's grommets. Traditional clevis pins and split rings are not needed (which always seem to come out or break 20 miles from a trailhead). You can make all the pack adjustments without tools. This is very handy when you have to do trailside alterations to get your pack fine-tuned for that long hike. The lash points (called "Lash Tabs") provide a simple way to attach shoulder straps and belts (and to secure extra gear). A tab at the end of a strap is inserted through a slot in the frame. You twist to secure it. The slotted edges are raised so it's easy to insert, but tough to pull out accidently.

The frame is tough (my pack, fully loaded, bounced out of a truck at 55 miles per hour with no ill effects beyond cosmetic scrapes). While the frame is rigid, it has controlled flexibility. What I like best is it "floats" with you when you're walking; the frame bends and flexes as you move. The standard comparison between a "flexible pack" and rigid frame is the difference between carrying a forty-pound child versus a forty-pound brick. This system is moderately priced and will last. In addition to backpacking use, I've removed the pack and used the frame for a meat board, lashing on eighty pounds of deer, elk, or moose.

This pack won't give you sticker shock, either. Models range from $94 to $175. The Peak will fit almost any body, from 4 feet 6 inches to 6 feet 5 inches. The numerous slots provide more than 2,000 configurations in even the standard-frame model. There is a handy set of instructions that show you how to tune it to your body. Be aware that some women need to upgrade the hip belt to attain the best fit. In fact, anyone planning to hike a long way may want to upgrade the hip belt.

As the name implies, an internal pack has no exposed frame.

Internal-Frame Backpacks

This pack has the frame built into it. It offers a low center of gravity, which is made to order for those who need to maintain good balance such as mountaineers, skiers, and climbers. This pack allows the wearer a greater freedom of movement because it is less bulky.

While this style had a more specialized use at its inception, it has become popular with many general packers. While it won't hold as much as a large external-frame pack, the fit can be customized. A lot of research has gone into this pack frame. Generally, more experienced packers use this style, but only after they really know what they want.

Price is one of the major drawbacks. Good internal-frame packs don't come cheaply. Another negative: This pack is hot! It fits snugly against your back and little, if any, air circulates. Your back will be wet with perspiration even on a cool day.

Getting a Pack to Fit

Making sure your pack fits is the most important thing you can do. If it fits you'll be happy; if it doesn't, you'll rue the day you were born, let alone the day you purchased your pack. Go with what's comfortable! Brand name will be important, but fit is your first consideration. A pack that fits your best friend may not fit you. Also be aware that packs fit women differently than men.

Don't buy a pack at a store that won't let you try it on and wear it for half an hour (or at least ten or fifteen minutes if you feel self-conscious wearing a full pack). Seek out an experienced clerk. If one is not available, come back later or find a different shop.

Take a close look at how the bag is stitched. Are any of the seams unraveling? Are the shoulder straps and the hip belt thickly padded? Are there a lot of pockets? Can you easily get at your map, water bottle, and other incidentals? Are there lower pouches or access zippers that let you reach your equipment on the trail without unpacking? Is there enough padding along the back side to protect your back from bumpy items?

It's often necessary to make adjustments on the trail. You should be able to fine-tune your pack easily.

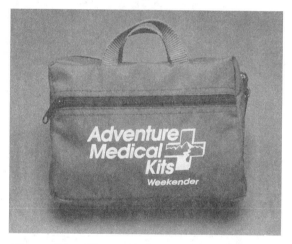

Throw a first-aid kit in a day pack or backpack and leave it there.

Load the pack with thirty to forty pounds, spreading the weight out as evenly as you can. A good backpacking store will have a supply of five-pound sand bags just for this purpose. Another thing to consider is will your own gear fit. If you aren't sure, bring in your equipment and stuff it in. You may decide to buy a bigger pack.

My advice is to go big. Go bigger than you think you need. You'll be glad down the line.

Fine-tuning Your Pack: See If It Fits

1. Loosen the straps. Put the weighted pack on and let it sit for a minute or two. Now cinch the shoulder straps rather tightly.

2. Loosen the shoulder straps and cinch the hip belt, which should ride comfortably on your hips. (A good hip belt, one that's nice and thick, will even out the load by shifting some of the weight to your hips.)

3. With a lot of the weight resting on your hips, cinch the shoulder straps again. The padded part of the shoulder straps should cover your entire shoulder.

4. Loosen the shoulder straps a bit. Is the shoulder padding still generously covering your shoulder? If it isn't, take the pack off and adjust.

5. The straps should be roughly 3 to 5 inches lower than the top of the pack itself. Does the pack have load lift straps that help shift the weight up from your shoulders? (These are very handy.)

6. Adjust the sternum straps, which should be just below your collar bone. These straps shouldn't get in the way of your breathing. Now readjust the hip and shoulder straps to comfort.

7. Wear the pack for half an hour and see how it fits. You'll certainly notice a thirty- or forty-pound load, but you can tell if the weight is distributed well. Can you hike 8 or 10 miles? When you walk around, lift your legs up high and see how it feels.

8. If you are looking at an internal-frame pack, some of the stays may have to be removed and bent to get an accurate idea of the pack's fit. Make the bends rather gently.

Loading Your Pack

Heavier Items: You will be more comfortable if you pack heavier items higher and closer to your back, because it will improve your center of gravity.

Lighter Items: Lighter items should be placed lower in your pack and farther from your back. Pack your sleeping bag and foam pad at the bottom.

Your pack will take a lot of abuse. Lee has used his pack for ten years; it's been down a lot of trails.

Chapter 7

Camp Cooking Gear:
Stoves, Pans, Pots, and Other Things

If you want to eat cold cereal, peanut-butter sandwiches, and pork-and-beans out of a can, you don't need to concern yourself with this chapter. All you need is a can opener, bowl, spoon, and an appetite without imagination.

Camp meals can be some of the best cooking on earth. There's nothing like a steak grilled slowly to perfection over aspen coals. There's nothing like waking up to the smell of pancakes, hash browns, and ham cooking on a sizzling grill. Is there anything better than Dutch-oven chicken and dumplings with fresh peach cobbler?

If my friend Alan is along to cook, who knows what this four-star camping chef will magically conjure up from coals, cast iron, aluminum, and the food box. The last time Lee and I camped with Alan, we put on five pounds. He spent $195 for three days worth of food. It was money well spent. The highlight dinner was Welsh rarebit and Cornish game hen, wilted spinach salad with Caesar dressing, Dutch-oven sourdough bread, fresh pasta, antipasto, and some cream dessert I can't pronounce.

Whether you want to camp a little or a lot, you'll need a few things to get the water boiling. Even if you're a backpacker who doesn't want to be bothered with much cooking, you'll at least need a stove, a pot, and eating utensils. If you're car camping with kids and want to spend as little time in the camp kitchen as possible, you'll need something to heat up cans.

Lunch never seems to cook fast enough when you're hungry. My son Jon-Michael is making split-pea soup on a one-burner backpacking stove. Children enjoy helping with the cooking chores.

When it comes to cooking, most of us are somewhere in the middle as far as culinary skills are concerned. Welsh rarebit and the trimmings are too much, yet we can't

Few things are more enjoyable than eating a fine meal with your family in the fresh air. Here we're eating breakfast before going on a nature hike.

Cooking over a campfire is fun, but a camp stove is still a necessity. Sometimes fires aren't allowed.

face the thought of peanut-butter sandwiches and warmed-up cans of beans and franks every day. We want to eat well, but sometimes we don't want to take much time getting meals ready. There's a lot to see and do, and we want to do it—not spend all our time cooking and cleaning.

There are other times when cooking a big meal in the open air is a lot of fun. I can still remember standing on a log stirring the pancake batter with my mother. We'd get up early and pick huckleberries or blueberries. What we didn't eat would go into the pancakes. My mom would cover leftover cakes with butter, sugar, or peanut butter and that would be our lunch.

Mom and Dad made cooking and cooking chores fun. We ate well. We all took turns on KP. Each day one child would help cook and clean up. Then he or she was free of kitchen chores until his or her turn rolled around again. There was a lot of one-on-one time with mom that we—and she—always liked it (unless the fish were jumping).

The Quest for Fire: The Camp Stove

Even if you like to cook on an open fire, there will be times you'll want to use a stove. It's true that you can cook about everything on coals, but some meal preparation can be a little bit delicate, so it's easier to have a stove to assist you perform your culinary creations. Other things you have to consider are fire restrictions, no firewood, or wet firewood. Some sort of a stove is a must. There are many stoves to consider: small stoves for backpacking; big stoves for family camping; and liquid-fuel and gas stoves.

There are a number of good brands on the

market. I've used Coleman and Peak 1 for years. They were all I could afford when I was in college, so they've earned my respect the hard way. I still find them to be a wonderful value. These are stoves for the working person because they're not expensive.

Light Stoves

Light stoves are single-burner models. You can fix a good meal on one, but you are limited by the number of burners. Many campers cook one-skillet meals. Or they cook one course and eat it, then cook the next course and eat it, and so on. Other camp cooks simply boil a pot of water, dump in the prescribed amount into freeze-dried packages, stir, let sit for five minutes, and eat.

Stoves like these aren't meant for elaborate cooking.

Lightweight Packing Self-contained Stoves: A self-contained stove's big advantages are that it's small and it's all right there. There aren't any tubes, hoses, fuel-feed systems, separate fuel bottles, or other attachments.

I've had good luck with this style of stove. I've used both Peak 1 Feather and Feather Dual-Fuel stoves for quite some time. They've been all I needed to fire up a yummy meal in the wilds. These stoves are a wonderful value for the camper's dollar. They tuck away handily in your pack. There are nifty little legs that fold out for stability. You fill them up and they're good for a weekend of packing. They're quite easy to use, too: Pump, turn the knob, and light.

We never miss a chance to toast marshmallows if an outside fire is allowed. My wife Shari has "mallow" roasting down to a science, so we have special sticks for the occasion.

This Svea packing stove is thirty-five-plus years old. When it was new it was state-of-the-art. Now it seems temperamental and sees little use. Camping stoves have come a long way in the past few years.

The Feather Dual-Fuel is one of the best "self-contained" backpacking stoves on the market. It will burn either Coleman fuel or unleaded gas. This makes it cheap to run. I've used this stove for years without incident.

In days past many backpackers used Sterno and a GI Canteen Cup to heat canned foods or boil water for coffee or dried soups. Such a heating method is obsolete these days. Sterno is heavy and an ineffective fuel for packing.

Peak 1 also makes a multi-fuel stove. It's convenient because it will burn unleaded fuel, Coleman fuel, or kerosene. The Feather Dual burns Coleman fuel or unleaded gas. The Feather burns stove fuel only. I lean toward the Dual, because I hate the smell of kerosene (kerosene doesn't burn as hot either). I don't mind burning unleaded gas, however, because it's about one-fourth the cost of regular stove fuel.

The Feather and Feather Dual carry about eleven ounces of fuel. The stoves weigh between twenty and twenty-three ounces depending on the model. Filled with fuel, they are just under two pounds. The Feather Dual will burn unleaded or Coleman fuel on high for about an hour and five minutes.

The drawback to this style of stove is that gas in the tank can leak if you put it in your pack upside down. It's never happened to me, but I've seen it happen to others, so I've been careful. I store my stove in a Ziploc bag inside a cushioned pouch. I also keep it away from my clothing or sleeping gear. The fuel tank isn't large enough to cover you on extended trips, so you'll have to carry extra fuel.

Lightweight Packing Stoves with Liquid-fuel Bottle: A liquid-gas aluminum "bottle" and stove is almost one-half pound lighter than a self-contained stove. Depending on the length of the trip, you can carry a single large or small fuel bottle to meet your needs. Another advantage is your fuel bottle can be snugly sealed so there's little risk of a leak.

It takes a minute or two to fire up because you must connect all the stove parts. The handy part is you can pack everything neatly in your kit. It's not as bulky as a self-contained stove. I have to admit, I've never been a really big fan of this style of stove. It's somewhat temperamental, and you have to do a lot of adjusting and keep the valves clean. I don't like to mess with things like this. I like to take them out and have them work without any fuss.

The Peak 1 Apex is a good stove at a very good price. MSR, which is very well made, is a good stove but the last one I used was more temperamental than a sow grizzly with cubs. You can, however, boil a quart of water in about four-and-one-half minutes with it.

Lightweight Packing Cartridge Stoves: These petite stoves are light, easy to use, and burn very hot. They take up little space in a pack and are mostly trouble free. The drawback—or advantage, depending on how you look at it—is you have to pack an easy-to-use fuel cartridge(s), and you have empties when you are done.

Sometimes cartridge stoves can be slow starting on very cold mornings and at high altitudes. Most campers aren't out in really cold weather or at really high altitudes, so these disadvantages may be somewhat mitigated. I've used my Peak 1 DLX stove at 11,000-plus feet without a problem. I've also used it in fifteen-degree-Fahrenheit weather without a hitch. I have no experience with it at higher altitudes or in colder weather.

My DLX Stove weighs just over seven ounces. With a large cartridge, it weighs twenty ounces. Its electronic ignition means you don't have to worry about finding a match on cold mornings. It will burn for fifty-five minutes on high. At twenty degrees Celsius it will boil a liter of water in three minutes. That's about eighteen liters of water per cartridge.

If you want a very small stove, the Peak 1 Micro Stove weighs a little more than five ounces and will fit in the palm of your hand. Connected to a small fuel cartridge it weighs twelve ounces and will boil a liter of water in three minutes and twenty-seven seconds.

This is an older version of my stove. It will burn only stove fuel. The plastic case is a handy way to store this unit, but it would take up too much room when backpacking. When you pack, a soft pouch is a better way to carry your stove. (It's advisable to keep the stove tucked in a heavy-duty plastic bag inside the pouch.) If you carry a small funnel with your stove you'll never regret it.

This stove is fueled from a separate bottle of fuel.

This handy stove has an electronic ignition. Without the propane cartridge, it weighs a little more than seven ounces. This is fast becoming one of my favorite stoves; I've used this stove under a number of conditions without a problem.

Peak 1 has a new fuel that is quite promising. The company has mixed 70 percent butane and 30 percent propane to provide a fuel to enhance operation in cold weather and at high altitude. The cartridges can be removed and reused later. The cartridge's bottom provides added stability, which earlier cartridge stoves didn't have.

Small Stove Wind Screens: Wind will lessen the stove's ability to heat quickly and you'll waste a lot of fuel. You can buy stove skirts that are beneficial. Or you can wrap a piece of foil around the stove, which is what I do.

Larger Stoves

Nowadays you can buy a full-size two- or three-burner stove that will burn unleaded fuel, traditional Coleman (stove) fuel, or propane.

Whichever fuel you choose, though, it's important to be consistent with your stove and lantern fuel. You want to use the same type for each. Having one stove burn one fuel and one burn another is a mess and a mistake waiting to happen.

There are many good meals waiting to be cooked. My parents have had their two-burner stove for nearly thirty-eight years. My sister Laura and I went to a store called the Big Y in Medford, Oregon, with my dad when he bought it.

That stove seemed a little bigger, boxier, and more wonderful than any stove I've owned or ever will. Nostalgic imagination is probably playing fanciful games with me. There was something mystical about that old two-burner. When the stove came out, it was a sure sign we were going

This is the Micro stove. With a fuel cartridge it weighs about twelve ounces. This is my personal favorite.

I like to use a piece of foil as a wind screen.

camping and when we went camping it was a lot of fun. All those dollar pancakes were cooked on that stove.

The Rutter family stove was a Coleman green and the fuel tank was a cheery cross between candy-apple and Christmas red. I can't see either color without thinking about my family when I was growing up. That stove is stored in the box it came in. At the end of every trip, it was carefully cleaned and put away.

A Coleman stove can and should last a long time, if not a lifetime. It's been a prominent fixture at campsites across this country for more than half a century. (The first Coleman stove was marketed in 1923). Today's stove is a great camping value. In real-dollar terms, a Coleman stove today is probably cheaper than the model my parents bought. You can buy models a little more compact and a little lighter, but the important things have stayed the same. The stove will cook a fine meal. Take your kids when you go stove shopping. Make them a part of that wonderful, mystical stove-buying experience that will live forever in their imaginations.

Two or Three Burners: Most families can easily get by with a two-burner stove. That extra burner, however, is convenient if you have a large family, you want several main dishes at once, or you'll be cooking for friends.

The Peak 1 Xpedition Stove is a two-burner model for backpacking. This is an especially handy unit if there are several people in your party. You can whip supper into shape in no time. It's also a great unit for car camping, too. You'll be very pleased at how fast the Xpedition boils water!

This gas stove has an electronic ignition. Other than this it's almost a dead ringer for the stove my folks have used for the past forty years. It has served three generations of campers.

When I worked as a guide and needed to feed a group of hungry men at once, I was glad we had an extra burner, even if the flame on the third burner was a little weak. You may find that when all the burners are on, one burner doesn't get as much gas as the others and, thus, doesn't get as hot. I've talked to a number of guides and outfitters with similar observations when they ran a three-burner Coleman. Still the

A Coleman Guide Series 3-burner propane stove is attached to a refillable propane tank. A refillable tank makes using this stove very inexpensive. Propane is an easy, somewhat trouble-free fuel.

For extra economy, we use a small propane tank to fuel our stove and lantern.

extra flame was advantageous for many cooking needs and so what if it didn't get as hot as it should.

I have several two-burner models, and we've done fine.

Liquid-fuel Stove: A liquid stove is a good choice if you're going to use it a lot. All things being equal, buy a stove that takes unleaded gas and Coleman fuel.

Whether you use stove fuel or unleaded gas, a few gallons will last you a long, long time. If you're camping in a remote area for an extended stay and not coming out for supplies, this might be a good choice. The drawback is you'll have to pack flammable fuel that is dangerous if you don't handle it carefully. It also stinks if you spill it. You have to pour the fuel into the stove tank and that can be a real mess. Be sure to carry a small funnel (the same one you use for your lantern).

Do your pouring outside and away from open flames and your gear. It's also messy, and possibly dangerous, if you fill the tank right before you need to light the stove. When I'm using liquid fuel, I top off the tank in the morning or afternoon long before I need the stove. This way I have a full tank for dinner and breakfast. Even if I've barely used the stove, I still fill it. I also store my liquid fuel about 20 yards from the nearest campfire, tent, or food. The other trick to this type of a stove is to keep the pressure pumped up so the flame burns consistently.

I'm fond of the new electronic-ignition models. What an easy way to fire up breakfast. If you've ever lost your matches, gotten them wet diving for your kid's reel, or faced a savage wind, you know what I mean. All you have to

The Coleman Kitchen is easy to set up; so easy that a child can do it in a couple of minutes. My son Jon-Michael's job is to put it up; he can't go fly fishing until he does.

These clever campers have made their kitchen center. The only drawbacks are it's not freestanding, it takes up table space, and there's no place for the stove. Nevertheless it's well made and organized.

do is click the knob and you have flames. For me, this feature is well worth having.

Propane-fueled Stoves: Propane-burning stoves are the easiest to use. The flame is consistent, there's no messy fuel, and no pumping the tank. All you do is turn on the gas and ignite. For the family that camps only a few times a year, propane cartridges are probably the best way to go. Convenience is more important than paying a little more for cooking time.

All you do is screw in the cylinder, turn the knob, and light. You'll go through a few cartridges on a family outing, but you'll have trouble-free cooking. Propane isn't that expensive, but it does add up if you cook a lot. You also have to dispose of the empties properly.

If you camp a lot, you might want to invest in a refillable propane tank. It's easier, cheaper, and more environmentally sound. You can get your propane

It's really convenient to have a place to cook and keep your stove. We've never found anything more handy than the Coleman Kitchen. It's light and easy to set up. It's made cooking a lot easier and more organized. It also frees the picnic table for eating and visiting.

very cheaply this way, and you won't be buying two-to-five-dollar propane cartridges that burn out quickly. Consider a distribution tree with an 8-foot propane hose. This way you can run your stove and lantern off your refillable tank. All you have to do is attach the tree to the tank, run the hose to your stove, and put the lantern on top of the tree.

Pots and Pans

I've always loved camp cooking ware.

Maybe the reasons are I like to cook and I like to eat. When I'm camping in one place for a while, there's nothing I like more than trying new recipes. It's fun to impress your family with creative meals.

Whether you love to cook for its own sake or whether you cook simply because you have to feed yourself or your family, you need some basic cookware. So let's look at a few items you may find useful. Unlike sleeping bags and tents, which you can use only when you camp, many of these cookware items cross over nicely for use in your home kitchen.

Cast-Iron Skillets and Dutch Ovens

Cast-iron skillets and Dutch ovens weigh a ton, but they're the best stuff in the world to cook with. Cast iron is heavy, traditional, and wonderful—as long as you don't have to carry it more than 100 feet or so. Backpacking gear this isn't!

This is my forty-year-old cast-iron skillet. It's my favorite pan despite its weight—it makes the best pancakes in the world.

My mom taught us that cast-iron cookery was what all the best chefs liked. It allows the heat to spread consistently so you don't have cold spots in the pan. Another advantage—short of letting cast iron rust—is that it's nearly impossible to damage. You can set it over almost any heat source without any ill effects. You can set it in the flames, on the coals, over the coals, buried in coals, on a grill, on a stove, and in a stove.

If you make a big mess, you can chisel out the failure easily with a screwdriver. About all you need to do when you're done cooking is to clean out the skillet with a little hot water and a dish rag. If you have a real mess, maybe use a mild scrubber or a wok brush.

The worst thing you can do to cast iron is use detergent or soap. This takes out the "seasoning." The pioneers rubbed a few handfuls of sand on it (this method still works quite well, incidentally). If the pioneers had the water they'd rinse it. Once the skillet or Dutch oven was dry, they'd run a light coat of oil or grease over the inside. If you keep your cast iron greased (run a coat over the outside when the camping trip is over), your cookware will last several generations.

Shari and I have a 12-inch skillet that we've had since we were married. We use it at home and for camping. It's been very adequate for our family of four, although someday we'd like to get a 14-inch model.

A griddle such as this is a great help if you're cooking for a lot of people. It fits nicely over both burners.

The long, heavy duty handle on this fry pan makes cooking on a campfire much easier. It weighs about 25 pounds.

A Dutch oven is a versatile camp pan and cooking with it is an art form. There's almost nothing you can't cook in it. About the only way you can hurt it is with detergent.

A Dutch oven looks like an iron fry skillet with high sides and a lid. Many have three short legs on the bottom. A Dutch oven comes in sizes ranging from 8 to 18 inches in diameter. The 12-inch model seems to be very popular. Anything you can cook in an iron skillet you can cook in a Dutch oven. Anything you can do in a crock-pot you can do in a Dutch oven. You can, however, do much more with a Dutch oven. You can bake all sorts of cobblers, pies, cakes, and breads. Dutch ovens are also famous for the chicken and dumplings, beans, stews, and pot roasts they produce.

Retired Kitchen Stuff

For general camping, you can pick up some good buys at discount stores, yard sales, or thrift shops. Or if you're going to buy some new pots and pans for the house, keep some of your old cookware for the camping box.

If you're family camping, just about anything will work.

Aluminum Ware

Aluminum cookware is very light, which makes it ideal for backpackers and others concerned with weight. Aluminum gets warm fast, conducting heat twelve times faster than stainless steel.

If you get less-expensive cookware— and aluminum is pretty inexpensive as it is— you can easily burn your food until you get used to cooking with it. If you have the money, don't buy the cheapest aluminum cookware. Upgrade and you won't be sorry. When we were first married, we bought a thirty-piece cook kit, including aluminum cookware, for about four dollars. We replaced most of it before long or used it for target practice.

Lee is cooking Canadian bacon on a nonstick pan that was recycled from the kitchen. It will serve the car camper for years.

We still have one or two pieces left; however, we always felt we'd made a mistake by going so low-end. Paying a little more gives you a better product, and you'll be happier down the road. The lids fit better and are better made, the handles actually work, the pots and pans nest better, and the aluminum won't bend in your hand.

I think it's a good idea to have a skillet with a nonstick coating. This will save headaches in the long run. Cooking will be easier and cleaning will be a cinch. If you take care of it, it will last for years. We have one skillet that's nineteen years old.

Look for a pan with a detachable potlifter (which can be used on other pans, too).

Some of the best nonstick camping stuff, for the camper or backpacker, is made by Evolution Cookware. I read about it in *Backpacker*, where it won the editor's choice award. I tried it, and I wasn't disappointed in the slightest. We even use it at home. Evolution Cookware also has a nonstick micro-groove bottom to keep your pan from slipping on the stove, which is nice if you're balancing it on a small single-burner backpacking grate. Most important to me, though, is it's hassle-free cleanup. All you have to do is wipe the pot out and that's it.

When you get aluminum cookware, you'll be well served to buy quality pots and pans (you'll get lids that actually fit). Camp gear takes a beating, so it doesn't pay to buy the cheapest equipment.

These pots come in sizes ranging from one to three liters. I use the small set when I pack. We use the larger stuff when we family camp. The pans come as a system. You get a lid that fits both pans, a potlifter, a packtowl scrub pad/scrub cloth, and a mesh storage bag. For less than forty dollars you can get a one-liter sauce pan, a 1½-liter sauce pan, lids, and potlifter—all weighing a little more than one pound. It's a great deal.

If you're going to backpack, consider procuring a nonstick pan without a handle. The problem with handles, even folding handles (which are popular on a lot of backpacking skillets), is that the weight of the handle can tip the pan on a single-burner stove.

Camping Ovens

I've tried a few outdoor ovens in my time, and they work pretty well. The one I like best, though, is the Outback Oven. Light and simple, it was originally designed for backpackers. Nevertheless, it's great for general

The Outback fits over a burner and turns your stove into an oven. It's one of the most exciting camping items I've discovered in years. We've used ours frequently in the short period we've had it.

camping, too. In addition to being very light, it takes up little space and is easy to use.

You can bake about anything you'd bake at home in this oven. You can use a backpacking oven or a regular camp oven in a temperature-controlled oven. An aluminized fiberglass convection dome sits over the baking pan. The dome circulates hot air and concentrates the heat, then vents air through the top. It has a thermometer that rests on the pan lid and a defuser plate that sits on the burner. It all breaks down into a handy little sack.

We've baked breads, pizzas, brownies, and cakes, among other goodies. This is a neat little plus if you like baking.

Use a wad of grass to scrape out your plates and pans.

Odds and Ends

There are a few other odds and ends that you may want to carry in your kit.

For family camping I like to use antibacterial soap for dish washing. Dawn is our favorite brand and it can also be used as a hand soap. It doesn't have much of a scent and it's concentrated. Many campgrounds provide places for you to dump dishwater; in some areas a biodegradable soap might be in order.

Don't forget a nylon scrubber. Take along a Brillo or an SOS pad, too. A scrub brush with a soap-filled handle is also nice to have along. And don't forget a couple of plastic washtubs.

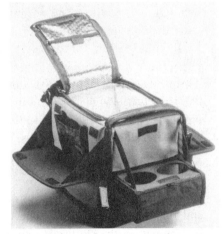

We've found soft-sided ice chests very handy. This Coleman Car Cooler, because there's some flex in the sides, fits very nicely into a cramped, overpacked vehicle.

Chapter 8

Knife, Hatchet, Saw, Flashlight, and Lantern: Equipment You Can't Do Without

There are pieces of equipment you can't do without. In this chapter, let's take a look at a few of the essentials that will make camping easier and more fun.

Knives and More Knives

Every camper needs at least one good knife.

There is nothing handier than a good blade. It's a tool every camper needs to carry with him or her at all times. You don't, however, need a sheath knife the size of a Roman sword: a simple pocket or folding knife will do just fine. The big sheath knives you see in frontier lore were carried more as weapons than as tools for camp chores. Jim Bowie might likely be disappointed, rolling over in his grave somewhere, but don't let it bother you. You don't need that much steel. Besides, you'll start limping to one side (big knives are heavy) and be the laughingstock of the campground if you go around with such ordnance. Go for something smaller.

My son Jon-Michael is getting a lesson on knife safety from Grandpa Rutter.

I've always loved a good knife and have the cuts and scars to prove it.

I got my first real pocketknife when I was seven years old, on my first official backpacking trip. It was a bone-handle Case pocketknife with four wonderful blades. My father honed one blade so sharp I could have shaved with it (if a seven-year-old had need of shaving). He told me not to use it unless he was around to supervise. The other three were pretty dull and were fair game for me to use anytime. I fancied myself quite a whittler.

As soon as he wasn't looking, I snuck away from camp, whipped out my forbidden blade, and started some serious cutting on a piece of pine. I wasn't watching what I was doing, and my hand slipped. I cut a neat 2-inch-long gash in the top of my

You can use the magnifying glass on a pocketknife to look at a leaf.

thigh. It didn't hurt much; the sharp blade did a clean job. Dad was good at sharpening.

I was a lot less worried about my lacerated leg, and possible infection, than about getting my knife confiscated. Besides, disobeying my father was a serious risk at best. I had no options I had to lie. 'Fessing up and telling the truth never entered my mind. I didn't want to lose that brand-new, now quite bloody, bone-handle, four-bladed Case pocketknife. Skin would heal.

I had only one pair of pants, so I dropped them to my ankles to keep the blood from staining them. I tied my bandanna over the "flesh" wound to stop the bleeding. My dad and uncle were fly fishing on the lake, so I snuck into the medical kit—clothed only in my undies—and doctored myself up. I dabbed the wound with disinfectant, gooped on some creamy stuff, and smothered the cut with bandages of various sizes.

I sewed up my pants with some butt leader for fly lines. It was so stiff I didn't need a needle. You could barely see the rip. Then I rubbed volcanic soil all over the front of my pants to hide the bloodstains. My mom discovered my nicely healing cut when we got home. She kept my dirty little secret.

I still have a wicked-looking scar from a wound that should have received about fifteen stitches, but I didn't lose that knife.

Pocket/Folding Knife

Every camper needs a pocketknife. It's your flagship tool, the thing you'll use more than any other.

I carry a small pocketknife on my person (in my left pocket next to a butane lighter). I've never been comfortable with a really large "pocket" knife. Besides wearing out pants, they're heavy.

A streamlined pocketknife with a 2-inch-long blade is my choice. For the past ten years, I've carried a Kershaw locking blade my father gave me for Christmas. It's too short to cut tomatoes well; I have, however, skinned and butchered with it. I've opened tin cans when I've been hungry and done about every

A knife is a tool no camper can do without. Find one that fits your personality.

other camp chore. It's easy to touch up on a steel or stone, and it keeps a razor-sharp edge.

There are a number of good knives on the market, and I've tried them all. In my old age, and after a lot of trial and error, I've settled on three brands that haven't disappointed me: Kershaw, Case, and Victorinox. My criteria for judgment are: Is it well made? Is it easy to sharpen? Will it hold an edge? Can working folk (like me) afford it? Will it take some abuse?

I'm a little skittish about knives with ultra-hard steel. I've owned Buck knives, for example, and I can sharpen them, but it takes a bit of effort. It's my belief that the average camper is better off with a softer blade that can be touched up with little effort.

I *always* carry an original Victorinox Swiss Army Knife on my belt or in my pack. Specifically I carry the Champ, the one with all the blades and gadgets. My buddies laughed when I first started carrying one. As each friend has had to borrow it for this or that, I've noticed that opinions have changed. In fact most of them are carrying a Champ these days themselves.

There are millions of uses for this knife. I discover more each time I use it. I wouldn't leave home without it. It's the handiest piece of hardware I own. I've started a fire with the magnifying glass, skinned an entire bear without sharpening the blades, even rebuilt spinning and fly reels, besides the obvious uses. The only thing I'm not sure about is the corkscrew because I don't drink. It's the only tool on the knife I'd replace.

You need a good knife. Carry it on your belt or in your pocket, but carry it. With the Champ you can saw wood, scale a fish, measure your index finger in inches or centimeters, trim your nails with the scissors, write a note with the pen, pull a splinter out with the tweezers, use the pliers to tighten the nuts on your tripod, and so on.

I always carry a knife, a lighter, and some sort of candle in my pocket. I like this knife because it's feather light and easy to sharpen.

I think a knife is the handiest tool a camper can carry. Except for the corkscrew, I've used every blade on this knife. I generally carry it on my belt in a leather sheath. It has a thousand uses. The blades hold an edge and are easy to sharpen.

Bigger Knives and Sheath Knives

Although a good pocket or folding knife will handle most situations, there are times when a large knife is in order. Simply put, you need a longer blade or a specialized blade to perform certain tasks. Try slicing a tomato delicately with a skinning knife or a two-inch-long pocketknife blade, for example.

An ax or hatchet has many uses besides cutting wood. Pounding in tent stakes is one of its many jobs.

Kitchen knives: A few good kitchen knives are handy if you're car camping or spending a lot of time preparing food. I don't think I'd rush out and buy new ones; instead, I'd borrow a few favorites from the kitchen drawer and let it go at that.

Campers who enjoy preparing gourmet camp meals will be lost without decent cutlery. Avoid a big Rambo-like sheath knife for your camp cooking kit. Such knives are too thick to be of much use for culinary purposes. They're meant for fighting bad guys.

If you're going to buy camp kitchen knives (or new ones for your home), look at those made by Chicago Cutlery. They're easy to sharpen and hold a good edge. I use them at home and while camping.

Fillet knife: If you catch and eat fish, a fillet knife is handy to have. A fillet knife has a thin, flexible blade designed for taking the fillets off fish. The blade is generally easy to sharpen and holds an edge rather well. If the blade is sharp, it also works well for kitchen use. I like a 6- to 8-inch-long blade. Rapala makes a good one.

Skinning knife: A skinning knife is designed to skin game. I've never been fond of long-bladed skinning knives; prefer shorter, easier-to-manage blades. My favorite skinning knives also have softer steel, so they're easy to sharpen.

Hatchets, Axes, Saws, and Shovels

Unless you're backpacking and weight is an issue, take along a hatchet or ax, a saw, and a shovel.

You can cut wood, shape a tent pole when your aluminum one snaps, pound in a stake, make a frame for a shower, construct a clothes-drying rack, clean up eye-poking branches, dig a latrine, level a tent area, dig a fire pit, and perform a hundred other chores with this equipment.

Furthermore, if you're going to camp in a single place for longer than three or four days, it's pretty hard to keep a fire going without the help of a hatchet. You'll have picked up all the easy wood that's close by. If it rains, it's downright difficult to get wood to burn without cutting or splitting it.

Hatchets and Axes

A good hatchet can last a lifetime. Select one that has a good piece of steel and a good handle. I prefer a wood handle because it feels good in my hand. A synthetic or a steel handle will serve you well, though, and you won't worry about replacing broken wood. Many old-timers, though, don't like anything but wood handles; if wood breaks you can carve yourself another handle in a pinch (something hard to do on those very rare occasions when something happens to your steel or synthetic handle).

A small folding saw is one of the most practical tools. It makes cutting firewood easy and safe. Remember to always use dead wood; it burns better and is easier on the forest.

I like a hatchet with a 14-inch-long handle, but you can effectively use one as short as 12 inches. I prefer also a curved handle, referred to as a "doe foot." This type gives me a better downward angle when chopping. I don't feel as comfortable with a straight handle. Pick up both types and see what you think. Select one that feels good in your hand. If you'd rather use an ax, select one with a 28- to 30-inch-long handle.

I like the steel wedge on either a hatchet or an ax to be on the thin side for the type of work I do. A thinner head is handy for camping, because it will cut deeply with less effort. I chopped wood every day from October until May when I was a kid, so I've learned what I like. You can get a good hatchet for less than $20 and a good ax for under $30.

If you aren't experienced with a hatchet or ax, cut wood with a saw. Then use your ax or hatchet as a wedge. Use a rock or another chunk of wood to pound the head of the hatchet into the wood.

Saws

A good-sized bow saw is a great joy in camp, but it's a little heavy and might eat up a lot of space in some camp settings. A big bow saw can do a bit of damage to a good-sized log, so you can keep a fire burning for a long time. If you're camping in one place for a long time, or it's very cold and you're burning a lot of wood, you'll appreciate a bow saw. Most outfitters, for example, have a big bow saw in camp.

A smaller saw, which is more practical for most camp settings, will work fine, but you won't be tackling the same size wood, nor will sawing be as easy. There are a number of small bow and folding saws on the market. Such saws will handily dispatch small wood, but you have to be a little more careful with the blades.

Coghlan's makes a lightweight folding saw that costs around $10. I've used mine for years. I carry a spare blade (which is inexpensive) in the truck for insurance. My saw is light enough to take backpacking, and I've used it all over this continent.

Cutting Wood

A hatchet or ax and a saw work in concert nicely. If you're car camping, take them both.

A hatchet is sometimes thought of as a dangerous instrument. I've heard of Boy Scout troop leaders not allowing their boys to use one. (I suppose they don't like skipping rocks, either.) Like any tool—a screwdriver, a gun, a power saw—a hatchet is only as safe or as dangerous as the person holding it.

I suggest that having a saw along makes using a hatchet safer. Most of the people I know who've been hurt with a hatchet have received injury while misusing it. To cut wood safely, consider the following:

1. With your saw cut pieces of wood (dead and fallen, of course) no thicker than your wrist and no longer than the length of your hatchet.

2. Use your hatchet as a wedge to split the wood.

3. Using another piece of wood or a rock, pound the butt of the hatchet— use it as a wedge—to split the wood.

Shovels

We use a folding shovel for all our camping needs. It collapses down into a compact unit and takes up little space. We keep the shovel stuck into the ground near the fire in case we need to reposition some coals or position a burning branch. It's also handy if a fire starts to get out of control. If you make your own latrine, a shovel is a valuable asset.

A folding shovel can be purchased at an army-surplus or sporting-goods store for less than $15. If you can, buy a case for it for a few dollars more. It will keep things in your kit from getting scratched up by the shovel blade.

Let There Be Light

You need something to light the way when the sun sets.

We'll break this discussion into flashlights and lanterns. Sooner or later you'll probably own both if you camp much. You can't survive, however, without a flashlight. A lantern is almost a necessity in a base camp, but you could do without it (at least for a while).

Flashlights

Stick with standard battery and bulb sizes; it's easier to find replacements. Buy high-end batteries, and carry some spares, along with a spare bulb or two. Some flashlights house a spare in the hilt. It's a good thing to check.

Small flashlights: I've owned a lot of flashlights over the years. I've lost my temper and thrown a lot of flashlights into the lake (metaphorically speaking, that is, because I'd never litter Eden). It's frustrating to depend on something only to have it let you down.

I've settled on Maglites because they've given me fewer headaches than any other brand. They cost a little more, but they're guaranteed. You don't worry about saving a few bucks when you're 9 miles from a trailhead on a moonless night and you can't find something. I also like Maglites because they have an

There are a number of different kinds of flashlights. Find one you like, and keep a spare set of batteries and a bulb nearby.

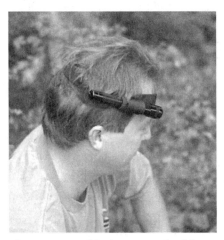

Strapping your Maglite to your head keeps your hands free. This is also a good way to read at night if the crickets are keeping you up.

adjustable focus, so you can make the beam tight or wide to suit your needs.

If you're a backpacker, you won't want the weight of a heavy light. I've used the Mini–Maglite AA (two AA batteries). It kicks out a really strong beam and weighs about four ounces. A few years ago I tried the Mini-Maglite AAA (two AAA batteries) to save weight. The AAA didn't have a satisfactory beam, but I thought I was saving ounces. I ended up weighing both lights and found only a one-half ounce difference. I switched back to the AA Mag. The only advantage was that the AAA light had a little longer staying power.

Obviously, the colder it gets the faster your battery juice dwindles. For the sake of comparison, let's say it's about sixty-five degrees Fahrenheit and you have brand-new batteries. According to my semi-scientific study, the Mini-Maglite AA will shine for about five hours fifteen minutes, and the Mini-Maglite AAA will shine for six hours seventeen minutes. At about ten degrees, each of the beams lasted just over an hour.

Larger flashlights: Although I like a small flashlight because it's so pocketable, there are times when a bigger flashlight is necessary. When weight isn't critical, I always pack a big flashlight.

Don't mix fuel supplies. Burn the same type of fuel for your lantern as you do for your stove. These are two of my favorites for backpacking.

When setting up a tent, looking for my daughter's lost doll in the grass, or searching for firewood, a powerful beam is nice. It's also nice to have a powerful beam if you have to check noises to reassure your kids that there's no bear in the campground.

I also use a Maglite for my large flashlight. I like the Maglite 3D (three D batteries). It lasts a little longer than the two-battery model. At about sixty-five degrees Fahrenheit the 3D Mag will light for almost seventeen hours; the 2D will shine for almost fifteen hours. At ten degrees the 3D will shine for just less than eight hours; the 2D light will shine for a little longer than six hours. The extra D battery also gives the 3D model almost thirty more units of candlepower. The 3D Mag has ninety-three candlepower. (Candle-power is the light's luminous intensity.)

During my informal tests, I've found any of the top batteries give me good service. If I have a choice, I'll reach for Duracell first, Eveready second (I don't like the bunny commercials).

Heavy-duty lights: Besides traditional flashlights, there are heavy-duty flashlights, lights that pack a six-volt battery. I have nothing against a bigger light. I've never needed one, though, with my 3D Maglite.

Lanterns

Since the early part of this century, the first and last word in lanterns has been Coleman. In 1902, the first Coleman lanterns revolutionized the industry. They're setting the standard today. Coleman has the market cornered whether you're considering propane, gas, or battery lanterns. It doesn't matter if you're looking at conventional-size or smaller packing lanterns; this company covers the playing field. Coleman brings you light at a price you can afford.

Let's take a look at large and small lanterns. Over the years, I've used every lantern in this discussion. I've had only one problem with a Coleman lantern, and that was about fifteen years ago. It was replaced instantly under warranty. Other than that one instance, I've never had a moment's complaint, and I've owned at least fifteen lanterns of different sizes and shapes over the years.

Lightweight packing lanterns: If several of us are backpacking—and we can spread out the weight among us—it's a given that we'll be taking a lantern. There's nothing cheerier than the light of a lantern, especially if you're hiking or fishing until dark and you need to set up camp or prepare a meal by moonlight. If you like to read a little at night, there's nothing better. In fact, several of these chapters were written by lantern light in Wyoming's Wind River Range and Utah's Uinta Mountains.

If you have to pack out at night, you have game down, or a person is lost, a strong light is a great joy. Peak 1, which is Coleman's backpacking line, has a couple

These lanterns light electronically—nice on a windy night or if your matches are wet.

This Coleman lantern is handy for instant light in a dark tent or when you come back to camp after dark. With the flick of the remote, you have light. It seemed almost too high-tech for me, but after I tried it (when my daughter had to go potty in the middle of the night and I couldn't find a flashlight), I liked it.

Store liquid fuel away from the camp fire and the cooking area.

of very good lanterns worth considering.

The first are fuel lanterns. Peak 1 has a model that burns stove fuel and another that burns both stove fuel and unleaded gas. (I'd get the dual model so that I could burn unleaded gas.) Both are well made and will give good service.

These lanterns weigh about twenty-eight ounces unfilled and hold eight ounces of fuel. Set on high, they'll give you a sizzling three-plus hours of light. Each has inner-coated tanks to resist corrosion. They both offer Instant Lite, which is nice because you don't have to struggle for matches to get the lantern going.

Very lightweight packing lanterns: Peak 1 also offers a couple of very light lanterns that attach to a fuel canister: the Micro Lantern and the Electronic Ignition Lantern.

The Micro Lantern stands 4.8 inches tall and weighs less than nine ounces. With the fuel cartridge, it's about 7 inches high and weighs about fifteen ounces. The light is equal to that of a seventy-five-watt bulb. It also has a rosette mantle that slides into place, so there's no tying.

The Electronic Ignition Lantern offers no-match lighting. Equal to an eighty-watt bulb, it weighs 13.1 ounces alone or 19.5 ounces with a cartridge. You get a touch more than four hours of light on the brightest setting.

Blended-fuel cartridges: In the old days I used to shy away from fuel cartridges. Once you had the cartridge attached to the appliance, you had to leave it there. Peak 1 has a triple-seal system between the resealable cartridge and the appliance, so the cartridge can be removed and attached later. This makes it really nice.

Another thing to consider: Peak 1 offers a fuel mixture of 70 percent butane and 30 percent propane. This makes firing up on cold days or at high altitude easier and more effective. You can get the cartridges in 6.5- and thirteen-ounce cans. The larger can is the better value, though; it costs about a buck more.

Bigger lanterns: I grew up with a battered Coleman lantern my parents bought in the 1950s.

I don't know how many mantles we used over the years, but our lantern was a

Set out your lantern early so you don't have to scramble for it at sundown.

workhorse. Many nights we did chores on our small farm when the electricity went out, or we looked for skunks lurking about the chicken coops. We used it whenever we had to work after dark or whenever a mare or cow needed our help during a difficult birth. We also managed to use it on numerous camping trips every year.

When you get a lantern, you can expect to get years of service from it. In a few years, my parents' lantern will be fifty years old. I think we've replaced about fifteen globes—which we seemed to break every couple of years—but the lantern itself is still in shining shape.

A lot of water has gone under the bridge since my folks bought their lantern. Nowadays, you have a lot of options to select from. You can get a lantern that uses kerosene, unleaded fuel, Coleman fuel, propane, or batteries. You can get the same basic model my mom and dad bought in the 1950s, or you can get one with all the bells and whistles.

You have a lot of options. The type of lantern you select will depend on your needs. How many times a year do you plan to camp? How long do you plan to camp in one area? While camping, how far will you be from supplies? How much are you willing to spend per hour to keep that lantern lit? How much hassle do you want to go through keeping your lantern lit?

Liquid-fuel lanterns: Liquid lanterns are probably the cheapest to run, especially if you buy one that burns unleaded gas. A single-mantle model, which is all I use in liquid-fuel lanterns, will burn a little longer than seven hours on high (about fourteen hours on low) on one tank (two pints). Thus it costs three to four dollars to run on high for fifteen hours (or twenty-eight hours on low). Burning your lantern on high costs about 25 cents an hour.

The basic design of the Coleman lantern was very good. There are, however, a few changes worth mentioning. For one thing, changing the mantle is now a lot easier. It clips on so you don't have to hassle with tying those awkward strings.

The NorthStar is my favorite model. It has a new electronic ignition that makes it easy to light. It also has a new pump system that's easy to use. It tells you when the right number of strokes has been achieved. Some other features are well thought out, too. The nut on the top plate stays attached so it won't get lost. (I don't have the original nut on any of my old lanterns.) There's also a wire guard on the globe to prevent it from breaking, and a wide skid-resistant bottom provides additional stability (this is really handy). Lastly, it's easier to change the mantle; the globe guard and the ventilator come off in one step.

A liquid lantern makes a lot of sense if you want to keep it running. A gallon or two of fuel will last you a long, long time. If you're camping in a remote area for a long time and not coming out for supplies, this might be a good choice. The drawback to this lantern is you have to pack flammable fuel, which is dangerous if you don't handle it carefully. It stinks if you spill it, too. You also have to pour the fuel into the lantern tank, so carry a small funnel to prevent messes.

Pour the fuel outside and away from open flames and your gear. When using liquid fuel, I top off every tank in the morning or afternoon long before I need them. That way I have a full tank come evening. It's a daily ritual I follow. I also store my liquid fuel about 20 yards from the nearest camp fire, tent, or food area.

Propane lanterns: Propane is the easiest and probably the safest fuel to use. It's also the most worry-free. You don't have to fool with pumping or pouring, and the light is constant until you run out of fuel.

You can fuel a propane lantern by attaching the lantern to a propane cartridge (there are various sizes) or by hooking a hose to a propane tank. The cartridge is an easy way to fuel your light. Cartridges aren't really expensive, but you burn through them quickly on high, so it's good to take a few spares. For the person camping a few times a year, this is a good setup. Using a cartridge makes your lantern mobile.

Propane is not as economical as liquid fuel, but it's not that expensive, either. My only caution is to dispose of your propane cartridges properly. They don't belong in the brush.

If you camp a little more often, as I mentioned in the stove discussion, you might consider purchasing a refillable propane tank and a distribution tree with an 8-foot propane hose. That way you can run your stove and lantern off the same fuel source. Attach the tree to the tank, run the hose to your stove, and hang the lantern at the top of the tree. The tank is refillable, so this is an inexpensive way to go. The only drawback is your lantern is stationary.

When we establish a base camp, we use a distribution tree. We have the lantern and stove in a central place, and cooking after dark is much easier. If we need to move about in the dark, we bring a second lantern or rely on flashlights.

Candle lanterns are popular among backpackers. Most are very light, and carrying a good supply of candlepower is no problem. These lanterns shed enough light to allow reading in a tent, but not enough to help you find the log where you left your reading glasses. The major drawback is they leak wax, and that's something you don't want to spill on your tent or expensive sleeping bag.

Chapter 9

Dressing for Comfort in the Outdoors:
The Age-Old Question of What to Wear

The key is comfort.

Dress for the weather you expect, but carry enough clothing so you'll be prepared if it's unseasonably hot or cold. In Yellowstone in June, for example, you need clothing suitable for temperatures ranging from twenty-five to ninety degrees Fahrenheit. It could be windy, wet, snowy, rainy, mild, or hot, or any combination of the above.

You have to be comfortable to enjoy the out-doors.

The trick is to have enough clothing to cover the situation, but not so much that you have to rent a U-haul to carry it. If you're car camping, of course, you have the luxury of packing a little more than you need. Our rule of thumb is to underpack for ourselves and overpack for the kids. Kids' clothes don't take up as much room anyway. It's better to have something than to wish you did.

Activities Help Determine the Clothes

What clothes you take depends partly on what you're doing when you get to camp. If you're going to canoe camp, for example, you'll want baggy clothing. If you're going to pack in on horses, you'll want heavy jeans. If you're going to backpack, you'll want shorts. If you're doing a lot of biking, you'll want bike shorts or tights. If you're rock hounding, you'll want sturdy clothing.

The Layering Concept

The best way to dress is in layers. Plan your clothing preparation around temperatures. That way you can balance and adjust your clothes to the weather. You don't want to be too hot or too cold; you want to adjust the layers as the temperature rises or falls or your physical activity increases or decreases. With layers, you can shed or add clothing as needed.

Remember that several light articles of clothing are equal to a heavy garment. The advantage is that layers are easier to manage and give you a wider comfort range. You aren't as likely to be too hot or too cold. You'll always have something appropriate for the conditions.

Always Have a Change of Clothes

You should always have at least one complete change of clothing in camp. If you take a watery spill, if a summer shower catches you away from your slicker, if your canoe turns over, or if your child potties all over you, you want something dry and—with luck—clean to wear.

An extra outfit will get some use if you're around water. This is doubly true for your kids. I've seen my daughter get several outfits wet in one morning.

What Clothes to Pack

No one agrees completely on clothing. I'll give you an idea of what my family takes on a general camping trip. You can use our suggestions as a guideline. If you're backpacking, you'll want to cut back because of weight concerns.

Don't get carried away, but have what it takes to handle the many faces of the environment. I don't mind dirty clothes, but I don't like to stink, even when I'm camping. I've never been so weight-conscious on a trip that I didn't have enough room for deodorant, soap, and shampoo. I swim whenever I can, and, unless it's really cold, I carry bottles, pans, and such into the bushes for some sort of shower every day.

Let me share some ideas.

The way to prepare for the weather is to dress in layers. It's better to have several layers than one heavy jacket.

To enjoy country such as this, you have to be ready for Mother Nature's mood swings. If you're prepared, you can weather about any storm.

Sometimes the natural look is the best. Always have a change of clothes for kids.

Clothes need to be comfortable. I've always liked a light long-sleeved cotton shirt for summer wear. I can roll up the sleeves if it's warm. If it's cool in the evening or the bugs are bad, however, I can roll the sleeves down.

Polypropylene Long Underwear

Don't leave home without 'em.

This article of clothing is often overlooked on summer trips and is one of the most important garments you can tuck into your kit. In the summer, I *always* carry a

Polypropylene

Polypropylene, a petroleum by-product, is hydrophobic, so it won't absorb water. It's a miracle fabric. It can be machine washed (usually in cold water) and will dry faster than polyester, cotton, or wool.

Polypropylene wicks water, sweat, and perspiration vapors away from your body. The heat from your body acts as a pump, pushing the moisture through the fabric into the next layer of clothing.

In addition to its wicking abilities, it provides some insulation, helping to prevent heat loss. Unlike cotton long johns, polypropylene won't act like an evaporative cooler.

pair or two of light to medium-weight polypropylene long johns. They weigh almost nothing and take up little room. The advantages are that polypropylene won't absorb moisture, it dries fast, and it wicks water and sweat away from your body (your body heat drives it out).

If a sudden snowstorm blows in, polypropylene long underwear goes under my regular pants or fleece pants. If I get cold sleeping, I slip them on to increase my bag's temperature range. If I wash my pants or they get wet and are drying, I wear long underwear.

There are a lot of poly manufacturers. They aren't all equal. I'm really impressed by Lifa, Helly-Hansen's long johns. (I'm not the only one impressed with Lifa; about 80 percent of my "extreme" hiker, skier, climber, and winter-camper friends wear Helly.) It's the best stuff on the market. And get this: It's guaranteed for life! A set might cost you two or three dollars more than those made by another manufacturer, but with a lifetime guarantee, I think they're worth it. I've heard that some Lifas are eighteen years old and still going.

Helly-Hansen spins about the best poly yarn out there. Many poly fibers retain odors. I've been on

Long underwear is the first key to staying warm. If you start to get warm, roll up the sleeves and open a few buttons. Polypropylene is the best material for wicking away moisture.

long, cold packing trips where I thought freezing to death was preferable to the water buffalo smell of my tentmates after ten days on the trail. Traditionally, poly fibers retained many salts and lots of foul smells. Lifa, however, during manufacturing removes some of the oils that absorb smells so it isn't as prone to "fragrance." Obviously you should wash your poly according to your manufacturer's instructions. If they're ripe, though, throw a cup of vinegar into the wash. That should take care of the smell.

One thing about poly is it will pill up. You have to live with it. It'll look pretty worn, but that's the nature of the beast. If you like to parade about in your underwear like the folks in fancy fly rod and shotgun ads, you'll look a bit worn down. Pilling won't hurt the performance, though.

In colder weather I take a pair or two of medium-weight long johns (such as Helly Life Thermal). In very cold weather I wear Life Prowool (a poly-wool blend). I wouldn't be caught dead with cotton long johns (in summer or winter) more than a

Long underwear is critical on a cold day. The temperature may be well below zero, but you can be comfortable if you layer properly.

On this pack trip in the redwoods, the climate changed on the hour. I like a thin cotton shirt with long sleeves I can roll up or down as the temperature or bugs dictate. I'm very fond of long pants that can zip into shorts when the conditions demand.

block from camp. Cotton absorbs water and will chill you when wet. If you're hanging around a car camp, the cotton stuff works fine. It's not good to wear it for any other kind of serious camping or outdoor activity.

I'll often wear long johns under my walking shorts on cool mornings. I'll sometimes throw in a pair of running tights, too. You can move easily in them, especially on days too cold for shorts. I've used my tights (which are a heavier poly) as long johns. I've also slipped my lightweight long underwear on underneath my tights.

Undies

Can I talk about this in a family book?

I'm not sure I want to—or should—but here goes: How about one pair per day! Or some way to wash 'em. You can live with dirty pants, but it's nice to have clean drawers.

If you have younger kids, especially if they're potty training, you might need a myriad of undies. When my daughter was potty training, she went through four to ten pairs a day.

Disposable Diapers/Training Pants

I guess these are clothes.

Buy more than enough before you leave home. If you get to Very-Small-Town, Montana, Wyoming, Arkansas, or North Carolina, don't expect to find your favorite Huggies or Pampers. Odds are most little towns won't have them. If they do, they'll likely be the wrong type. Your little boy will be wearing pink before the trip is over. You can also expect to pay about double the price.

Shari's rule of thumb is this: If you think you need two packs of diapers, get three. (The same holds true for formula.)

Socks

I talk about socks in detail in Chapter 11. Let me say,

though, that good socks are expensive but worth-while if you're doing much hiking, especially if you're backpacking. I'm partial to the Rohner brand. They're very soft and made for hiking comfort. They wick moisture and can be worn for a couple of days without washing. Even though these socks can be worn alone, I prefer wearing polypropylene liners.

Pants

Long pants for summer: In the summer I always pack jeans or cargo pants. Yes, they're cotton. Experts tell you never to wear that "damn killer" cotton. There are drawbacks to cotton, but I like it. I wear cotton while car camping, backpacking, canoeing, horse packing, and so on. I've worn cotton pants from Alaska to Colorado to Texas. I once wore the same pair of Levi's on a packing trip for three weeks without washing them (that's scary to reflect upon).

If I get my pants wet and it's cool out, I'll slip on poly long underwear. That way the wet cotton does not act like an ice pack on my legs. If the day is wet, I wear knee gaiters. I've had a few problems, and I like how cotton feels. It also breathes well in hot weather.

Tip: I prefer darker colors that won't show dirt. Spray your cargo pants or jeans with Scotchguard before leaving on a long trip. It will make them water- and stain-resistant.

In the past few years I've switched to cargo pants because the cotton is fairly thin and it dries quickly if wet or washed streamside. Cargo pants have a lot of pockets and are loose and comfortable. They're also very compactable. I can easily pack two pairs for every pair of Levi's. They can be purchased from any out-door catalogue (Cabella's, Orvis, L. L. Bean, Bass Pro). Some have zip-off legs and become shorts. Traditional Levi's can act like a sponge, but are useful if you need a heavy pant such as in brush or thorns, for rocky terrain, or in snake country. I've worn Levi's for years.

If it's cold, you can spend the day in the sleeping bag. An early snowstorm and an accompanying chill caught us by surprise, so my wife Shari spent a lot of the day huddled in her bag.

My son Jon-Michael reels in an 18-inch-long cutthroat on Yellowstone Lake. It's mid-June but quite cool, especially with the lake wind. He's wearing a double set of long johns and thick socks.

A friend fell into the lake trying to get into a canoe. All his clothes were wet and he didn't have anything to change into. Fortunately he was able to borrow a set of sweats while his pants dried.

If you have kids in diapers or training pants, take more than you think you'll need on your camping trip. They may be hard to come by in a small town, and they'll certainly be more expensive.

Tip: If you roll your pants up tightly, you'll save space when you pack your kit bag.

Tip: Save tight pants for your local disco. When you're camping, loose pants will be more comfortable and more practical. This is especially critical if you're hiking or canoeing. Get 'em loose and buy a belt. Don't forget you need enough room to slip long johns on underneath.

Cooler-weather pants: If the weather is cool or cold, I'll switch to wool pants. I like worsted wool; the tighter the weave the better. Such a weave will prevent a lot of grasses, sticks, and weeds from collecting on your pants, too. Wool can be a bit heavy when wet, but even completely wet (absorbing about 33 percent of its own weight), wool will retain almost half of its insulating value.

Sweats: Sweats are handy to have around camp. They're great to sleep in, and they make handy runabout garb. I normally wear 100 percent cotton sweats at home, but for camping, I use sweats that are at least 50 percent acrylic. Not only are they cheaper, they make a lot more sense for camp wear. Sweats are like sponges when they get wet. If you get an acrylic blend, they dry quickly. They're also about half the weight and half the price as all-cotton.

Lately, I've become partial to fleece. They weigh almost nothing, they're very warm as long as you're not exposed to the wind, and they dry quickly. Fleece is also nice to slip into on a cold night. Wear your fleece under your rain or regular pants on a cold or wet day.

Shorts: In the summer I pack a couple of pairs of shorts. For me anything above freezing can be shorts weather if I'm hiking. I usually wear the light cotton cargo-type design or cutoff Levi's. Shorts don't take up much space and are a great way to beat the heat. Besides, shorts are the hiker's and backpacker's traditional garb.

If you wear shorts, smear on the sunscreen. You'll get fried if you don't.

Shirts

Light summer shirts: Even in the summer I like very thin cotton long-sleeved cargo shirts with lots of pockets (handy for film, fly boxes, baby's pacifier, notebooks, peanut-butter sandwiches, and small teddy bears). You can order shirts like these from any outdoor catalogue. They cost about $25 and last forever. If the catalog has a fishing model, which has a high, flip-out collar for protection against the sun, you might want to consider buying it.

A thin shirt is very cool and dries quickly if wet. If you roll up the sleeves, it's like a short-sleeved model. I like long sleeves for a number of reasons. They provide good sunscreen, good bug protection, and a hedge against an evening breeze.

T-shirts: I love cotton T-shirts. They're an important part of my summer camping wardrobe. I always take along a couple of my Ts from country or rock concerts I've been to. They bring me luck. My favorite Ts (I've caught very large fish or have seen bears while wearing them) include the following: Jethro Tull, Reba, Led Zeppelin, Willie Nelson, Neil Young, Garth Brooks, George Jones, Dave Matthews. You get quirky about your favorite shirts when you camp. They're good-luck charms, and you're sad when they wear out. My Led Zeppelin shirt is now retired. I wore it as I floated in a pod of killer whales (or, more politically correct, orcas), when I caught a seventy-pound salmon on Alaska's Kenai River, and when I saw two big Kodiak bears.

Heavier shirts: I love flannel shirts and wear them if I'm car camping. They feel good, but they're not going to do you any good if you get them wet. When I pack, I always include a heavy wool, acrylic, or fleece shirt.

I've used wool shirts for years, but lately I've shifted to fleece. Both come with a

Having extra clothes, especially an extra pair of thick socks, can make life outdoors very pleasant.

Shorts are a must if you are going to do much wading. Make sure you bring sunscreen so you don't get sunburned. If you're around water a broad-brimmed hat and sunglasses are a must.

Levi's are great summer wear. They breathe and are great around thorns or, in this case, marsh grass. Our good friend, Dave Card, co-author of Fly Fishing Made Easy, *with bass.*

Shorts, sandals, and not another person in 100 miles. There's nothing like camping in the desert.

price tag. I like fleece because it's lighter and has great insulating qualities if it's worn under a windbreaker. Without a windbreaker, wool will keep you warmer in the wind. Wool will also insulate when wet, but it's heavier and takes forever to dry. Wet fleece can be wrung out and dries quickly (it's also light). It insulates when wet, too. Acrylic shirts are not as expensive. They're pretty warm and dry quickly.

Even in the summer, I always take a heavy shirt. In colder weather I pack at least two heavy shirts.

Shoes

You'll want a change of footwear. I like to hike in boots, but around camp, I enjoy wearing a pair of running or deck shoes. If I'm near water, I wear Tevas or an old pair of sneakers. Unless I'm in a swimming pool, I like to have something on my feet. When I go backpacking, I always have a pair of Tevas strapped to my pack. I wear them around camp, when I go for a short hike, or when I swim.

There are a number of good walking shoes. You need to get what's comfortable. I wear New Balance because they fit my feet well and offer excellent support. New Balance accommodates foot sizes that other manufacturers, such as Nike, have ignored.

Tip: If you're canoeing, wear shoes that can be tightened or laced. You don't want them to come off in the water or when you're walking on muddy banks (details in chapter 11).

Windbreakers

A light windbreaker is an important part of every camper's kit. A windbreaker protects you from the wind so your body heat isn't sapped.

A breaker over a shirt might be enough. You might want to wear it over a sweater, fleece, or down vest. My light Helly-Hansen rain jacket is my windbreaker (and rain gear). If you have only a poncho or a heavier rain parka, a separate windbreaker is a very good idea. Windbreakers need to be very light, and they're inexpensive.

As a rule of thumb, you can figure a good windbreaker/rain shell will add about fifteen degrees of warmth to whatever is under it. If you're in a Yukon windstorm where you figure in the wind chill factor, a windbreaker will add more warmth.

Down Vest

Nothing beats a down vest. Every camper needs one sooner or later (unless you're allergic to down, like my wife). A down vest is warm and will be an appreciated part of your kit. It will scrunch to nothing and fit almost anywhere. It will keep you toasty under a windbreaker or jacket. It's a jewel in a sleeping bag on a cold night. I can't sing its praises enough.

You don't need to buy an expensive vest, even a cheap one will work nicely. If you're allergic to down, consider a Micro-loft (synthetic down) vest. You can get a Hollofil or another synthetic fill vest, but they're heavier and not as compactable.

Stocking Caps, Hats, and Gloves

In the winter it's certain that you'll need all of the above. I suggest, though, that they're handy anytime you're camping. If you're camping with your kids, it's very important that each child be equipped accordingly.

Stocking caps: No matter what type of camping you're doing, a warm cap is a must. I learned how valuable these items were a few years ago in Canada in the mountain country. I was chasing bears in a T-shirt during late May. The weather was in the high

A good walking/running shoe is okay for gentle trails or short hikes. For longer hikes a heavy boot is more comfortable.

A down vest or a down sweater as pictured here, is a nice addition to your layering.

When it's warm, cotton is the fabric of choice because it will hold moisture and keep you cool.

T-shirts are standard garb during summer.

Abbey dabs suds on her nose while working on the wash.

seventies or low eighties, and the nights were mild. The next morning the wind came up, and a cold front shot in from the Arctic. The temperature dropped radically. By midnight the water in my aluminum pot was mostly frozen solid.

I woke up as cold as a polar bear on ice; my feet were especially chilled. I had set up a spike camp in the bush, and most of my gear was back at the main camp on the Clearwater River. My bag wasn't warm enough for that weather. I put on a pair of gloves, socks, and a cap. They made all the difference.

You lose a lot of body heat from your head.

Tip: Remember what Mom used to say, "If your feet are cold, put on a hat." If your kids get cold, have them put on a hat. If you get cold, do likewise.

An inexpensive stocking cap works great. Dollar for dollar it's one of the best camping investments you can make. It works wonders under a hood, inside a sleeping bag, or worn alone. Most of the less-expensive hats are made of acrylic, which works well, or you can spend a little more and get wool. I'd recommend that whatever you get, try to find a hat with a tight weave.

I've used both acrylic and wool hats for years. As I mentioned earlier, I've shifted to polar fleece. Fleece is light, doesn't absorb water, and is very soft on my delicate ears. I'm also slightly allergic to wool. Fleece doesn't make me sneeze or itch.

A good windbreaker, such as this rain parka from Helly-Hansen, will provide about fifteen degrees of additional warmth.

Nothing beats a fleece jacket. It keeps you warm while waiting for that perfect shot.

Tip: Don't overlook a balaclava or a full-coverage cap for sleeping. I have a fleece balaclava I wear in cold weather.

Hats: You want a good hat. It keeps you cool or warm. Most important, it keeps the sun out of your eyes, which is as important in winter as in summer. Wear whatever's comfortable—a baseball cap, cowboy hat, or fly-fishing hat—and keeps the sun off.

Kids should all have hats that fit; encourage them to wear them during the sunny part of the day.

Gloves: Every camper should have a pair of gloves. Inexpensive cotton jersey ones will do. Light wool gloves are even better. Cover up your hands when it gets cold. I always pack a light set of army wool gloves.

I frequently take a pair of leather gloves, too. Besides keeping your hands warm, they're great for unloading gear, collecting firewood, or camp cooking.

Chapter 10

A Camper's Rain Gear:
What You Need to Know about Staying Dry

Having rain gear handy is as important to the camper as the ark was to Noah.

You never know when you're going to need it; it's a necessary piece of equipment for any outdoor adventurer. Rain can put a "damper" on anything you want to do unless you're prepared to meet it on its own terms.

You Must Have Rain Gear

How good your rain gear has to be, however, depends entirely on where you plan to camp, how much you plan to do in the rain, and the current state of your checkbook. Although some might disagree, I believe that any rain gear is better than none at all.

You'll know how good your rain gear is if you spend much time in the Pacific Northwest. My wife, Shari, is walking the Oregon dunes in a summer drizzle that lasted several days.

Even the cheap plastic stuff, which lasts only hours (instead of days), is better than nothing. Even a plastic garbage sack can pinch-hit in an emergency.

If you love the outdoors and you plan to do much camping, decent rain gear is something that you'll consider sooner or later. Although the cheapest rain suits will work, in the long run they cost more, weigh too much, and won't be as dependable—or as ecologically sound. You use them once, maybe twice, and then they're trashed.

One summer at Glacier Park several years ago, we experienced an unseasonable amount of rain for several days. I noticed that every $16 plastic rain suit at every convenience store, gift shop, and concessionaire had been purchased by anxious tourists who didn't want the wet to keep them from seeing the sights. The park looked as if it had been invaded by an alien troop in clear plastic. On the morning that it cleared up for good, we slept in and were getting a late start. Most folks in the campground had pulled out. I took a load of garbage to a bin and found it stuffed with shredded rain suits. Later at a picnic spot I found the garbage so full of dead $16 rain suits that I had to find another can. If I had to pay $16 every time it rained, I couldn't afford to leave my house in Utah.

You'll do some serious thinking about false economy and rain gear when you have to pitch a tent by flashlight in the driving rain. You'll reflect pensively when nature calls at 3:00 A.M. and you have to face a gushing deluge and 6-foot-wide puddles when you do a 200-yard dash for the campground's outdoor toilet.

Disposable Rain Wear

A plastic rain suit will run you from $9.00 to $16.00, but you'd better carry some duct or electrician's tape to fix the numerous rips. Plastic suits fall somewhere between a garbage sack and a shower curtain. They have those awful plastic buttons that hardly snap without pliers. When you do get them buttoned, they're welded for life. They'll rip before they come undone. The legs are always a foot too long, so you have to roll them up (no matter what size you buy). Most don't have hoods, so your head gets wet. And never try to put one back in the cute little pouch it came in. Once you take it out it magically multiplies in mass, defying any sort of future folding. When you chuck your suit in desperation, you'll note that it takes half a garbage can to hold what at one time fit neatly, albeit heavily, in your pack.

This rain wear is stiff and restrictive; an Apollo space suit would be more maneuverable. Plastic suits rip easily on anything larger than a grass blade but are rather heavy for what you're getting. If you look at them wrong they tear, and they always tear in the best spots for getting you really wet. You always resolve after you wear one of these things that you're going to get some real rain gear as soon as you get home.

In an emergency such stuff is better than nothing, for a short time. Don't plan on its lasting or being very effective over several rainy days.

I'm not a fan of plastic rain suits, but I think highly of the disposable, petite plastic rain poncho. It doesn't pretend to be any more than it is: an emergency poncho. It's about as thick as a thin garbage sack. It's about the same size, but it has a hood and it's poncho shaped. It costs

A light poncho is inexpensive and will keep you dry. It also serves as a windbreaker, a ground cloth, and a mosquito shield.

about a dollar (Quick-cover Poncho by Rainfair is the brand I use), fits into your shirt pocket, and weighs as much as a large pack of gum. All Rutter day packs and backpacks carry one. Plastic ponchos are made for emergencies—when it rains cats and dogs but the sky was blue when you left (and the weatherperson said no showers).

If I go camping or backpacking, I always have some sort of rain gear. This sort of product wasn't designed to be a full-time rain poncho. It's the perfect product for getting caught in a shower when you're hiking. The plastic is thin and tears easily, but it does have a hood and it's long enough to work. I've used one all day and didn't get wet, but by evening I'd torn a few holes in it. Unlike the rain suit, the poncho can be disposed of handily.

Rain Suit versus Poncho

You can go two ways. You can use a rain suit (jacket and pants) or a poncho.

Rain Suit

It doesn't matter where you go, a good dose of rain can shut your camping party down if you aren't prepared to meet it.

If you camp frequently in the Northwest or the Northeast, or you're planning a trip to Alaska or British Columbia, good rain gear is a necessity. If you camp at higher altitudes, even in more arid states such as Utah, rain gear is a must. Big mountains attract a lot of water.

This is a Helly-Hansen Deep Water Jacket. Not only is it breathable and waterproof, making it a fine raincoat, but it's also an excellent windbreaker. I use the garment as my outer shell during the winter. Notice the mesh inside; it will keep you cool in the summer.

I use an unlined rain shell (which will add ten to fifteen degrees of warmth). As I mentioned in the clothing discussion, my rain parka doubles as a windbreaker to save on weight. I've learned that it's best to buy your parka fairly large so it fits nicely over all your clothes, including your jacket. Not only will it keep you dry, it will act as a final shell, and it won't hamper the loft of your other clothing.

I generally want my raincoat to be extra, extra, extra large. I'd rather have it too long than too small. Besides, I like a lot of air to circulate down the arms and the neck and up the bottom of my coat. That way I can wear it on warm, wet days. If the rain jacket isn't breathable, the looseness helps keep me from being wetter inside than out.

I use a Helly-Hansen Deep Water Jacket. I've worn it in Alaska for day after day of rain without a leak. It's about the best thing I've ever owned. It's not made from Gore-Tex, but from Helly-tech. The fabric has been treated with a microporous coating that lets body-heat vapor escape but keeps out rain, snow, and wind. My jacket was designed for fishermen. The sleeves shut with Velcro, the zippers are very durable, the hood has a bill. After all the rain and snow I've worn it in, I can't sing its praises enough. It didn't come cheap, but I'll have it for years.

A while back, I bought a set of Deep Water bibs to go with it. There's not much I can't weather now. I feel like a duck in a rainstorm. I ski in the bibs and wear them inside my waders when I fish.

Another outfit I recommend is the Hansen Impertech rain suit. It was designed for fishing, but it's a great all-around rain suit. Shari has one and it's very comfortable. It's a waterproof stretch fabric: a soft knit backing and elastic polyurethane coating. It has a 200 percent stretch factor. It's very soft and offers wonderful movement. The material is very light and quiet and will stand up to a lot of washings (don't use Deet insect repellent around it, however). The coating won't wear out. Machine wash and put in a *low*-heat drier for about seven minutes and it's re-waterproofed.

Here are a few things to look for if you want bells and whistles in your rain jacket. You want one with a good hood: a hood with some sort of a brim, a hood that will cinch down if necessary. You don't want to pack a rain hat. You want a jacket with lots of pockets so you can store stuff—such as candy bars, fresh diapers, stuffed toys, gloves.

Another thing to look for is a mesh liner inside your jacket, which will help keep you cool. Pit zippers are also nice. I like lots of Velcro and cinch cords to batten down the hatches. Even if your jacket is rather large, you can still cinch it up to keep out a cold wind or a driving rain.

Poncho

A poncho is a handy piece of gear, a good second best, but it will never be as handy as a good rain suit. A lot of writers, I've noted, don't like them. A poncho is good for that afternoon rainstorm, for the

During a rainstorm, this yurt looked inviting. A yurt is a round tent with hard sides. The campers at this site spent several days inside; they had no rain gear.

occasional day of rain, and for a drizzle.

A poncho isn't the rain gear you want if you have to be out in the weather all day. If ponchos were great for working outdoors, you'd see workmen wearing them instead of rain suits. If you have to hike all day in a poncho, your pants will be wet thigh-high before long (never mind how fast you'll get wet if you have to go through wet brush or grass).

I've used a poncho for years. If you hike the high mountains, where a thunderstorm is a possibility any afternoon, it's good insurance. Alpine thunderstorms are fierce in the summer, but they usually don't last long. Sitting huddled in your poncho will keep you dry. A poncho will also double as a small ground cloth (especially if it has grommets), a lean-to, or a sun shield.

When it rains continually, you'll wear your rain gear even when the rain has stopped. Every branch and blade of grass is moist and waiting to get you wet.

It's also a good piece of survival gear. On more than one night I've sat huddled in my poncho next to a fire. A poncho can serve as a good emergency windbreak.

A good lightweight polyurethane nylon poncho weighs about fourteen ounces and costs less than $20. Make sure the poncho you select is made of rip-stop nylon. Some ponchos are heavy duty; the nylon is thick, so the weight factor is increased substantially. They wear a little longer, but I'd rather have a very light, thin garment that I'm more likely to carry. Besides, rip-stop nylon—even thin stuff—is pretty tough.

You'll also find some ponchos that are a little longer in front and quite a bit longer in back. In fact the back section is so long that it snaps back inside itself. These are so-called backpacking ponchos. The back flap is extra long so that it can fit over a backpack. There are a number of sizes; don't get one too long, as I did. Even with a backpack, the back dragged on the trail. When I wore it without a pack, with the extra length snapped up, it caught on every low branch and stick and came undone.

Chapter 11

On the Trail of Outdoor Footwear: Boots, Boots, and Walking Shoes

For some people, locating a perfect pair of hiking boots is more difficult than finding true love. I'm glad to report that I've been fortunate in both departments. Shari and I have camped happily together for the past twenty-five years and we're still best friends. Coincidentally, we've been wearing Vasque hiking boots about that long, too.

A Boot Must Feel Good

There's a lot of hype about footwear (and love for that matter). When you get down to it, *comfort is everything!* A good pair of boots is an important part of your outdoor gear, especially if you like to walk. Good footwear increases your outdoor enjoyment.

You don't, however, want to overdo a good thing. Every pound you wear on your feet is equal to five pounds carried on your back. Besides comfort, you want a boot that is lightweight, gives good support, and is sturdy.

It doesn't matter what Madison Avenue is selling or what's the latest boot trend. You must have something on your feet that feels good and treats your 250,000 sweat pores with respect. A boot is like a policeman; it's there to protect and serve. A pair of good boots isn't cheap and must be a good value. If you take good care of your boots, they'll last you faithfully for years.

Select a Boot That Meets Your Hiking Needs

The style you select will depend on where you hike, how often you hike, and how much you carry in your pack. For instance, if your outdoor game plan calls for hikes over various types of trails and some backpacking, you want a good general-purpose trail boot that's designed for medium to heavy-duty hiking and back-

A hiking shoe must feel good. This packing trip was the first time my son Jon-Michael wore tennis shoes and not boots. Although his pack wasn't very heavy, he complained of sore feet the entire trip. He didn't have the support he needed to walk comfortably along a rocky trail.

Without proper footwear, you might spend more time resting on a comfortable rock than hiking. Even children need a shoe that gives them good support.

packing; such a boot will be somewhat rigid, with good support, yet not too heavy. There are a host of other more specialized boots, too, designed for technical extremes, climbing, scrambling, mountaineering, glaciers, trail running, and so on. Manufacturers have footwear to fit just about every outdoor niche.

If you spend a lot of time around camp and hike only gentle trails, a good running shoe or a soft high-top trail boot might be a suitable choice. If you plan to do heavy backpacking with a large load over tough terrain, you need a stout boot that gives you a great deal of support and is rather rigid (understandably, such a shoe will weigh a little more).

I'd like to make an observation regarding running or athletic shoes. They work very well on trails as long as you don't push their limits. If you're hiking up steeper trails or trails that are strewn with sharp rocks, running shoes have drawbacks.

Let me explain. I'm writing this chapter after taking a long hike with my good friend Kirby Cochran. We just returned from hiking the trail to Mt. Timpanogos near our homes in Orem, Utah. There is quite a lot of vertical climb to reach the 11,800-foot peak.

I asked Kirby to wear an excellent pair of running shoes as we hiked the trail. I

Help Your Boots Last

❑ Keep your boots well oiled. This keeps the leather soft and happy!

❑ Don't dry your boots too close to the camp fire, and don't warm your feet by sticking your boots close to the fire. Your boot should never get too hot to touch comfortably. Not only will too much heat dry out the leather and harden it, such heat can also be detrimental to the glue in your boot.

❑ Don't allow dried mud to stay on your boots. It dries out and hardens the leather.

❑ Clean your boots after every trip and apply a coat of oil.

wore my boots. A few days before, he'd climbed the same trail in hiking boots. I wanted him to compare the two. I need ankle support on the trail so I declined to do this experiment with him.

Kirby is in fantastic shape, a veritable mountain goat on the trail. The fact that he's always training for a marathon and is about 6 feet 5 inches tall may have a lot to do with why I run to keep up with his stride. As an interesting aside, I found that after a mile or two, I was keeping up better than usual.

Here are Kirby Cochran's observations after hiking the steep trail in running shoes.

"On the first part of the trail, where it stays fairly flat, I didn't notice much difference. Once it turned steep and rocky, I bumped my ankles a few times, and I noticed in the shade where the soil was damp, I wasn't getting very much traction. I found my legs getting tired, and I wasn't making good time.

"After a few more miles, I was starting to feel the sharp rocks more acutely, and I was walking more cautiously than I normally do; I was afraid of getting an injury 7 miles from the trailhead. At about 9,000 feet we started to get into snow and I was slipping all over. I had to tiptoe over the 30 or 40 streams that crossed the trail so I wouldn't get my feet wet. Coming down the steep stuff, I needed more stiffness. Once I hit the flat part of the trail, it was easy going."

Most of us have tender feet, and we feel inclined to take care of them. If your feet hurt, you're not having a good day. There are a few

New Balance makes a good hiking shoe that absorbs a lot of shock. For gentle trails, it's a good choice. Several of us sort the flies we'll use for that day on our shoes or boots (it's good luck).

Tevas are great for knocking about camp and near water. For longer hikes, though, they might not provide enough ankle support. With the added weight of a child on my back, I need to be extra careful not to turn an ankle.

To hike to the farthest mountain, you need a great hiking boot—a shoe that's comfortable and will take the abuse a rough trail can dish out.

folks, though, who don't seem to have any nerves below their knees. I have such a friend, Lee, who maybe has ten nerve endings in his entire body. He climbed the Grand (13,770 feet), a wonderful peak in the Tetons, and King's Peak (13,529 feet), the highest mountain in Utah, in Acme Cowboy Boots.

Explain that one to me!

Lightweight Hiking Boots

Boots have come a long way in the past twenty-five years. When I first started college, "mountain climbing" boots were in vogue, both on campus and in the field. Such footwear took about three months to "break in," if it ever really did. It also weighed in at slightly less than a mountain bike. Those boots were foot coffins, blister makers for most hikers. They were heavy-duty technical boots, not really designed for what we were using them for, which was general hiking.

During the 1980s the boot industry went through a synthetic phase, and the lightweight boot was born. Bootmaking was looked upon as a science, and the once-fashionable heavy "mountain climbing" boot was once again placed back in the "technical" niche where it belonged. Many of these synthetic boot fabrics were good. I heartily applauded the trend toward lighter footwear. I've always been fond of leather, however. For me it has a little more give and seems to mold to my foot, giving it a glovelike feel after it's been worn. Synthetic fabric doesn't have as much give, but it's tough and trailworthy for all but the toughest terrains or heavy backpacking on an extended trip.

Choosing a Boot

The pendulum has moved back to leather again, but it's a leather boot that uses all the technological advances. It's a redesigned shoe that's lighter and more pleasant to wear.

I give my friends who are interested in boots the same advice I'd give them if they were buying a new fly rod. Take your time, visit a lot of shops, and don't get talked into anything right away. After you've played the field, you'll have a good idea about what you need.

A boot must be light, made from sturdy materials, and have a good deal of support. I also like a Gore-Tex liner so it's theoretically waterproof. I've tried literally every boot on the market. For me the Vasque Sundowner is about the best all-purpose boot for the money. It's light and sturdy, and you don't have to take out a bank loan to purchase a pair. It's also a boot that lasts.

The Sundowner, by the way, is a leader in popular backpacking magazine field tests. It's been *Backpacker*'s Shoe of the Year. It's a shoe where everything comes together. It's made

Vasque makes a great hiking boot. Our family has worn Vasque boots for years. Today this boot collected a set of wet flies for the day's fly-fishing adventure.

Breaking In Your Boots

❏ Get the boot to fit comfortably before you buy it. If that boot doesn't feel well in the store, it's never going to feel very good anywhere, no matter what the salesperson promises.

❏ If there are a few tight spots, work a little oil into the areas before you hike.

❏ There will be some give as the leather molds to your foot and you work some of the stiffness out of it.

❏ Wear your boots to work for a week to loosen them up.

❏ Take a couple of short hikes, maybe 2 to 3 miles, to see how they're breaking in before you take them on that long-awaited backpacking trip.

Getting a Good Boot Fit

Make the rounds, go to a number of reputable shops, and see what they have to offer. Make sure they measure your feet with a Brannock, a device that gives you a complete measurement.

Don't let a salesperson tell you how a boot should feel, and keep in mind this eight-point checklist.

1. Wear the same pair of socks to the store that you plan to wear hiking. I wear a polypropylene sock liner and a medium wool sock. Don't change the sock combination while you're shopping. It's your constant.

2. When you stand up, your toes should not touch the front of the boot. If they do, try the next size up.

3. When you stand up, have the sales clerk put pressure around the instep. The boot should feel somewhat snug, and you shouldn't be able to move around much.

4. Get a boot that fits now; not one that you hope you'll grow into.

5. How does your heel feel when you stand up and walk around? It should remain stationary.

6. Walk down an incline (you'll be doing plenty of this in the field). Does your heel stay in place? Does your toe hit the front of the shoe? If it does, try a different size or another brand.

7. In time, your boot will stretch out a little. It will get a little wider, but it will not get any longer.

8. Some boot manufacturers, such as Vasque, provide inserts with the boot to ensure a custom fit: one insert is for wide feet; another for medium feet; the third one for narrow feet. Take some time and try each insert to see which one gives you a good fit. This is also useful if one of your feet is larger than the other.

The Vasque Sundowner is the best boot on the market for the money. Besides winning about every award a boot can win, the Sundowner is comfortable, waterproof, and lasts forever. This pair is getting worn, but they've logged thousands of trail miles. There's not a Western state or major Western mountain range where they haven't been worn. They've also been worn in several Canadian provinces and Alaska. They fit like old gloves.

Don't get talked into something you don't want. A pair of shoes must feel good in the store. You know your shoe fits well when you start hiking over rocks or going downhill.

from a single-cut piece of leather that extends about the foot. The leather is "mulled" longer for a soft, pliable feel. It also has a minimum number of seams (which is an advantage in wet weather and when you encounter a snag or sharp rock). It has a natural flex when you hike trails, too.

I've recommended this boot to dozens of friends and have never had a bad report. You want a boot that fits your feet and feels comfortable. Somewhere along the line, try this one on for size and see how it fits.

Children's Footwear

If your kids are like mine, you dread growth spurts. We bought our nine-year-old son several pairs of new jeans at the start of the summer. He had to roll them up because they were too long. By the end of the summer they didn't need to be rolled up, and by Thanksgiving they were high-water pants.

Shoes are the same story. We buy them and before long they're hurting his toes. It's hard to spend a lot of money on a child's shoe when you know he or she will outgrow it in a few months. If you're going family camping and don't plan to do more than hike a few miles down the local trails of interest, a child's regular shoe will do just fine, so don't worry about specialized footwear.

If you're going to do some serious hiking with your kids, especially if there are sharp rocks and rough terrain, you may need to consider a better shoe. Tennis shoes get torn up pretty fast on sharp rocks. Besides offering little trail-hazard protection, there is little support in a shoe made for basketball or jogging. Most discount boots I've seen aren't much better. If you're going to have your child carry a backpack any longer than a day or two, a sturdy boot is in order.

Last summer my son and I backpacked into Utah's High Uintas for a couple of days. It was not a difficult trail, but several stretches were fairly steep and rocky. He was carrying about twenty pounds, which is about a third of his body weight. We were in between "good" boots, so I had him wear his high-top basketball shoes. He never complained on the trail before, but this time his feet were hurting, and I could tell he wasn't getting the support he needed. His shoes were made for the court, not for the trail and a pack. We shortened our trip.

If your kids don't have boots, a pair of high-top athletic shoes will provide ankle support for a mountain trail.

My wife and I have had great success buying Vasque children's shoes. They cost less than most athletic shoes and provide excellent support on the trail. We buy ours on sale in September and try to get them at half price.

Hiking along a trail is a bad time to discover that your shoes don't fit properly. When you're 10 miles from the trailhead, there's not much you can do about a bad fit.

As more adults start taking their kids camping and packing, they're caught in a dilemma. The kid needs a good pair of footwear, but is it worth the expense when a kid's feet grow faster than garden tomatoes? I've found good boots worth the money, and if we're careful, we can get a lot of wear out of them, not just as serious hiking and backpacking shoes, but also as school shoes.

A good hiking boot costs about as much as a middle-of-the-road athletic shoe. To stretch our dollars further, we have our kids wear two pairs of hiking socks when we go shoe shopping, so we buy boots almost a size too big. As feet grow, we trim back on the socks. We can usually get a year's worth of wear from a pair of boots (unless they wear out sooner).

Some of the better shoe manufacturers have tried to meet the challenge. Vasque's children's boot, the Kids Klimber, has a child growth insole. A "Child Growth Plate" on the bottom of the insole not only gives extra shock absorption and cushion, but when more room is needed, you can remove the insole and peel off the child growth platform. Put the insole back and there's more growing room and more life left in the boot.

We keep an eye on the shops. The boots we like cost between $50 and $100 dollars. We watch for sales, though, and get a much better deal. Several of the shops we frequent have sales in late September or early October. The price of a pair of boots will often drop considerably.

Between the child growth insole and double socks, we can usually wear out our kid's hiking boots.

Hiking shoes are very important. After an 8-mile hike in the High Uintas, Abbey's feet are very sore. Jon-Michael's did very well in Vasque Sundowners. Abbey's feet grew so fast she'd outgrown her heavy hiking shoes; we didn't realize it until we were trailside. She was a trouper, and wore her light sneakers, but she scuffed her ankles, and the lack of support was very apparent.

Socks

If you're hanging about camp and hiking gentle trails, about any shoe or sock will do just fine. If you're hiking hard or backpacking, however, not only will a specialized shoe help you, but so will a specialized set of socks. My favorite combination is a mid-to heavyweight wool-blend sock with a light poly sock underneath to wick away moisture. Even in hot weather, two pairs of socks will keep your feet cooler and more comfortable.

Your feet take a lot of abuse and a fair amount of strain. With the exception of your brain, your poor dogs might be the hardest working part of your body when you're seeing new country. You need to take care of—even pamper—your feet.

Socks are your first line of defense. A lot of thinking has gone into the newest generation of socks. My favorites are made in Switzerland by Rohner and are called Fiber Tech Trekking Socks. I wear them

You get what you pay for with socks. We are very partial to Rohners made in Switzerland. While they wick moisture, I still wear a poly liner to ensure that my feet stay dry.

over a Thermex liner because wool, even soft wool, makes my feet itch. The Fiber Tech transfers moisture from skin to the virgin wool. Then the vapor wicks out through the membrane of my boot. I also like two socks because this system prevents blisters.

My long-time packing buddy, Kirby, doesn't like away from the foot while the terry knit absorbs its weight in moisture. I like a heavy sock such as the Summit Thermal for cold camping.

You want a sock that won't bunch up or slip inside your boot and one that will wick away the moisture so your feet stay warm or cool. I look for a plush heel, to protect tendons and reduce friction. I like the plush to extend over the toe. This is nice because it helps absorb shock on the balls of your feet when you're coming down hard or walking on hard surfaces. Plush also allows your foot to breathe.

Boot socks are a good trail value. I usually take two or three pairs of heavy socks and five light Thermax liners. I switch pairs daily, letting the previous day's socks dry. After two days of wear, I do some washing in the nearest stream (perhaps with a little biodegradable soap). I can go on this way for several weeks if necessary.

My children, Jon-Michael and Abbey, are watching a moose in a willow thicket several miles from the trailhead. Young children can enjoy hiking; half the challenge is making sure their feet feel comfortable on the trail.

This was an overcast August day in Yellowstone National Park. An early snow turned the trail slushy. I had Gore-Tex boots, so my feet stayed dry. My hiking partner, however, was wearing light summer boots that quickly became soaked. He slipped into his Gore-Tex booties and was able to forget that the trail was slush and his boots wet through. His feet stayed dry.

A rocky trail is hard on your feet and ankles without adequate foot support. If your child has a light pair of shoes, you can make the conditions a little better by having him or her put on a thin pair of socks under a thicker pair. This will help prevent blisters and cushion ankles and shins.

Keeping Your Feet Dry

You want to keep your feet dry from the outside in and the inside out. There are several other things to consider.

Foot Spray

I must admit that I tried this just last month. A friend had me do it while I was on a camping trip in Montana. He gave me a can of Desenex Foot & Sneaker Deodorant spray. He told me it keeps your feet warmer in the winter and cooler in the summer.

It wasn't that my feet stank; that would never happen. Rather, it's a way to cut down on taking so many socks on a long trip while keeping your feet cool at the same time. He has been doing this for years. I've tried it on only one trip, but the results looked favorable. Spray your feet in the morning before you put on your socks. Your feet get covered with a fine powder, which feels very nice and keeps them from sweating. In the winter it keeps them warm because the sweat can't freeze. In the summer, it keeps them cooler, or if not cooler, at least a lot less wet. My friend backpacks a lot, and he says he takes only two pairs of socks on his trips.

Gore-Tex Booties

If you don't have a waterproof shoe, you may want to consider carrying a pair of Gore-Tex booties. They're just Gore-Tex socks.

They're especially handy if you're wearing a light pair of nonwaterproof boots in the summer and you encounter a sudden rainstorm and soak your boots. You can still wear your boots and comfortably keep your feet dry even though your boots get soaked.

I've use Gore-Tex socks in rubber-bottomed pacs. They allow my feet to sweat, which they'll surely do in rubber shoes, but they wick away the moisture.

Section Two

Camp Craft—The Art of Camping

Chapter 12

Setting Up a Comfortable Camp:
Camp Craft and Other Considerations

A successful camper in days of yore needed to know a fair share of camp craft, camp craft that wasn't learned overnight. Beyond a few blankets, a sheet of canvas, a knife, an ax, and a coal oil lantern, there were relatively few modern camping conveniences.

Campers literally hacked their camps out of the wilderness. Camping was usually, at best, a consumptive endeavor. And since there was plenty of wilderness, why not?

Few worried about the effects of chopping narrow young trees for tent poles, tent stakes, or camp racks. If you felled a convenient tree to serve as a seat or a table near the camp fire, there was a forest of others ready to take its place. You cut trees, dug into the earth, caught fish, or shot birds and deer as your pleasure demanded, thinking little about tomorrow. There was always more forest if resources were exhausted. There were always more game animals and land around the next bend.

Setting up camp means having a few of the right tools so your impact on the land will be lessened.

Not long ago it dawned on us that our wild lands had dwindled at an alarming rate. We can't simply move on to the next site if things run out. Commercial and urban growing pains have strained our forests, grasslands, mountains, prairies, and swamps to the limits. It would be wrong to say we planned for the future carefully. Pioneers hacked a living out of the wilderness, knowing they could move on once the game, the fish, the soil, the forest, the pure water, or the mining claim played out. This consumptive attitude has followed us into the space age. We're changing, but slowly.

Gratefully we've come to view our natural resources from a posture that is more than monetary. We've discovered that such wild lands are valued recreational areas, more important than short-term financial gain. Outdoor use has proliferated. Almost 50 million Americans will camp at least once this year.

The sort of outdoor craft one needed to know at the turn of the century is different from the craft a camper needs to know as we enter the second millennium. Except in survival situations or perhaps in the vast woods of the Canadian North, there is little call to chop wooden tent stakes or cut boughs for a soft bed. Modern technology has taken care of many of the needs we used to meet through consumptive camp craft. No bed of boughs, for example, is better than a self-inflating Therm-a-Rest. Technology has allowed us to be outdoors and environmentally responsible at the same time.

We need open places.

The camper of the twenty-first century needs a different set of skills. In this section, I'll cover how to have a minimal impact on the land we enjoy. I'll also talk about how to have fun. I'll discuss:

- planning a successful camp;
- choosing a campsite;
- reducing the impact on the land;
- how to start a fire and keep it going;
- camping with children and surviving it;
- living with bugs, snakes, bears, and other creatures; and
- what to do if you get lost.

Chapter 13

Planning Your Trip:
Taking the Guesswork out of Camping

When I was a boy, my Cub Scout leader had us say: "Proper Prior Planning Prevents Poor Performance." Or put in other terms: Proper Prior Planning Prevents a Rotten Camping Trip!

A little preparation makes for a good camping experience.

Planning the Gear You'll Need

There's nothing I love more than planning and laying out my gear before a trip. It's half the fun.

For a family trip, I jot down an "essential stuff" list: sleeping bags, pads, tent, stove, lantern, propane (gas), cooking box, water containers, ice chests, and so on. Then I make a "misc. stuff" list for the important things that make camp life comfortable: ax, first-aid kit, folding chairs, solar shower, etc. Then I make a "food stuff" list that includes some basic meals and what foods we'll need to get at the store: salad fixings, pancake batter, syrup, 97 percent fat-free ham, and so on.

What is the most important piece of camping gear in this picture? If you guessed the potty you might be right. Being prepared is the first step to enjoying your trip.

A few days before a trip, I start to pile our gear either in my basement office or the garage. I make a pile for each list and check off each item as I put it in the pile. As I think of things I need, I write them down, stack them in the pile, and check them off. I do it a little bit at a time so it doesn't seem like work. I get my kids to help, too, and let them scratch things off.

It may seem a bit obvious to write down "tent" and "sleeping bag" and then cross them off, but if I had a dollar for every time I've seen a camper on site without an essential, you'd become a believer. Making a list in advance gives you time to add or delete as the need arises.

I keep most of my gear in a central "camping area," so it's not hard to locate my equipment unless one of my friends has borrowed it. Big Rubber-maid boxes or plastic tubs are handy for storing supplies because they have a lid that seals. We put a masking-tape label on the box's top and side so we can reach the contents quickly.

We made one into a "chop box" where we store cooking staples: oil, sugar, hot chocolate, dried soups, salt, pepper, flour, basic canned goods, and so on. We always keep it stocked. In another box we store flatware, matches, pots, pans, plates, cups, paper plates and cups, plastic bags, and the like. In a miscellaneous box we store toilet paper, hatchet, small ax, solar shower, potty seat, and plastic garbage sacks. And, remember, before you leave take down the plastic boxes and check to make sure the gear that's supposed to be there is.

This is a handy way to keep your gear organized both at home and when you are camping. The boxes fit nicely in your vehicle and your gear stays a little more protected. When it's time to load the vehicle, you have it all in one place and there is little last-minute scrambling.

We always shop the night before a trip so we have fresh food. We place these groceries in separate plastic boxes.

Being somewhat impulsive about outdoor opportunities, I've learned to keep my camping gear in a central location so I can pack quickly if necessary. In addition, I keep a small tent, sleeping bag, change of clothes, toothbrush, week's worth of food, and loaded fly-fishing rod in my trooper. If the salmon are running, if the geese are flying, if

A good camp takes planning.

It doesn't matter how good the food is if you've forgotten the toilet paper. Life just isn't as pleasant as it might have been.

Don't forget the fun stuff; your Sage rod to catch that trophy-size trout and your Pentex camera to take a verifying photograph.

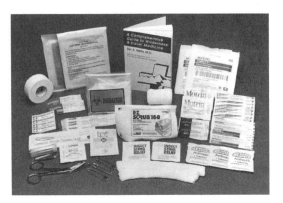

It's important to be prepared.

the elk are in rut, or if the fishing is good, I can be gone in ten minutes.

First-Aid Kits

Every camp—and every camper—needs some type of first-aid kit. You never know when you'll face an emergency. It's good to be prepared. It's also a good idea to have a little first-aid training. If it's been a few years since you earned that first-aid merit badge, take a refresher course.

Growing up in a medical family, it was easy to go to my dad's office and borrow the essentials for a kit. Now that dad's retired from medicine, I've found it's pretty cheap to buy an already assembled first-aid kit and add extra supplies as I see fit. It's certainly easier. Whether you buy a kit or make one, however, it must be accessible in case of an outdoor emergency.

For nearly twenty years, I roamed outdoors without incident. Other than minor cuts and bruises, perhaps a few blisters, I was lucky. But that changed a few years ago when I was in a canoeing accident while shooting some rapids. I green-stick fractured and badly lacerated my left leg. A sharp rock scraped across the bone of my right leg, then gouged my calf muscle when the canoe rolled over in shallow water and pinned my poor leg. We were two hours from a pull-out so first aid was necessary. My "informally adopted son," Kasey Kox, took charge, helped with first aid, and stopped the bleeding.

We used every bandage and drop of antiseptic in my kit. My leg did get infected, and I spent the next five weeks on my back. But the doctor said it would have been worse if we hadn't cared for it on the spot.

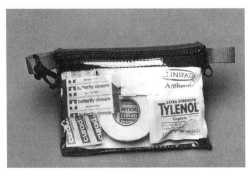

The Optimist by Adventure Medical is a great first-aid kit for the backpacker or hiker. It weighs six ounces.

At the least your trail kit needs something to stop bleeding (large and small wounds); antiseptic; something for pain; prescriptions and medicines. If you're backpacking or hiking, you'll probably want blister protection and an Ace bandage or two (if you have a trick knee or weak ankles). Keep a more complete kit in your car.

I'm impressed with first-aid kits put out by Adventure Medical. The company has a variety of packages to meet about any camper's or outdoorperson's needs. We use the Optimist and the Family II first-aid kits for our camping trips.

Hiking First-Aid Kit

The Optimist weighs only six ounces and is perfect for hiking and backpacking. It costs about $15. *A Guide to Wilderness Medicine* also comes with this kit and it's excellent! It's about the best, most concise treatment on outdoor medicine I've ever read. (You can buy this book separately for less than $5.00.) The kit comes with the supplies listed below (use them as a guideline if you're building your own kit).

The Family II by Adventure Medical is an ideal first-aid kit for a camping family. There's also room in the kit for you to add other items so it specifically meets your needs.

- Splinter picker/tick remover
- Wound management: butterfly closures (two); tincture of benzoin; antibiotic ointment; antiseptic towelettes; moleskin
- Medications: Motrin; antihistamines; Secta Soothing Sting Relief swabs
- Bandage materials: 3-by-3-inch sterile dressings (four); non-adherent dressings (two); conforming gauze bandages (two); tape; strip and knuckle bandage; Q-tips
- Infection control: latex surgical gloves; Sani-Dex antimicrobial Hand Wipe; bio-hazard waste bags
- Safety pins

To my own kit, I add a few extra Band-Aids, hay fever and headache medication, extra moleskin, and an Ace bandage for my knee.

Family First-Aid Kit

The Family II kit has clear vinyl compartments to keep things sterile and dry and to make everything visible. This kit weighs just less than two pounds. The following items are from the Family II and will give you an idea if you want to make your own kit.

- Basic medical instruments: digital thermometer; bandage scissors; splinter picker/tick remover

- Wound management: butterfly closures (four); tincture of benzoin; antibiotic ointment; antiseptic toweletts; 7-by-4-inch moleskin; instant cold pack
- Medications: Motrin; ipecac syrup; acetaminophen chewable tablets; Extra-Strength Tylenol; cortisone itch cream; A and D Ointment; antihistamines; Secta Soothing Sting Relief swabs
- Bandage materials: 3-by-3-inch sterile dressings (six); non-adherent 3-by-4-inch dressings (four); conforming gauze bandages (two); adhesive tape; strip and knuckle bandage; Q-tips
- Infection control: latex surgical gloves; Sani-Dex antimicrobial Hand Wipe; bio-hazard waste bags
- Safety pins; plastic bag

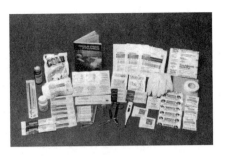

The contents of the Family II.

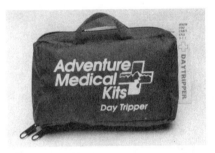

A light first-aid kit should be a part of every hiker's or packer's gear.

The Family II kit also has *Caring for Children in the Outdoors*, which is wonderful if you are camping with kids. This booklet also can be ordered separately for less than five dollars. It's a must have. The author deals with all the common ailments from diarrhea to dehydration to diaper rash; she also talks about what to do in life-threatening situations such as choking and poisoning. The book is important reading before you take off to the wilds.

The Family II also provides enough room to add a few of your own favorite medical necessities. Some of the things we've chosen to include are: lotion, lip balm, sunburn medication, and extra insect sting relief. Shari also has put together a few extras in case one of us

Safe water is critical. Many medical experts, including my father, a doctor, feel a water-purification system is an essential part of your family's health preparation. The PUR Explorer is an excellent water purifier. We've been a PUR family for some time.

gets sick. We throw these in a Ziploc bag. We're often gone for weeks at a time so we like to be prepared. We generally use generic brands because they cost about half the price. So you don't get confused, however, here are the specific names. We take Dramamine, Chewable Tylenol, Triaminic, Anacin, Immodium-AD, and Pepto Bismol. You'll also want to bring your favorite cough syrup.

Getting Ready to Go

I'll admit it's fun to simply take off and drive, setting up camp at sundown wherever I happen to be. It's just as much fun to take off down a trail and camp somewhere that looks nice.

Camping gives you a lot of freedom. Nevertheless, you still need to do a little planning.

Some campers love the unplanned. They ramble about and camp where they happen to light. Others don't feel comfortable with this carefree drifting. Such campers like a firm schedule and plan with precision. No matter how you like to camp, you'll need to do some planning if you want to visit certain places during peak seasons.

A good pocketknife is part of your preparation. My wife Shari's choice is a Huntsman (which she thinks should be renamed Huntswoman) with a pouch.

Camping in National Parks during Peak Season

The United States has some wonderful national parks. That's the good news. Here's the bad news: If you want to visit them during the peak tourist season, you're going to need to plan ahead. Don't show up at Glacier, Yellowstone, or Yosemite parks in July or August without a reserved camp spot. You'll be disappointed. I confess without shame that the Rutter family has an Odyssean wanderlust. We love to take off and go. But we'd no sooner think of going to Yellowstone or Yosemite in mid-summer without reservations than we would leave our toothbrushes at home.

It's my wife's job to get campsites for the summer trips during the winter. All the magnificent spontaneity in the world becomes very annoying when it's 4:00 P.M., your kids are hungry and cranky from being in the car all day, and every campsite within 100 square miles is full.

Camper's Checklist

General Camping Checklist

Every camper's needs are different. Use this list as a guideline for your camp preparation. Some of the items listed may not fit your needs. Take a highlighter and mark those items you need. There are blanks provided to add extra items you might need. As you collect your gear, check off each piece as you load it.

Sleeping System
___ tent
___ tent poles
___ tent stakes
___ ground cloth
___ sleeping bag
___ sleeping pad
___ pillow
___ _____
___ _____

Light/Fire
___ flashlight
___ batteries/bulb
___ lantern
___ fuel/mantles
___ candles
___ matches
___ fire starter
___ hatchet (ax)
___ folding or bow saw
___ shovel
___ _____
___ _____

Water/Drinking
___ large water container
___ smaller water container
___ canteen
___ bucket
___ water-purification system
___ _____

Kitchen
___ ice chest
___ plastic dish tub
___ can opener

___ dish washing soap
___ dish washing cloth(s)
___ tablecloth
___ fire grill
___ plates
___ bowls
___ cups
___ utensils
___ plastic utensils
___ paper plates
___ aluminum foil
___ plastic storage box
___ paper towels
___ thermos
___ _____
___ _____
___ _____
___ _____

Pots/Pans
___ cast-iron skillet
___ nonstick skillet
___ Dutch oven
___ coffeepot
___ small pot
___ large pot
___ aluminum pots
___ plastic bowls
___ spatula
___ cooking spoon(s)
___ large fork
___ knives (various sizes)
___ _____
___ _____

Food Staples
___ salt

___ pepper
___ sugar
___ coffee
___ chocolate
___ spices
___ flour
___ cooking oil
___ peanut butter
___ _____
___ _____

Odds and Ends
___ pocketknife
___ hand soap
___ toilet paper
___ first-aid kit
___ portable toilet
___ solar shower
___ leather gloves
___ wire
___ duct tape
___ rope
___ heavy string/twine
___ _____
___ _____

Hiking
___ day pack
___ canteen
___ compass
___ hiking stick
___ guidebooks (animals, birds, plants)
___ emergency kit
___ Counter Assault bear spray

Fishing

___ license
___ rod
___ reel
___ tackle, flies (Gulp, Powerbait)
___ extra line
___ tackle box, fishing vest

Photography Gear

___ camera
___ lenses
___ film
___ more film
___ cleaning kit
___ camera bag
___ _____
___ _____

Personal Items Checklist

___ camping permits (reservations)
___ sunglasses
___ toilet kit
___ mending kit
___ medication
___ insurance information
___ insurance card
___ small first-aid kit
___ bug dope
___ sunscreen
___ playing cards (games)
___ soap
___ pocketknife
___ sharpening steel/stone
___ Swiss Army knife (The Champ)
___ favorite candy
___ field guide
___ notebook
___ novel
___ extra money
___ small flashlight
___ batteries/bulb
___ bath towel (pack towel)
___ camera/film/lenses

___ gun and ammo
___ hunting license
___ day pack
___ field glasses
___ topographic maps
___ canteen
___ _____

Clothing Checklist

___ one or two complete changes of clothing
___ extra socks and underwear
___ two or three pairs of footwear
___ rain suit or poncho
___ polar fleece, sweater, hooded sweatshirt
___ heavier coat
___ stocking cap
___ hat
___ gloves (for warmth and camp chores)
___ swimming suit

If you are around water, or if the weather is wet, consider taking more clothing than you think you need. (Beyond this, clothing needs will be determined by season, location, and length of camping trip.)

Optional Gear Checklist

___ ground cloth
___ cot
___ pillow
___ duct tape
___ tools
___ folding shovel
___ folding camp chairs
___ camp kitchen system

Backpacking Gear Checklist

All gear should be lightweight.
___ backpack

___ sleeping bag (lightweight)
___ sleeping pad (repair kit if self-inflated)
___ tent (lightweight)
___ stove (lightweight)
___ fuel
___ waterproof matches
___ butane lighter
___ fire starter/candles
___ pack lantern
___ cooking kit
___ cooking pot(s)
___ fry pan
___ mixing bowls
___ large fork/spoon/spatula
___ plates
___ bowl
___ cup
___ water bottle(s)
___ water-purification system
___ 100 feet of parachute cord
___ compass
___ topographic map
___ sewing kit
___ electrician's tape
___ biodegradable soap
___ pack towel
___ toilet paper
___ first-aid kit
___ medications
___ sunglasses
___ pocketknife
___ penlight
___ batteries/bulbs
___ aluminum foil
___ rain gear
___ folding saw
___ toilet items

My wife, Shari, plans our national park adventures. She's the "official" camping coordinator. Many of the more popular parks start to fill up by spring.

If you're a first-time camper, here are a few items to consider *before* you leave on your trip. You can always alter your itinerary as the need arises.

Money: Decide how much you want to spend, and how much you can afford. Plan your trip around your budget. If money is tight, stay close to home and camp in less-developed campgrounds. Assess how much campground and park fees, gasoline, food, supplies, and entertainment will cost. Fees vary widely.

Dates: Plan when you'll be leaving and when you'll be back. Also plan when you'll see what. You'll camp at Mt. Rushmore on Monday. On Tuesday, you'll travel to Custer's Last Stand and camp at a KOA near the monument. On Wednesday you'll drive to Yellowstone National Park and camp at your reserved site at Bridge Bay. On Thursday and Friday, you'll camp at Canyon Campground, and so on.

Time: How far will you travel each day? How much time will you spend in each area? (Don't forget to allow for camp chores when you plan your day, then allow a little more.)

Chapter 14

Selecting a Campsite: Setting Up Camp

I'll never forget 1966 for a number of reasons. It was the year I went to junior high, bought my first Beatles LP, and had a crush on Valerie Something-or-Another (can't remember her last name these days). It was also my first year as an official Boy Scout.

We were setting up camp at Blue Rock near Mt. Pitt. My scoutmaster, a crusty old logger, said something to me as I pitched his tent: "Boy, they tell me there's no such thing as a perfect campsite. But, this here spot, well son, she's as close as we'll get to heaven on this earth."

I've made a lot of camps over the years. From time to time I've stumbled across a campsite that was almost perfect—and pretty close to heaven— especially in Wyoming's Wind River Range. I've been about as close to pitching a tent in Eden as you can get.

While *ideal* or *perfect* campsites exist, you won't have the luxury of camping in them every time. Beyond the aesthetics there are a number of char-

Choosing a campsite isn't like choosing a marriage partner, but it is important that you select a location that will make you happy.

acteristics that make a campsite comfortable. Let's consider them.

Find a level place to pitch your tent: There is nothing worse than waking up in a twisted wad on the lee side of your nylon house, a house that was pitched on a crooked piece of ground. Not only will you sleep badly, but the ensuing shoulder/neck ache will also put a damper on the day and do nothing for your trailside temper.

You may not find a place that's perfectly level, but if you aren't too anxious to pitch your tent, you'll find a place to lie down that's relatively flat. If you can't find a spot that flat, select a patch of land where your head is a little higher than your feet.

Lay out your tent before you pitch it and lie down. See how the ground feels. It's sometimes difficult to tell if the real estate is going to work without actually testing it.

Pitch your tent on ground that will drain: Some meadows turn into swamps after a summer shower. Pitching your tent on grass or pine needles will keep off the mud if

Before you pitch your tent, lie down and see if the ground is even. There is no substitute for getting down and doing it the old-fashioned way.

it turns soggy. You don't want to end up in a mud puddle.

Keep to higher ground: Remember the old cliche, "go high and stay dry!" Pitch your tent on a slight rise or a hill, not in a depression. Select a place that will dry fast after a shower.

Being higher keeps some of the mosquitoes away, too. If you are higher you're more likely to catch a little wind to blow off those blood suckers. Being higher might be a problem if it gets really cold, but in the summer it can be heaven-sent, because it will keep bugs at bay and cool you off with an evening breeze.

Get a good exposure: You want sun in the morning for warmth and shade in the afternoon. The trees should also protect you from any strong afternoon winds. Pitching your tent on the northeast side of a stately group of trees will probably give you afternoon shade. If you set up your camp on the easterly side of a slope or rise, you're more likely to get a warm morning sun and some shade during the hottest part of the day.

Camp near the water (but not too close): You need to be able to reach drinking, cooking, and bathing water easily. (In my case I also need to be close enough to fish without a long hike.) If you camp too close to the water, or in a valley, you'll discover that the nights and mornings will be colder.

Make sure plenty of firewood is nearby: This isn't so critical if you're going to cook on portable stoves. If you want a cheery evening fire, or if you're going to cook over open flames, though, you'll need a handy supply of wood. Make a practice of using only fallen dead wood (it burns better anyway).

Pitch your tent on high ground that will drain.

Set up camp where it's safe: Pitch your tent away from snags (dead trees) that could become widow makers. (A widow maker is a tree that falls down and kills you thus making your wife a widow.) Pitch your tent away from game trails. This is especially important if you are

Why Camps Next to Water Are Colder

If you camp at water's edge or in the bottom of a small valley, you'll have a colder camp (as much as fifteen degrees colder!). This will be a problem if you have marginal gear or if the weather turns unseasonably frigid.

Remember that cooler evening air settles into valleys and about bodies of water. With good equipment, you can camp near the water without much problem. Your mornings, however, will be cold and damp.

camping near water. Animals need to drink, too, and it can disrupt them if you are on their forest thoroughfare. Avoid gullies and overhanging rocks. If there is poison oak or ivy about, know what it looks like. Don't camp in the middle of it. Don't camp under a lone pine in a lightening storm, stay about 100 feet off any bear trail, and camp no closer than 20 feet from the high-water mark.

Campground Camping

If you're camping in a campground, you'll still want to follow the suggestions we've talked about in the previous section on open camping.

There are advantages to campgrounds. First, you can camp *right there* (never mind that in many high-use areas, camping, except in organized campgrounds, is forbidden). The greatest advantage is that you are in a wonderful national park, by a famous trout river, next to a beautiful lake, or at a site of historical interest. There's something about the immediacy of the location that gives the experience magic. I always wonder if someone has really done Yellowstone or Glacier without camping in one of its campgrounds.

There are other advantages, too. One is you don't have to hunt for a camping spot. In addition, you'll find tables, running water, a safe fire pit, toilets, security in numbers, and pre-cut firewood.

There are drawbacks, however. With crowded campgrounds, there's bound to be noise and not too much privacy. And frankly, some campgrounds are maintained better than others.

Up the trail the flash flood wiped out the road.

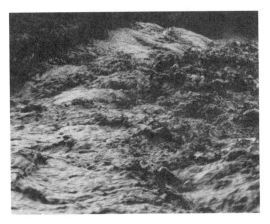

Never camp in a dry gully on the desert. We were camping on the Utah desert near the Deep Creek Mountains. A little after dawn we heard an awful rumbling and clattering of boulders. It must have rained in the mountains that night. About 20 yards away the gully, which was empty the night before, was a raging torrent. The water was at least 20 feet deep and moving boulders the size of Volkswagens.

Campground Tips

Here are a few ideas on getting the most out of organized campgrounds. In hot weather select a camp that has lots of trees around it. You'll have the benefit of shade most of the day. Direct sun beating down on you can get pretty miserable. If the weather is rainy, select a location that is open so any available sun will dry out your equipment. If you are camped under thick trees, it will stay damp longer.

It's nice to have nearby water. Some campgrounds have water taps conveniently located; others have them in a central location. If you are doing a lot of cooking, and especially if you have a few kids in the picture, you'll be making a lot of trips. Look for restroom locations. My family likes to be close but not right next to them. In some areas, all gray water (soapy dish water, rinse water, personal washing water) must be dumped in specific locations. This is often near the restroom facilities. If you're doing a lot of dishes, this might be something to consider.

Developed campgrounds sometimes have lighted areas, especially near restrooms—very handy for hitting the toilet after dark, but terrible if you're in a tent and that artificial neon moon is shining above, keeping you awake. Avoid areas near "group" camping sites. Such areas tend to be rather noisy even after quiet hours. It's almost certain that there will be a lot more people concentrated in a small place. The bathroom and water facilities are liable to be overtaxed, too.

Good Attitude

At times you won't have a choice where you camp. You'll be given a site and that's that. With demand for campsites very high, you might be placed in a site that has the

It's nice to be near the potty, but because of noise and lights you don't want to be too near.

Avoid camping near the dumpster (especially one that needs dumping). It won't smell like lilies of the valley.

aesthetic appeal of a used-car lot. If the place you are given is very awful, you might ask if there's another site. You might get lucky; it doesn't hurt to ask. Don't get your hopes up, though. You could try someplace else, but if it's peak time, don't hold your breath. Instead have a good attitude; invent it if necessary.

You might be assigned a spot at Bay Bridge Campground in Yellowstone Park (and feel darn lucky to get it if it's July or August). The spot might have all the charm of acne, so tell yourself that you're in a national park to see the park, not spend a lot of time in a campground. It doesn't do any good to argue or get mad at the folks assigning spots. Many of the national parks, Yellowstone included, subcontract their campgrounds to vendors who manage and run them. I can't say I've been thrilled by such campground services. In my opinion they're not run particularly well. The problems, however, are usually caused by administrative policy and not the local folks.

Of course the aesthetics won't be as important if you're driving across country, you're tired, all you can think of is flopping up your tent and rolling out your bag, and you have to be on the road again by dawn.

Chapter 15

Low-Impact Camping: Comfort in the Great Outdoors

I come from a long line of people who consider camping a way of life.

My parents, of course, were camping enthusiasts. They camped for fun and taught us to love and respect the outdoors. My other ancestors a few generations removed, the Nelsens and Rutters, were professional campers out of necessity.

They haunted the Eastern woods, dodging woodland Indians and copperheads, spending many nights in the forest. They camped one winter in brush lean-tos in the hills of Pennsylvania before building a squatter's cabin. Later they headed west. Some wandered the Rockies looking for furs, gold, and quick fortunes. Others crossed the Great Plains in clumsy wagons. Some were hung for stealing horses.

Back then there were a lot more trees and fewer people. If you chopped down a tree or tore up some land, it didn't matter—you moved on. If you farmed or logged out a section of land, you moved west. There was always a lot more land. The resources seemed never-ending. The land was vast, fertile, and harsh. It could easily be taken for granted. To some degree, we still subscribe to this attitude.

Part of my long line of campers. We're setting up a camp near Crater Lake National Park in Oregon.

We have a lot of wonderful open land left, but the recreational pressures (not considering the commercial pressures) we are placing on our forests, waters, and wildlands are starting to show.

If you're careful when you're afield, you can help ensure that your favorite forest, wetland, lake, or plain will be around for your children. The key words are *Tread Lightly!*

Wilderness has a restorative value that is critical. It puts us back in touch with something modern society has leached out. The value of our wildland is far more important than any amount of short-term commercial gain. Campers, hunters, fisherpersons, backpackers, boaters, animal lovers, Boy Scouts, bird-watchers, and other outdoor enthusiasts need to unite to save the real estate. We can worry about the minor details and who gets what and does what later. First, we have to save it.

Minimal impact is the key to careful camping. It's absurd to assume we can have a zero impact: We can't. So we must adopt a posture of minimal impact. I once had a friend chew me out for walking across a lovely field of wildflowers. If I had been in Yellowstone Park, where one hundred other persons could follow and blaze a trail, it might be different. I wasn't going to worry about this field 5 miles off the trailhead in the middle of blissful nowhere.

The first thing to remember is *leave no trace, just tracks!* In other words, leave your campsite as if you'd never been there. My father's admonition was to leave the campsite better than we found it. In some places I've camped, this was impossible; you can't improve upon nature. We often camped in campgrounds, so it wasn't always hard to improve on the site. He'd give each of us a garbage sack and have us police the area before we could fish or play. Then before we left, we'd clean up again.

A favorite saying of Mom and Dad is: *Leave the campground the way you'd like to find it.* They would sooner cut off an arm than leave a piece of trash. We were taught that the land was our responsibility and we needed to all do our part.

In his 70s, my father is still a dyed-in-the-wool camper. He keeps the back of his Blazer stocked and ready to go at the drop of a hat.

It's hard to imagine how many thousands of campers have stayed at this campsite in Yellowstone National Park. If you take care of your camping area, it will last a long time.

To maintain—or improve—our wild and recreational areas, we need to establish the following good habits.

- If you enjoy riding in motorboats or on motorcycles, snowmobiles, or ATVs, be careful with gas and oil. There's nothing more unpleasant than an oil slick or gas-killed grass.

- Pick up empty oil or gas cans.

- Pack out used propane or butane fuel cartridges for cooking stoves.

When you use ropes to tie tents or lean-tos to trees, be sure the tree isn't damaged. Use a soft rope that won't bite into the tree and wrap a piece of cloth about the tree so it won't hurt the bark. Trees can last a lifetime, and another lifetime, and another lifetime.

Don't cut live trees. Use deadfall for campfires; you might have to drive a way to find a place that hasn't been picked over. It's sometimes difficult to find firewood in a popular campground.

•Pick up all litter.

•Pack it in, pack it out! Don't bury your trash, carry it out; this applies even when backpacking.

•Pack up someone else's garbage. Leave your camp area better than you found it. There is nothing worse than pulling into a campground and finding half-burned garbage in the fire pit. Take all your garbage with you!

•Keep on established roads and trails. There are plenty of roads and trails for four-wheeling. Don't cut any more. It will cause erosion. (I'm a big four-wheel-drive enthusiast, but I'm proud to say I stay on existing tracks.)

•Don't hurt live trees. Use fallen dead wood for fuel. There is plenty of deadfall for fuel, but you might have to walk a few hundred yards from camp to find it.

•Except when it's a life-or-death situation, don't cut pine boughs for your bed or for the front of the tent. A long while ago, this might

Potty-Time

1. Obviously, use a toilet if one is handy.
2. If you are car camping outside a campground, use either a Port-a-Potty or make a proper latrine (cut up the sod carefully so you can replace it).
3. Bury your waste 6 to 8 inches deep so animals won't dig it up (but not so deep that it won't decompose).

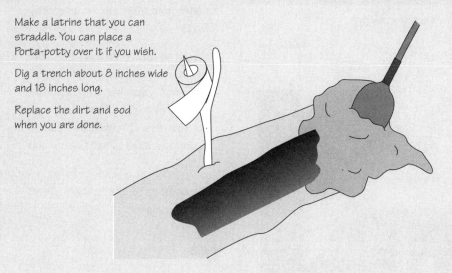

Make a latrine that you can straddle. You can place a Porta-potty over it if you wish.

Dig a trench about 8 inches wide and 18 inches long.

Replace the dirt and sod when you are done.

have had a minimal impact, but no longer. If everyone did this, every tree this side of the Atlantic Ocean area would be naked from the ground to head level.

- If there is a fire pit or ring, use it. Don't create another one.

- Be careful with your bathroom habits. Bad potty habits are responsible for a lot of contaminated water. Most folks agree that the widespread contamination of giardia (beaver fever) is a direct result of campers' and backpackers' poor sanitation habits. (Maybe we shouldn't call it beaver fever at all.)

- Don't stay so long in unimproved campsites that you have a negative impact on the land.

Dried driftwood makes a nice fire.

You want to look up from your oatmeal and see a scene like this; not a bunch of sawed trees and garbage.

- It's fun to make shelters away from campgrounds in wilderness settings. Making shelters, wood tent poles, and such are traditional campcraft skills. Confine your woodworking to deadfall. Take a picture of your creation, and enjoy it on photo paper. When you are done, tear down your structure and scatter the logs.

- We were bushwhacking to a lake and were about 20 miles from the trailhead when we came across a wood structure with a plastic tarp on the top. It looked hideous. Leave the land as pristine as you found it.

- Remember don't trench about your tent.

Fire

I love a nice fire.

I always have one whenever I can. If my wife or kids are with me, it's a must. Marshmallows are a family tradition. I prize the smell of wood smoke and appreciate how it gets into my clothes. I relish the ceremonial toasting of my hands over the flames after the sun goes down. In many ways it's the essence of camping. There are times, though, when a fire isn't practical.

More than once, some of my favorite backpacking areas have been over-baked by the summer's heat. The Forest Service prohibited open fires in the area. We packed days on end, fireless, doing all our cooking from pack stoves. About all we had to do was boil water for drinks and dehydrated food.

The sputter of a pack stove isn't as aesthetic as a crackling fire, but it's a whole lot better than going to work. The truth is, you can easily survive camping or backpacking without a fire. Some campers I know haven't had a traditional fire in years.

You can feed three people for a weekend by using a pack stove and about ten ounces of fuel. All you have to do is boil and pour and you've cooked. Dehydrated food is wonderful (sort of).

If you have a fire, build it safely. Generations are counting on you not to burn the forest down. To quote my little boy when he was five, "A burned forest has a severe impact on my plans to camp there."

Chapter 16

The Quest for Fire:
Starting Campfires (Keeping Them Safe)

Okay, it sounds rather obvious, but the first thing you have to remember is *don't burn down the pretty forest!*

Fire is a sacred trust. Look what happened to the Greek demigod Prometheus for giving this sacred gift, supposedly reserved for the gods, to man. The other Olympians were so annoyed that they chained him to a rock and had eagles eat his liver (which grew back) every day. Used wisely fire is a wonderful tool. Used carelessly its power is awesome.

Before You Strike That Match

Know what the fire laws are before you ignite your kindling!

In some areas—especially during summer or during a dry spell—open fires are prohibited. Under these conditions you can use only your camp or pack stove or the pit fireplace in improved campgrounds.

Unless you are in an approved campsite, you should always check the regulations because they change according to conditions. Sometimes you need a fire permit (this is particularly true if you are trekking into the back country). You might be required to have a shovel and a bucket of water near the fire. Different regulations are in place in different areas, and it's your job to know them.

Depending upon where you are camping, you can get up-to-date information by calling any local office of the Forest Service, Bureau of Land Management, national park, or state forestry department. Fire regs are also often posted in campgrounds or at trailheads.

Protect Your Right

Being a responsible fire user means more than not burning down the forest.

It means using existing fire rings or sites. There are usually plenty to pick from. You can do this, of course, by camping in existing campsites. This will naturally diminish the impact.

You also don't need a bonfire that can be seen from 14 miles away. A modest fire

Your first responsibility is don't burn the forest. Fire is both a great tool and an awesome responsibility.

There's nothing like a cheery fire to warm your hands or to cook a meal.

will do. It burns less wood, and it's more manageable. Being responsible also means using live wood or your trusty hatchet to scar up every tree in sight. Instead, burn deadfall. Collect it in such a fashion so it's not offensive. Lastly, don't leave cans of half-burned garbage in your fire for the next responsible person to clean up.

There's a movement afoot by some overconcerned do-gooders to limit campfires. So if you'll excuse the lack of tact—don't be one of those "slob" campers who helps ruin it for the rest of us. Members of the anti-fire group argue that beyond the fire danger, fire users are often irresponsible. They feel that fires scorch rocks and earth and use up fuel that should be allowed to decompose. They argue that fires aren't necessary or efficient because cooking can be done more effectively on a stove. Further, they contend if you wear miracle fabrics such as Gore-Tex and other high-tech clothes, you don't need the warmth or the protection from the elements that a fire provides.

I understand their argument, but I respectfully disagree. You can draw your own opinion. In the meanwhile, however, be a careful fire user.

Using a fire ring in a campground is a safe way to have a fire. Nevertheless, you still have to be careful with sparks. Make sure your fire is out before you leave.

Make sure you have enough wood before you start your fire. If you run off to collect more fuel, your fire might go out (or worse, get out of control). You need to be there to nurse it.

Making a Safe Fire

Making a fire, especially under adverse conditions, is an art form. Employing flint and steel, hitting two rocks together, and using a fire bow takes a good bit of skill. There have been times that getting a fire started during an Alaskan drizzle with stout wind, even with matches, pushed my skills to the limit.

For most of us, a butane lighter or matches ensures that we are going to get a flame. It takes some camp craft (unless you have a quart of lighter fluid). When wood is dry, or you have a bit of gasoline (which can blow your head off), the job is pretty simple. It also helps if you have a fire starter.

Most of the time, a book of paper matches will work just fine. In your kit, however, you should always have a supply of waterproof matches and a butane lighter. You need some fire starter that will light easily and burn effectively.

Fire Starter

There are a number of natural—and unnatural—fire starters that will make your life easier.

If you can't have a fire, it's a good idea to have a stove and lantern. An open fire will not be allowed in some places you camp.

❏ Don't overlook very tiny twigs, dry weeds, or small match-size sticks. Test the twigs by breaking; if they snap they are dry enough. Depending on where you are, paper-thin birch bark is wonderful. So is cedar bark or wood with pitch.

❏ Use a stub of candle; then carefully remove it after the fire has started.

❏ Wrap up newspaper until it's the diameter of your index finger. Cinch it tight with pieces of string about every inch. Cut it in inch strips. Soak in melted paraffin. When dried, store in a plastic bag. This fire starter is waterproof.

❏ Mix sawdust and paraffin, then form in an egg carton. When the mixture dries take it out and put it in a plastic bag. This fire starter is waterproof.

❏ Buy commercial sticks of fire starter or fire ribbon in a tube.

Fire Starter

Make a fire starter out of a rolled up newspaper

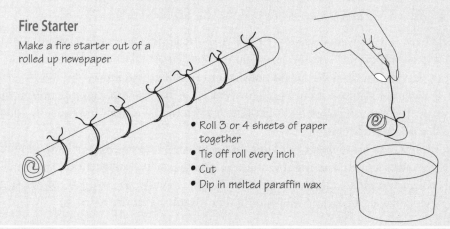

- Roll 3 or 4 sheets of paper together
- Tie off roll every inch
- Cut
- Dip in melted paraffin wax

Where to Make a Fire

Use an existing fire ring or a fire pit.

If that isn't available, make sure you have all flammable materials (twigs, pine needles, leaves, dry grasses, overhanging branches, and the like) cleared 5 or 6 feet away from the fire ring. Carefully dig a pit. Keep the sod in one piece so that you can replace it later. Circle the fire with rocks to act as a windbreak and keep the fire in place.

Now collect the wood you need. If everything is dry, getting a fire started will be easy. If the wood is wet, you'll have to be patient. (Review the discussion on axes and saws.) Collect enough small wood so you can feed the fire.

A saw is a great help. Saw arm-length pieces of dead wood about the diameter of your wrist to burn in your fire.

The Wood "Get" List

1. Get out your fire starter if you have it or collect tinder such as pine cones, nests, dried grasses, mosses, or bark. A dry piece of paper will help.
2. Get several handfuls of twigs the size of a matchstick.
3. Get several handfuls of wood the size of your little finger.
4. Get several handfuls of wood the size of your thumb.
5. Get several armloads of wood half the size of your wrist.
6. Get several armloads of wood the size of your wrist.

Now you are ready to start your fire. Too often folks gather a little wood, start the fire, and run off into the forest for more wood. Under ideal conditions, you can do this. Under less-than-ideal conditions, your fire will go out miserably.

You need to nurse it during its first stages, so you can't go running off for more wood. You want all your wood right there so you can build your fire properly and get a bed of coals burning.

There are a number of different ways to get a fire started, including building either a tepee, with the tiny twigs in the middle, or a box structure, with kindling between two larger pieces of wood. The trick is always to have enough air so the growing flame can breathe and another branch for the flames to eat.

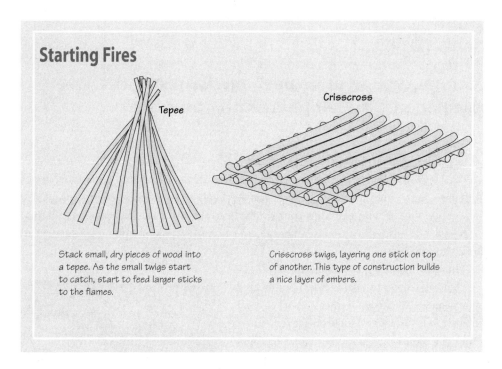

Starting Fires

Tepee

Crisscross

Stack small, dry pieces of wood into a tepee. As the small twigs start to catch, start to feed larger sticks to the flames.

Crisscross twigs, layering one stick on top of another. This type of construction builds a nice layer of embers.

If you are cooking with coals, you'll want an additional area where you can scoop the coals. I like having a trench near the fire circle so I can shovel in the coals and start burning more wood to replace them.

Chapter 17

Camp Cooking at Its Best and Easiest: Meal Ideas for Campers on the Go

Camp food needs to be tasty and nutritious.

Some people live to eat; others eat to live. If you love eating and good food, cooking may be the highlight of your trip. You are likely to spend a lot of time preparing your shopping list and planning your meals. If you think of camp cooking as a necessary evil, and eating as a way to recharge your batteries, your shopping list may be an afterthought.

In which group do you belong?

It is up to you to decide how complicated you want to make your meals. You can eat fresh foods. You can lunch on frozen foods. You can consume canned goods. You can dine on freeze-dried delights. You can sup on MREs (Made Ready to Eat). You can live on cattails, bass fillets, and wild berries. You can feast on any combination of the above.

The types of food you prepare are, in some degree, limited by the kind of camping you choose. It's not realistic, for example, to consider fresh steaks or Dutch-oven cooking when you're on a backpacking trip. We've

My son Jon-Michael eats a breakfast that he helped prepare.

had steaks the first evening out, but fresh food is pretty much out of the question after the first day. As far as a Dutch oven goes, I wouldn't want to stuff one in my pack.

On some camping trips, cooking is a big part of the fun. It's fun to try to outcook your camping companions. (One time our good friend Alan topped all our efforts with a main course of trout almondine on a bed of spinach fettuccine with grilled onions and pesto followed by blueberry crepes flambé.)

Camp cooking is sheer poetry unless you would rather be doing something else. There are times you just don't want to spend a lot of time slaving behind a hot Coleman. Maybe the salmon are running, the sites in the park are waiting, or there are trails calling. It's no sin to grab a quick bite and be on your way.

My daughter Abbey isn't shy about eating. Abbey can't shovel enough in with a fork, so she resorts to a more effective method: her fingers.

My wife Shari whips up a snack for brunch. It's fun cooking in the open air.

Meal Ideas for Backpacking and Day Packing

You're going to eat a lot more food while camping—especially if you hike or backpack—than you do at home. There's something about the fresh air that stimulates an appetite. At home I can hardly stand the thought of breakfast in the morning. I almost never eat meat, eggs, or anything greasy. When I'm camping, though, I eat a lot of food.

Being outdoors takes a lot of energy. It's fun, but it's a lot of work at the same time. That energy has to come from somewhere. If you are packing or hiking, a good rule of thumb is to take double the amount of food

Lee is taking his dinner seriously. He's eating it as fast as it's ready. For many campers, food is one of the high points of a camping trip.

you think you'll eat. You can't use at-home criteria for measuring your food consumption. Leave your diet at home, too; you need plenty of calories to enjoy all the other activities. Camping is not a desk job.

Foil is a quick and easy way to prepare a meal. Meat and vegetables cooked in their own juices are delicious. Double- or triple-wrap your entree and put over coals. Turn about every five minutes. Be prepared for a very satisfying dinner.

Nuts make an excellent trail snack. Mix up your favorite combination of snacks and store in a heavy Ziploc bag. Nuts are high energy and gratifying.

Day Packing

Take along an extra sandwich and some snacks. I wouldn't touch a bit of peanut butter at home for love or money. It's fattening, has too many grams of fat, and I'm not sure I like it that well. When I'm hiking, wheat bread with peanut butter and strawberry jam is my standard food. I love it.

For munching trailside, you can eat what you like. I personally don't eat a lot of candy, but a candy bar or two might be good to have. I prefer to snack on a Powerbar and dried fruit. I also like to eat lightly salted nuts. Nuts are high energy. I buy mixed nuts or cashews (I know I'm indulging myself) then divide them among small Ziploc bags along with dried fruit (so I won't eat them all at once).

Fresh fruit is also a great trailside snack but a bunch of apples and oranges can get heavy if you take too many.

I stuff in a few extra snacks in my day pack in case I get stuck on the trail or have an emergency. I try to have two extra Powerbars and a pack of dried fruit. Those few times I've spent the night away from camp for one reason or another, I was really glad I had a little something for dinner and breakfast the next morning.

Backpacking

Weight is an issue; so is getting enough to eat.

Water is an important part of your preparation. Culinary water should be treated.

It's fun to have a few snacks around.

If this is your first packing trip or you're going for a long time, commercial freeze-dried food is a good choice. It's easy to fix and you can control the weight effectively. Make sure the menus you select have adequate nutritional amounts to keep your body stoked. If you're doing heavy physical activity—and laboring under a fifty-pound pack up steep trails qualifies—daily menus need to have 3,000 to 4,000 calories. If your trails are extra rugged and steep, you will need more calories. Add 500 to 1,000 more calories to your menu.

Go on a few trial hikes to determine your caloric needs. Consult your doctor to fine-tune your planning. There's a limit to how much you can take with you. Some backpackers lose weight no matter what they do. Don't skimp on proteins or fat. Your body is a machine and you have to keep it powered. You'll burn up those fat grams. If the weather is cool or cold, it's even more critical that you take in some fat grams. They'll keep you warm. If it's really cold, you'll sleep much warmer if the last meal of the day is rich in calories and laced with some fat grams.

I like to start my day with a daily protein amount of fifty grams. Obviously a schedule of heavy hiking will burn up more energy, and you'll need a higher protein amount. Keep in mind that bodies and metabolisms are different and you must be sensitive to yours.

Backpacking means going light. Usually a hiker uses freeze-dried foods to keep

The last few years have seen great strides in freeze-dried foods. Mountain House is by far our family favorite and the only freeze-dried food I'll buy. It comes in a wide variety of flavors and options. Freeze-dried foods are light and a staple for backpacking. However, don't overlook them for any camping purpose. All you have to do is add boiling water and wait a few minutes, and you have a tasty meal.

Dried fruits are superb trail foods and camp snacks. You can buy them dried or prepare them yourself in a food dehydrator.

the weight down. Many consider two pounds of food per day about right. Once again, though, this is a choice you must make. It depends on how much you want to eat. I would consider two pounds a marginal limit for a man carrying a heavy pack or anyone on a rough, steep trail. I still get hungry on two pounds of food in high altitude under a heavy load. I need some bulk and often carry Oriental noodle packages (tasty and cheap but limited food value).

An important consideration if you're using freeze-dried food is your water source. In alpine settings, water is usually not a problem. It's a different consideration on a desert hike. If water is a marginal resource, you must calculate how much water you'll need to reconstitute your food. A sweet-and-sour pork meal for two requires two-and-one-half cups of boiling water.

Freeze-dried meals are great, but you pay a little more for the convenience. After you've been around the block, you can shave the price of your meals by supplementing. Don't forget to pack crackers such as Wheat Thins, Triscuits, or soda crackers. Bring along tubes of peanut butter, jam, and cheese spread. Some cheeses, salami, powdered milk, trail mix, cereal, and granola will go a long way. Grape Nuts, instant oatmeal, and Cream of Wheat are also good packing foods. Don't forget that dried soups, Minute Rice, and pastas are nice additions to your meals.

Don't forget drinks. If you want to

Making Camp Bread

Twist

Make your own camp bread
called twist. Fashion the dough and
twist it on a stick and hold it over the coals.
Turn the stick from time to time to cook evenly.

Making Twist

- Take a healthy handful of flour

- Add a pinch of salt

- Add two pinches of baking soda

- Add a pat of butter (or two)

- Mix all the ingredients, blending in the butter

- Put some flour on your hands and pour in some water. Stiffen and mix.

- When the dough is ready, twist around a willow stick

Bannock

- Bannock is made the same way as twist (although
  you may want to increase the size depending on
  the pan)

- Place the stiffened dough in a well-greased pan

- Hold the pan over the fire to cook the bottom

- Next, prop next to the fire to cook the top

flavor your water, there are a number of good mixes available. We use Crystal Lite because a little bit goes a long way. Instant coffee, tea, or hot chocolate are great to help get you going on cold mornings.

It's always a smart idea to pack trail snacks. Dried fruits, nuts, hard candies, and Powerbars are all good. Instant pudding is also nice. My wife always smuggles in a box or two of red vines and black licorice.

The following is a sample meal for two packers on a four-day-long hike.

Most of the meals come from Mountain House. I've supplemented with some extras. There is no need to fire up the stove for lunch in this meal schedule.

Day One

Breakfast: eggs and bacon, pilot biscuits or crackers with jelly, dried fruit, hot drink
Lunch: cheddar-cheese spread, hard salami on bread, granola/candy bar, dried fruit/nuts, powdered orange drink
Dinner: spaghetti and meat sauce, carrots, instant pudding, hot drink

Day Two

Breakfast: granola cereal with dried milk, dried fruit, hot drink
Lunch: peanut butter and crackers (soup if it's cold), granola/candy bar, dried fruit/nuts, powdered orange drink
Dinner: beef stroganoff, peas, hot apple cobbler, hot drink

Day Three

Breakfast: cheese omelette, fruit juice drink, hot drink
Lunch: cheese spread, hard salami, crackers (soup if it's cold), dried fruit/nuts, powdered lemon drink
Dinner: sweet and sour pork, green beans, instant pudding, hot drink

Day Four

Breakfast: scrambled eggs, sausage, orange juice drink, hot drink
Lunch: cheese spread and/or peanut butter crackers, granola/candy, dried fruits/nuts, powdered drink
Dinner: beef stew, corn, raspberry crumble, hot drink

Freeze-dried foods have come a long way since I started backpacking. Mountain House's sweet and sour pork is pretty good.

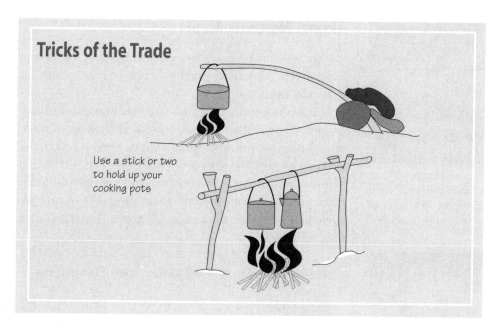

Tricks of the Trade

Use a stick or two to hold up your cooking pots

Cereal Ideas

You can buy trail mix, granola, or cereal. It's a lot cheaper however, to make it yourself plus you'll get it how you want it. For a healthy cereal that will stay with you, try my mother's muselix. It's a good way to start the morning. Mom put this together after she and Dad had something like it in Copenhagen. No wonder the Danes are healthy people. Modify the recipe to suit your needs. (I leave out raisins because I hate them.) This makes a pretty large batch.

Josie's Muselix

14 cups of regular oatmeal
2 cups of corn flakes
2 cups of raisin bran
2 cups of golden raisins
½ cup of shelled sunflower seeds
½ cup of chopped almonds
1 cup of sliced filberts
4 cups of dried, chopped apples
½ cup of sesame seeds

Mix and bag. This is our trail mix cereal.

You can take your favorite cereals camping. Take more than you'd eat at home because everyone will be extra hungry. Cereal also makes a very good snack.

You can make your own granola, which I prefer to do because I hate raisins. I make my granola raisin-free, of course, and add extra nuts and dried fruits.

For campers who want to play and spend almost no time cooking, canned goods provide a quick, palatable food source.

Almost No-Cook Meals

I've borrowed my father's famous "No Brainer" easy menu for campers who don't want to cook any more than is absolutely necessary.

There's not much cooking—only opening and warming up cans. My dad used this menu when all we wanted to do was to hunt or fish and spend as little time cooking and cleaning as possible. Of course, we used paper plates and plastic utensils. This isn't fancy food, but it keeps you fueled when you don't want to hang about camp. (Of course we could add a few fish dinners to this menu. We didn't turn them all loose.)

Paul's No-Effort No-Brainer Four-Day Menu

Day One

Breakfast: cold cereal (Wheaties, Grape Nuts), one-third cup dried fruit (raisins, apples, apricots), one cup instant dried milk for cereal; hot drink

Day's snacks: Trail mix, granola bars, fruit

Lunch: sliced ham, cheese, bread, instant pudding, instant orange drinks or soda

Dinner: canned beans, canned veggies, bread and peanut butter, cookies, hot drink.

Day Two

Breakfast: instant oatmeal and raisins, instant milk for cereal, apple, or other fruit, hot drink

Day's snacks: trail mix, jerky, candy bar

Lunch: dry salami, cheese, bread, fruit, soda or flavored drink

Dinner: canned beef stew, bread, instant pudding, hot drink.

Day Three

Breakfast: cold cereal (Wheaties, Grape Nuts), one-third cup dried fruit (raisins, apples, apricots), one cup instant dried milk for cereal, hot drink

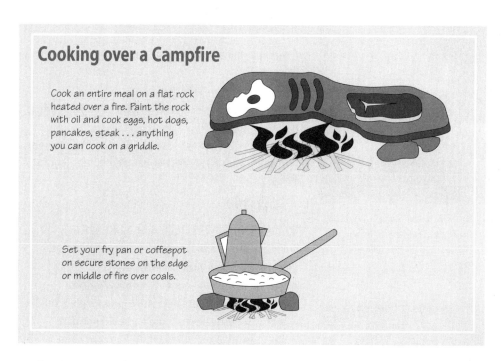

Cooking over a Campfire

Cook an entire meal on a flat rock heated over a fire. Paint the rock with oil and cook eggs, hot dogs, pancakes, steak . . . anything you can cook on a griddle.

Set your fry pan or coffeepot on secure stones on the edge or middle of fire over coals.

Day's snacks: trail mix, granola bar, candy bar, jerky

Lunch: canned spaghetti, crackers, carrots and celery, instant fruit drink

Dinner: tin-foil meal: hamburger or ham, potatoes, carrots, onions. (If this is too much work, open another can of beans and eat the last of the bread), fruit cocktail, drink

Day Four

Breakfast: instant oatmeal and raisins, instant milk for cereal, apple or other fruit, hot drink

Day's snacks: trail mix, granola bar, candy bar, jerky

Lunch: dried salami, cheese sandwich, crackers, fruit, soda

Dinner: eat all the leftovers

No-effort meals do not have to be skimpy. You have many options. Try MREs. Check the dates; old MREs have a tendency to be soupy!

Minimum of Cooking Meals

With a little more effort, which means a little bit of cooking, you can upgrade your meals. Here is another four-day menu.

If you're not going to be around camp for lunch, pack a plastic tub with your food and your ice chest. You can have a wonderful picnic wherever you happen to be at noon.

Walking around giant redwoods makes you hungry. What's for lunch?

Day One

Breakfast: ham and eggs, toast, applesauce, hot chocolate

Day's snacks: trail mix, jerky

Lunch: peanut butter sandwiches, instant pudding, instant orange drink

Dinner: steak cooked over the coals, potatoes (wrapped in foil), carrot sticks and celery, cookies, drink

Day Two

Breakfast: instant rolled oats (add raisins), powdered milk for oats, toast with jelly, drink

Day's snacks: trail mix, granola bars

Lunch: grilled-cheese sandwiches, oranges

Dinner: Dutch-oven beef stew, bread or crackers, instant pudding with cookies, hot chocolate

Day Three

Breakfast: berry pancakes and syrup, bacon strips, oranges, hot chocolate

Day's snacks: trail mix, candy bars

Lunch: tuna-fish sandwiches, apple, drink

Dinner: Dutch-oven spaghetti, garlic bread, carrot sticks and celery, cookies, raspberry tea

Day Four

Breakfast: ham and scrambled eggs, toast and jelly, apples, hot chocolate

Day's snacks: cookies, jerky

Lunch: peanut butter sandwiches, dried salami, oranges, drink

Dinner (the last night, do it right!): steaks, potatoes, tomatoes, toast, carrot sticks and celery, try making a cake before dinner in reflector oven, drink

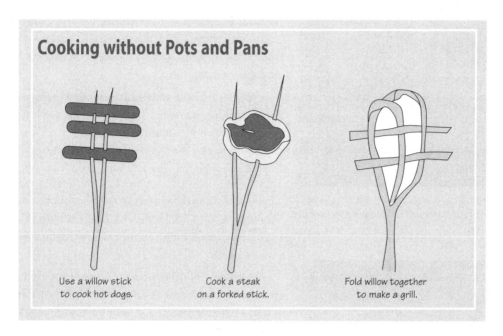

Cooking without Pots and Pans

Use a willow stick
to cook hot dogs.

Cook a steak
on a forked stick.

Fold willow together
to make a grill.

A Few of Alan's Favorite Camp Recipes

For those with an epicurean penchant, consider a few of Alan Baumgarten's favorite camp meals. On our last trip to Montana, I wrote down the recipes when he wasn't looking. If you like to cook or have a more sophisticated palette, these might be fun. Alan showed me it didn't take a lot of extra effort and time to come up with a really fine meal. He's a fly fisherman, after all, so he's not going to spend a lot of his fishing time cooking. Some of his dishes, however, could be served in the finest restaurants. To the serious camp chef, any meal that can be prepared indoors can be prepared outdoors.

Mountain Fajitas

What you need: Fajitas seasoning packet (Shilling); onion; bell pepper; oil; flour tortillas; fresh chicken, beef, venison, or fish (or all four); salsa and/or avocado.

To prepare: Slice the onions and pepper, then stir fry in hot cast-iron skillet until crisp or soft (your call). Remove the

For car camping Coleman's Propane Griddle Grill is a handy addition to your camp kit. Fueled by a propane canister, it'll have you cooking in seconds. (And it makes great pancakes.)

Dutch-oven cooking is a quick easy way to prepare food outdoors. Few dishes are better than those cooked in a Dutch oven.

Setting up the kitchen.

Don't overcook your fish!

veggies but leave the juice in the pan. Cut the meat into strips. Add the seasoning packets to the oil and fry the meats. Add veggies and cook for another minute.

To serve: Roll the meat/veggies combination in flour tortillas. Top with salsa or—my favorite—avocado chunks.

Trout Almondine

What you need: Fresh trout fillets (hope the fishing's good); McCormick's pesto mix (package); pasta (any kind); onion; slivered almonds; oil or butter.

To prepare: Boil the pasta. Prepare the pesto mix (add oil and water as directed). In a hot frying pan or skillet, sauté sliced onion and almonds in butter or oil until the onions are light brown. Add trout fillets to the pan. *Trout cooks fast, usually two or three minutes per side (when it starts to flake it's done).* To quote Alan, "You can't overcook fish or it's just dead." Drain the pasta and stir in the pesto mix.

To serve: Start with a generous serving of pasta on the plate. Lay one or two trout fillets on the noodles. Top with onions and almonds.

Chicken Cordon Bleu

What you need: Chicken breast fillets; sliced ham; sliced Swiss cheese; crackers (any kind); McCormick's alfredo sauce mix (package); oil or butter.

To prepare: Prepare the alfredo sauce mix as directed. Butterfly slice (cut down the middle) each chicken fillet. Sandwich a slice of ham and cheese between the chicken halves. Toothpicks work well for keeping everything together.

Crumble a handful of crackers into a fine meal. Oil (or butter) the chicken and then roll in the crackers to coat the outside. Fry in a medium hot oiled skillet, turning occasionally. Make sure the chicken is cooked thoroughly.

To serve: Top each cordon bleu with plenty of alfredo sauce and enjoy. Serve with pasta or, even better, mushrooms sautéed in butter.

My daughter Abbey sneaks a few licks of cake batter while my wife Shari bakes a cake on our Outback Oven.

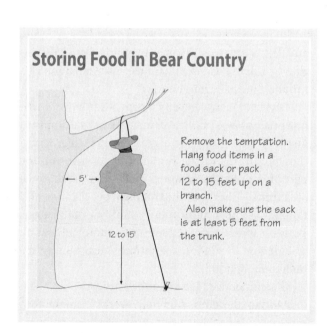

Storing Food in Bear Country

Remove the temptation. Hang food items in a food sack or pack 12 to 15 feet up on a branch.

Also make sure the sack is at least 5 feet from the trunk.

5'

12 to 15'

This is the best system we've found for keeping our picnic organized.

Chapter 18

Drinking Water:
Water Water Everywhere, but Is It Fit to Drink?

Not long ago, the federal Environmental Protection Agency reported that nearly 90 percent of the world's freshwater was not safe to drink. While giardia comes to mind for most seasoned outdoor sorts in this country, global studies have shown that 65 percent of water-related maladies were instead caused by bacteria or viruses.

The bottom line is you need to be careful what you drink.

Most of the water we enjoy isn't safe to drink. Unless you get your water from an approved tap, you must treat water so it is safe to drink.

When I was younger, and not as smart as I am today, I used to drop down and drink in whatever puddle, stream, river, or lake was handy. I was young and led a charmed, if not a foolish, life. If I was thirsty, I drank water with all the discrimination of a bird dog flushed from hunting.

My father, the country doctor, warned me that my practice was foolish if not downright stupid. I knew all the rules for making water safe, but I thought all this worry was alarmist behavior on the part of the older generation. It was fun to fall down and drink. I was rarely troubled by a canteen; I thought all that purification stuff was for sissies. Besides, there was a certain amount of charm in drinking at all the local watering holes the way the mountain men did.

Then it ended. I learned the hard way.

During the course of four years, I caught four cases of giardia, that nasty little parasite that produces beaver fever, an awful stomach ache. Being shot in the gut with a twelve-bore shotgun would have been preferable. I've repented and changed my ways, and I haven't had a problem since. Unless water is coming out of a mountainside or out of a tap, I'm not going to drink it if I haven't treated it myself. It may be attractive, if not romantic, to fall down on all fours and suck up natural water, but all that charm is meaningless when giardia, or some other nasty bug, starts hatching in your gut. You'll fall down all right, but it'll be for all the wrong reasons and all the while you'll be praying for death.

The only time I'd suggest drinking untreated water would be in an emergency, such as if you're lost and seriously suffering from thirst. If you get in a pinch in the backcountry and you find yourself without water, most experts suggest you go ahead and drink up. "The worst thing that can happen is a sore gut," one survival expert wrote. (He'd obviously never had a case of giardia.) Nevertheless, the effects of dehydration can be very serious and the results worse than the effects of a belly full of bad water. If you drink suspect water in an emergency, visit a doctor the second you feel an unaccountable stomach twitch.

Whiskey Springs in southern Oregon is a cold stream that gushes out of the mountain. The water is cold, sweet, and safe to drink. Usually water coming out of the earth is potable.

The Culprits in Drinking Water

Let's take a look at the major culprits in unsafe water.

Protozoa

These little creeps are probably the worst offenders, and the ones with which I've personally done battle. I was once so doubled over I prayed someone would put me out of my misery. Protozoa, like giardia or cryptosporidia, are single, hard-shelled cysts that reduce grown men to tears. Such cysts are from 4 to 15 microns, which is relatively large, and can be screened out by nearly all filtration systems.

As a point of interest, giardia won't nail you at once. It won't show up for at least fourteen days; sometimes it might take a couple of months. You'll the experience the worst stomach cramps in the universe along with diarrhea, vomiting, and so on. Because the effects can be delayed, pinning down the ailment as giardia might be complicated.

Bacteria

These gut-wrenching fauna-like creatures are relatively small; much smaller than protozoa. Generally they are from 1 to 9 microns. You've heard about some of these in the news: belly bending, sometimes life-threatening microscopic organisms such as E. coli, salmonella, and cholera. Bacteria also cause other stomach problems such as "Montezuma's revenge," typhoid, and streptococcus.

Chemical Pollutants

Some chemicals—for whatever reasons—get into water. Pesticide oversprays, herbicides, and diesel fuel can all taint water. Don't forget that water from mining areas should always be suspect and treated. Such stuff isn't good to drink.

Viruses

It's a good idea to carry a canteen with you. This is a Platypus, a collapsible canteen. As you drink it gets smaller and takes up less space. The Platypus will ride on your belt, but I prefer to keep it in my pack.

These little buggers are the smallest elements you'll come up against and probably the most dangerous. Water-borne viruses can exist any place animals or humans have visited. Some of the offenders are hepatitis A and B. Polio is another. In industrialized countries, there is little danger from water-borne viruses. In third-world countries, however, beware.

Types of Water Treatments

There are a number of effective ways to treat the water you drink. See which method is best for your situation.

Chlorine

In a pinch, chlorine is better than nothing, but it's poor under uncontrolled conditions. It just won't nail some water-borne bugs that will make you wish you were dead.

Where to Collect Drinking Water

While all water you drink should be treated, you need to know that some of the places you collect water are safer than others. This is good information to know if you have to drink untreated water in an emergency. Even though I treat my water, I make a habit of collecting it from the safest place I can find.

It's a good idea to get your water from the coldest, deepest source available. If you can, get away from shore. Get your water several hundred yards upstream from any camp or trail.

Areas to avoid include the following.

Beaver dams: Don't collect water from beaver dams or near a beaver lodge. Beaver are carriers of the wicked little giardia protozoan, which is why giardia is often called beaver fever.

Brackish stagnant backwater: Such water is likely to hold more microscopic creatures than a zoo.

Water with a lot of algae: This water will be green or bluish-green. It is more likely to contain harmful organisms.

Shallow water: Shallow water is warmer and more likely to hold harmful bugs; there is more decaying matter to feed organisms.

Water might look pure, but you can't tell by looking. Chemicals, mining runoff, pesticides, or human contamination might be present.

Iodine

Using iodine, if done correctly, is a good water-purification method. It will clear up most water-borne problems. One drawback is that iodined water tastes like a bottle of disinfectant. The bad taste can be mitigated by adding neutralizing tablets.

You can get your water iodine-safe by using tablets, liquid, or crystals. Either way it's easy and effective if you follow a few simple steps:

1. Add more iodine to cloudy water, or better yet, filter or strain it through a cloth first.
2. Water has to be at least sixty-nine degrees Fahrenheit for the chemical to kill giardia. Heat it up on a stove if you have to, set the bottle in the sun, or put the

You can treat water with iodine. (Polar Pure sells an iodine water-purification system.) The drawbacks of iodine are that you have to let it sit for at least twenty minutes and it leaves a chemical taste in the water unless you neutralize it.

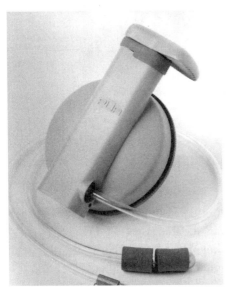

Perhaps the best way to make your water safe to drink is to filter it and then treat it chemically. A good purification system will do both steps at the same time.

bottle next to your person so your body heat can warm it.

3. Wait at least thirty minutes before drinking.

4. Neutralize the taste with tablets then shake for better-tasting drinking water.

5. Follow the instructions. If you open a bottle of iodine tablets, remember they have a short shelf life once exposed to air.

Boiling

Not many gut-busting bugs can withstand 212 degrees Fahrenheit and a rolling boil. Most experts, if cornered, will tell you bringing your water to a rolling boil will be enough. Then they add, though, to let it boil for at least three to five minutes just to be safe.

The problem is fuel supply. It's also a mess to boil a pot of water for a refreshing drink on a hot day. You have to slave over a hot stove, then wait an hour or two for it to get it cool—not to mention some places have burning restrictions.

Filtration

In a filtration system a mechanical filter strains out some or all the bad stuff. Not all filter systems are equal, however. You get what you pay for.

The key to any filtration is the filter. Some systems have cleanable filters (that can be somewhat fragile). Other systems have replaceable filters.

I think the best water purification is achieved by a filtration system coupled with a chemical treatment such as the water systems sold by PUR. For my money this brand is the easiest and safest way to get drinking water in the field.

When I backpack I *always* carry the PUR Scout. It weighs only twelve ounces and is compact so it easily tucks into a backpack, day pack, fanny pack, or jacket pocket. The purification filter lasts for about one hundred gallons, and I can purify nearly a liter of water per minute.

When I'm camping with my family I take the twenty-ounce PUR Explorer, one of the most advanced water-purification systems you can buy. It has the highest rating for total microbiological protection, and it's self-cleaning. It has a double-action pump that works easily. In independent tests both of these PUR units have met or exceeded federal Environmental Protection Agency purification standards.

I've become so dependent on my PUR systems that I've taken to carrying less water with me (unless I'm hiking on the desert where there is little water available). I carry a medium-sized canteen and my PUR. If I need a drink, I find a water source and use my purifier. It weighs a lot less than a second canteen.

While most filter manufacturers say you can filter muddy water, I like to strain it as much as possible. It makes the filters go a lot farther. Don't overtax your filter if you can help it. Keep the intake hose off the bottom so it will suck up less gunk. Wrap a bandanna or a coffee filter around the intake to filter out sediment. Collect the water and let it sit for an hour, or better yet, overnight, so all the floating matter settles to the bottom. If I usually get ninety to one hundred gallons out of a normal filter, I've found I get only fifty to sixty gallons if I use unstrained, cloudy water.

Before you buy a system, consider some of the following questions.

- How long will your camping trip be? At some point you'll need to replace or clean your filter. Some systems can be cleaned on site; others require a new filter. Find out the life of a filter. Even if it's cleanable, carry a spare.

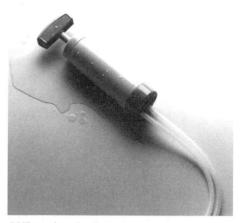

PUR makes the best water-purification systems I've found. The PUR Scout is a great system to take when hiking. It weighs only twelve ounces and will tuck into a day pack or a pocket easily. It will give you a liter of water in a minute.

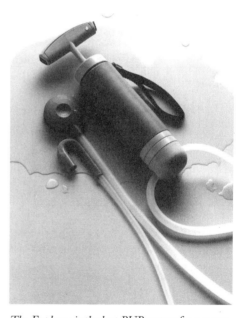

The Explorer is the best PUR system for a camping family. It weighs twenty ounces, it's self-cleaning, and the resulting drinking water meets or exceeds federal Environmental Protection Agency standards.

Collecting drinking water is so simple a child can do it. My son Jon-Michael is gathering stream water for the evening meal.

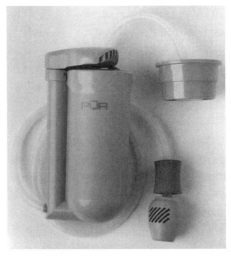

Several of my friends carry the PUR Hiker. It's a fine unit.

- How many gallons of water will you need on your trip? If there are a number of people who need water, buy a system that produces a high volume.
- Where will you be camping? Most systems remove giardia, the worst offender in our country. If you are heading off to a third-world country, however,

Water-System Tips

❑ Store your purification system in a mesh bag so it can dry out.

❑ Run a solution of bleach water through your system after every trip.

❑ Keep the tip of the output hose covered with a plastic bag to prevent contamination.

❑ Carry a spare filter for trips lasting longer than one night.

❑ Carry iodine so you can treat your water if the system fails.

❑ If you need to treat cloudy, muddy, water, carry coffee filters to place over the end of the input tube with a rubber band.

A water system and a collapsible canteen. If you are hiking on trails that are close to streams, carrying a purification system will be lighter than an average-size canteen, and you won't have to limit your water intake.

Pure water coming out of the mountain isn't something you can always count on when you hike.

you'll need a more specialized filter that strains and chemically treats your water.

Unless you have safe water in your campground, invest in a purification system. Even with my health insurance, my co-payments on my giardia medication would easily have purchased several PUR Scouts with some money left over. (It would have been a lot less painful, too.)

Chapter 19

Tips on Camping with Children: Camping with your Kids

Camping with kids is rewarding. Nothing is more delightful than sharing the outdoors with a child. I have many heartwarming recollections from my own childhood camping experiences. I have wonderful memories camping with my children Jon-Michael and Abbey.

For me camping is more than escaping suburbia and embracing nature, it's about developing relationships that last lifetimes.

Passing On the Camping Tradition

It's been thirty-some years, but I can almost taste those scrumptious stacks of dollar-size pancakes my mom made on our Coleman stove. She'd smother them with wild berries and syrup and serve them with Canadian bacon, scrambled eggs, and hot chocolate. While I cringe thinking about those cholesterol levels now, I'll never forget those tasty camping breakfasts. We still talk about them.

Every August we camped on the shores of Diamond Lake in southern Oregon. I remember catching my first trout while camping with my father on a weekend trip to Four-bit Crick. Dad tied a piece of orange yarn to a salmon-egg hook. He cut a willow pole and spliced on monofilament. The rest was up to me. I was only six years old, but this experience, this camping adventure with my dad, was one of the outstanding episodes of my life. I've written

Camping builds family bonds that last a life-time. Make camping meals fun, not complicated.

fishing articles for nearly twenty years now, but my career as a professional fishing bum, a paid liar my mother calls it, started on that camping trip with my dad when I was six.

My sisters and brother and I will never forget the cross-country camping trips we took, either. Camping from state to state, we called on the mighty Mississippi River. I'm not sure why, we just wanted to see where Huck Finn lived. On other camping–sight-seeing trips, we visited Glacier and Yellowstone national parks, Mt. Rushmore, San Francisco, Alberta, Victoria Island, the Wind River Range, Crater Lake, Lava Hot Springs, the Badlands, and a couple of dozen other places.

We camped to camp, and we camped to get somewhere. It was a family thing.

It was a blast and I wouldn't change a thing. We pulled together as a family in sun, wind, and rain. In Starr Valley, Wyoming, something happened one night and the sleeping bags got wet. We sat up most of the night playing Old Maid, eating endless handfuls of popcorn my dad popped over the sputtering fire. It was a time of sharing and fun. We drew together and learned something about the outdoors and about ourselves.

Create memories for your kids. Create memories for yourself. Do yourself a favor, go camping with kids.

Teach a Kid Conservation

Kids take to camping.

If you've never camped, you might find the younger generation acclimates faster than you think. Besides the family fun, you'll be able to teach your children lessons about the physical world they'll never learn in any classroom. Kids who take an interest in the outdoors are less likely to get involved with gangs, drugs, or other negatives. Looking up into a sky full of stars, stretching out under an august pine, or sitting

Kids love the campfire. My daughter is waiting for evening so we can sing songs and roast marshmallows. Abbey has about five more hours to wait.

We took a father-and-son trip to Yellowstone to hike and fish. We're sitting on a deck overlooking Yellowstone Lake.

The Coleman Xcursion is an excellent small lantern. At 6.5 inches, it will shed light on any subject. It's great for reading bedtime stories or for trips to the potty.

about a fire roasting marshmallows—gives children a new perspective and reverence.

Be a teacher of conservation. Pick up your garbage. Make a point of having your kids help while you cheerfully pick up someone else's garbage, too. Teach them not to trash the earth. Take a few minutes to study the flora and fauna of the area. Take occasion to point out the moose, a redrock formation, a circling redtail hawk, and an Indian paintbrush in full bloom. Teach your kid something wild.

Whether you go on an overnighter or camp for a week, you need to keep a few things in mind. Kids require a little extra care, but they're worth it. They're delightfully high-maintenance. Every now and then children and camping can be a challenge, maybe even trying, but with a few tips from someone who's been around the block, you can have a memorable experience and keep frustrations to a minimum. I remember my mother saying when there was a handful of us under age ten, she needed a vacation from our vacations. She now admits it sometimes got hectic, but she wouldn't change it.

Equipment

Let's look a few things to make camping with kids a little easier. I want to make sure your first trip is memorable and successful. In addition to your regular gear, you'll want a few extras to make your kid's life, and yours, a little happier.

Toys

Younger children get very attached to a favorite doll, blanket, stuffed animal, or some other toy. My wife and I have always allowed our kids to take along that special thing (or two). Avoid the temptation to go overboard with toys.

We take a stuffed animal and a favorite blanket and pillow (Shari is worse than the kids; she has to have her pillow). We feel it's a small concession. Our kids have never had a problem adjusting to camp life. We always bring along a supply of books and a family game or two (a card game, a Frisbee, a ball).

As Jon-Michael has gotten a little older, we've tried to focus on more educational "toys" such as guidebooks, educational coloring books, pencils, papers, pens, paints, and the like. Each of our kids has a day pack, which is handy for hikes or other personal items. If we go on long car-camping trips, where they spend a lot of time in the back seat, we let each kid fill up the knapsack half way with whatever possessions he or she chooses. We also rent and play cassette tapes featuring children's stories to make the long drives go more quickly.

It's a good idea to let your kids take a few favorite toys on your camping trip. A favorite doll or stuffed animal will give a child comfort.

Include the Kids Before You Leave Home

Clothes

What do you take?

If you take too much stuff, you'll swim in a sea of clutter. If you don't take enough, it's not like you can go back to the closet and restock.

If you're car camping or camping as you travel across country, packing a few extra things won't be a problem. If you're backpacking, canoe camping, or if space is tight, you must be a little more careful. If you have children in diapers, you need to pack more things than you would for an eight-year-old. The good news is toddler clothing doesn't weigh that much.

Kids get dirty, too, and if you change their clothes each time they dive into a mud puddle, you'll go through ten sets of clothes in one day. Camping and getting dirty seem to go hand in hand. It's like the wind; you can't really fight it. Don't stress over keeping your kids, especially the young ones, too clean.

Over the years we've learned what to do for the types of camping we like to do. We go around June 15 every summer to Yellowstone National Park, to see the sights and catch cutthroat trout. We spend about a week. This is our clothing list to give you an idea. Remember, we are car camping, so space isn't a major problem.

Children's Clothing List:

- eight pairs underwear
- one pair long underwear
- seven pairs socks
- two pairs long pants
- two pairs shorts
- three T-shirts
- two long-sleeve shirts

A child's pack needn't be expensive. Check the zippers, however, and make sure your child can use it without help.

Planning and Packing

Before we'd go on a trip, my dad used to gather us all together and have us look at maps of our destination. We'd go to the library and look at books and magazines about that place. He also invited our input on places we could stop at along the way.

When we camped our way across country to Mt. Rushmore, my sister (I think it was Laura) asked if we could stop at the Crazy Horse Monument. He said sure. We liked it better than Rushmore. When we went to Victoria, I found an article on the Rose Gardens and asked if we could stop. We did.

We felt ownership in our trips because we helped plan them. Everyone was excited, and it was a fun family activity. Get your kids involved. Show them where you plan to take them. Look at the library, surf the Internet, write for maps. Planning a camping trip is fun and educational.

While we're traveling we get books on tapes or music CDs to entertain our kids. If it's something we all want to listen to, we plug it into the car system; otherwise each person has his or her own earphones.

Get your kids involved in the packing process, too. Depending on their age, they'll be more or less underfoot (and more or less helpful). Getting ready to camp is infectious. Be patient and let those kids help even if it takes you an hour longer to load the car (and it likely will).

Yes, it would be easier if you left them home (or secured them in your closet with duct tape). That would defeat the purpose, however. No matter how young your kids are, have them help pack their clothes. You'll have to do a little sidestepping, but their involvement is the best way to learn.

Menus, Meals, and Cooking

Get everyone involved when you plan meals and do the cooking. Have a child select a favorite meal to have

While I drag the wood in, Jon-Michael cuts it into campfire-size chunks.

My mother helps Jon-Michael unpack the tent.

when you are camping. Each child can help arrange the food that will be needed for that meal, then help in the preparations. Kids need to be involved in all the aspects of camp life.

As they get older have them, under your supervision, prepare a meal. It may be sandwiches at lunch for a younger child or pancakes and eggs if the child is a little bit older. I've always been a little cautious around a gas stove. Even with older kids I still light the stove. If we're cooking over an open fire, I carefully monitor the progress.

Take the kids shopping for the camping trip and have them pick out items you'll need.

Watch That Sun

Keep a hat on your kids and watch them when it's warm. Youngsters are more likely to overheat than adults. Remember they don't sweat as much as an adult. Some pediatricians feel that kids don't acclimate as fast as adults either.

Keep your kids well hydrated with plenty to drink in warm weather. We have our kids drink every hour whether they're thirsty or not. We usually give them water or

Kids burn a lot of fuel in the great outdoors. Keep them well fed. On backpacking trips and on longer day hikes, I carry a few Mountain House freeze-dried meals in my pack. I boil water in my Micro Peak 1 stove, and we have a hot meal. Here Abbey is eating at timberline. My kids love Mountain House stew.

Give your kids plenty of water. If they're not peeing every two hours, you're not giving them enough. I'm a big fan of Gatorade; I carry powdered Gatorade when packing. When hiking I have each kid carry a quart bottle (in addition to water). Kids dry out fast and you have to watch them carefully. Jon-Michael will often carry two quarts on long hikes.

boxed juices, but if the weather is really warm we give them Gatorade or Poweraid. Shari dresses them in baggy clothes and each is required to wear a hat during peak sun. Each of our kids has a pair of sunglasses (to protect their eyes from cataracts, which can show up in later life). They lose them a lot.

Children dehydrate faster than adults so look for tell-tale signs. A child who is dehydrated might appear lethargic, listless, flushed, and whiny. Urine that is dark yellow and not clear also signals this problem.

Every hour or two Shari dabs each kid (and me) with a coating of thirty SPF sunscreen when we're in the sun. Remember that most skin problems come from too much sun during childhood, so protect your kid's skin. When you apply sunscreen, take care to keep it off your child's eyes because it really burns. Avoid eyelids and getting too close to the bottom of the eye. Keep the lotion off little fingers so the kids won't rub it into their eyes accidentally.

If your child does get a sunburn, treat it quickly.

Bites and Stings

Things That Buzz and Fly

Mosquitoes love to prey on young children. Prevent as many bites as you can. While repellents with deet in them work well, most experts recommend not using it on your kids; if you do, use a very low-percentage deet formula. Sun and Bug Stuff and Deet-Plus are two nonabsorbing, low-percentage deet repellents that you might try. If you want to avoid deet products entirely, consider Bygone Bugs, Buzz Away, or Natrapel, which all use natural ingredients.

Itchy Bites

If a child gets a bug bite, clean it and put a salve on it. Telling a kid not to scratch is pretty tough. Scratching will only make things worse. Give them some help. No More Itchies is a good choice, as are a number of other hydrocortisone products.

Poisonous Things

Keeping your kids out of rocks, logs, and creeks is easier said than done. You want them to have fun, yet you want them to be safe. The truth is you run a greater risk of getting into an automobile accident on your way to the campground than you do of having a serious mishap with a poisonous creature. Still, a little caution goes a long way.

A chair is a joy on any camping trip. If you have small kids you need to feed or hold, it's a necessary piece of gear. This Coleman rocking chair is very handy if you have a baby. It's also nice for watching sunsets.

Teach kids about the outdoor world so they can exercise judgment. Then keep an eye on them. We'll talk more about this in the next chapter.

Teach children to identify poisonous snakes or spiders in the area in which you are camping. Most important, teach them not to pick up and play with snakes until they are old enough to identify the species. More than half the snake-bite victims in this country are children; more than half the snake bites occur because the victim is trying to pick up a snake or play with it.

Most snakes, especially poisonous ones, will try to slither away when they sense you coming. They won't bother you if they are left alone.

Don't make your kids paranoid about snakes when you are in snake country but do keep a close eye on them. Teach them to look first before they step and reach. During the heat of the day, watch out for shady areas such as overhanging ledges and caves. In the evening, when it's cool and snakes are out hunting, carry a flashlight and watch where you step. Teach your children to appreciate a glimpse of a serpent.

Chapter 20

Things That Buzz, Slither, or Go Bump in the Night: Dealing Gracefully with the Natural World

I've spent a good many days and nights outdoors, and hope, God willing, to spend many more. I've only been really frightened a couple of times.

Once in northern British Columbia, a myopic cow moose walked through camp in the middle of the night. I was in a sound sleep. She caught her leg on a tent guy line and dragged the tent (with two friends and me in it) a foot or two. She then ran into the cooking stuff and knocked over pots and pans to create more of a racket. She scared herself and me to death.

You never saw anyone come out of a sleeping bag faster.   We didn't get much sleep that night. Mostly we stayed up and laughed about our moose adventure. It was funny after she was gone. At the time I was tempted to shoot her.

The worst scare came when I was fourteen years old and camping on Abbott Creek with my parents. We were very tired and got to camp well after dark, so we left the dishes for the next morning. This was the only time in all our years outdoors we ever kept an untidy camp.

About midnight I heard a very raspy sound and the rattle of pots and pans. My parents were still sleeping, and not wanting to be an alarmist, I crept to the tent door and carefully unzipped it. I shone the light on a big old she-bear licking out our fry pan. She must have heard me, but she didn't seem to care because she was enjoying the hardened bacon grease.

Not only do you share the world with creatures, you share it with plants such as this poison oak. You do not want to set your tent up in the middle of poison oak, ivy, or sumac.

I chambered a round in our old military-issue Colt .45 and slipped out. The bear was about 20 feet away. I aimed the pistol in the air and shot off four rounds into the stillness of the night as quickly as I could. It just so happened that she was finished with the grease about the time I fired in the air. In two seconds she was gone and my

If the bugs are really out in force, you may want to invest in a screen that encloses your picnic table and offers rain/sun protection, too.

parents were up. We discovered that sow had licked our plates clean and the cast-iron frying pan, too.

That was the last time we went to bed with dirty dishes.

You need to share the outdoors with other creatures. Sometimes your paths will cross when you're not expecting it. I've long felt that my family is safer outdoors than at home. There is very little to fear in the wild. Most encounters with animals are chance meetings. If you don't run, they will.

I'm more concerned about taking my family to New York City, Chicago, or even Disney World than I am about letting them wander in the wilds. The only animal that's really mean is a human; the rest act on instinct. You have to respect the wild, but you don't have to fear it.

The three questions asked most by a new or less experienced camper are what about bugs? what about bears? and what about snakes? There have been some horror stories about these but most are quite exaggerated. Again, you're safer in bear country or snake country than in any city.

Getting Bugged

Insects can be annoying to a camper; for that matter they can be annoying to anyone. If they're not biting, they're buzzing and being pesky. Perhaps I shouldn't admit this, but I rarely, if ever, get bug bites. Nevertheless, for as much as flying bloodsuckers hate me, they love my wife. More than once I've seen a hungry herd of mosquitoes home in on my arms and legs, give me a quick look, then beeline for Shari. I don't blame them.

While I don't get bug bites, I'm easily bugged (pun intended) by the whining hum, the relentless buzzing, and the dive-bombing sorties. I don't care much for bugs or flies unless they're tied on a hook and cast to hungry trout.

I'm especially bothered by blackflies and no-see-ums. These little beasts seem to get so thick you can't breathe without taking a dozen or so into your lungs.

Ticks

I pick up a tick every now and then. Of all insects, these little buggers make me the most nervous. When I was growing up, I managed to get drilled by two or three a year.

These little devils liked to bore into my skin and suck my semi-sweet blood. Spring was always the worst time. My mom, a registered nurse, always pulled them out. I had only one bite get infected.

Besides getting an infection from the festering bug's head, the most frightening thing about ticks is getting sick, most notably with Lyme disease or Rocky Mountain spotted fever. Lyme disease has serious effects. If you feel arthritis-like or flu-like symptoms, get a red rash near the bite, or feel feverish, you need to see a doctor *ASAP*. A good dose of antibiotics should clear up Lyme disease. Spotted fever can be treated with a medication from your doctor, too.

Keep a sharp eye for ticks on your person. Inspect each child at night before bed.

When you pull out a tick, you must be careful to get the head of the insect, otherwise it could fester. Use tweezers to get a good grip on the tick. The tweezers on your Swiss Army knife will do nicely.

Most tick problems can be prevented by wearing long pants and high socks. Ticks are usually on the lower bushes waiting to embrace a warm body. It's good practice, especially in the spring, to inspect your legs every hour or two. It takes two to six hours for a tick to settle, get comfy, and dig in.

One year on our annual camping trip to the Wind Rivers, we found seven or eight ticks on Abbey and four on Jon-Michael. They had been on the children for several hours without finding the perfect lunch spot. We inspected them every few hours from then on, but if a person will search his or her body at least twice a day (behind the knees, the arm pits, the private parts, below the knees) most lodging can be prevented. If you check your body on a regular basis, even if the tick has started to embed, it likely will be only halfway in and thus easier to get out.

There are a lot of country remedies for removing an embedded tick. One is to cover the area with butter, margarine, or cooking oil. The theory is that by smothering the pore, the tick will back out because it begins to suffocate. Another hearsay remedy is to put a drop or two of stove fuel on the back of the tick. A third is to use the glowing embers of a recently extinguished match to force the tick to back out. I've also

Be alert for ticks in thick foliage during the spring.

heard you can splash the tick with deet or insect repellent and the smell will drive it away. I'm not sure which way is best (probably the aforementioned tweezers). I do know you have to be careful to get the head out. Then you need to cover the area with antiseptic.

Besides long pants, a good dose of preventative deet or repellent on your legs from the knee down will be good insurance. And don't forget to spary your pants and socks with a repellent, too.

Mosquitoes

These bloodsuckers are mostly a nuisance, even if they are a part of the landscape. Pray for a good breeze to blow them into the next camp. In the extreme South, mosquitos may be responsible for malaria, but for the most part, they pose no real threat other than itching.

Where you set up camp will make some difference in the size of the mosquito population. Stay away from swampy areas and get on higher ground where you can pick up a breeze.

Bees and Wasps

For most of us, the sting of a wasp or bee is annoying, if not a little painful. A bit of ice or a rag dipped in cold water is usually helpful. There are also sprays that help relieve the pain of the sting—a good investment if you have young kids. A sting can be frightening.

For a few people, however, the sting of a bee or wasp can be deadly.

About 5,000 people have died from bee and wasp bites over the past few years. About ten times more people die a year from these stings than from snake bites. If you're the person who really swells up from a sting, or if a sting makes breathing difficult, your next sting could be your last. There are varying degrees of allergic reactions, but some are really bad—even fatal.

You should visit your doctor and get an adrenaline kit to carry with you everywhere you go. My good friend, Kasey, has had a more severe reaction to each progressive sting over the years. I watched his arm swell up to double the normal size and heard his breathing become rough. A shot of adrenaline did the trick.

Bug Dope

I wear deet by the ounce even though it's not good for you in large quantities. Like everything else, it *might* cause cancer. When the bugs get bad, usually in the morning or evening when the wind has died down, swatting is futile. Besides going home, jumping in a lake, or being bitten, you can crawl in your tent, stand in the smoke of a campfire, or wear a mesh headpiece and lots of clothes (then you'll resemble a beekeeper). You can also smear on bug dope, which really helps. The deet stuff makes you smell a little like a combination of old gym socks and a doctor's office.

Most of us opt for some kind of bug dope. If the bugs are bad, I like something with 100 percent deet such as Otters or Cutters. The odor isn't pleasant, but the bugs hate it. There are a lot of products that contain varying amounts of deet. There are also other lotions, liquids, and sprays. A favorite is Avon's Skin So Soft; it works well but it doesn't last long and you have to reapply it. It also makes you smell like a rose. Most men don't like smelling like the perfume counter at Bloomingdale's (even if it does make their skin soft, young-looking, and supple). I'd be a little worried about smelling so sweet in bear country.

My wife and children wear deet substitutes. For me oil types stay on the longest and need fewer touch-ups. After smearing down, we spray our hats with OFF. Then we have our kids shut their eyes while we spray them about the neck and collar, giving their clothing a good dose. Next we spray about their shoes and socks.

Every hour or so, we reapply the lotion. If this doesn't work, we play cards in the tent.

Bears, Bears, and Bears

Bears are soft, cuddly, and cute; they have clown-like manners. Help make the land safe for the bears. Don't be responsible for turning a wild bear into a problem bear. This happens when you feed a bear or you tempt a bear to rob your camp. Keep your food and cooking items locked up or stored high in a tree sling.

As sure as God made red apples, a bear that robs a campground is going to be a dead bear.

The summer quest for the Rutters is to see bears. We prefer seeing them on our terms, and that's during the daylight hours and from a safe vantage point. We don't want to catch them by flashlight gutting our food larders or breaking open the Coleman ice chest. We don't want them sticking their cold noses in our tent.

In bear country we keep our food locked in the car when we're not eating. If we're ATV, horse, or canoe camping or backpacking, we hang food from a branch at least 10 to 12 feet off the ground and a good distance from the trunk of the tree.

A good clean camp will do more to insulate you from bears than anything else. If there are no tempting smells or foods, bears will pretty much leave you alone.

Hiking in Bear Country

It's hard to stumble onto a bear but it does happen once in a while. I've seen lots of bears while hiking, and I've never had a close call. Like many hikers, I'm most afraid of national park bears. These are bears that have been around humans and may have lost some of their fear.

I'm also a little more cautious around grizzlies than black bears. Grizzlies have a shorter fuse and are less likely to get out of my way. They seem to be more territorial, too.

You need to be particularly cautious if you encounter a momma bear and her cubs. You'll rarely have a problem, however, unless you get between her and her furry family. If you encounter a bear, especially a sow and cubs, at close range, back up slowly. I like to sing softly as I retreat. You run little risk from bears, but there is some slight danger.

A bear is a wonderful animal to see but you don't want to come upon one at dusk on a narrow trail at 20 feet. This one was viewed through a 500-millimeter lens.

Many campers carry a gun in bear country, especially grizzly country. If this is your choice, I'd recommend you know how to use it expertly. Otherwise, all you'll do is wound a bear and then you'll have real problems. If the weapon is a handgun, a .357 magnum is about as light as I'd go for a black bear, a .44 magnum for grizzly. Make sure you use fully jacketed bullets and not hollowpoints. A charging bear is a hard target to hit.

You can't carry a weapon in national parks. Instead, many hikers carry a bear spray

If you are going to carry a handgun in bear country, know how to use it.

made from pepper. The only spray I'd recommend is Counter Assault. This stuff works. I haven't used it on an angry bear, but I know several photographer friends who have. One stopped a charging grizzly sow at 10 feet. Counter Assault is made in Montana, and it's been thoroughly tested. I carry it in Yellowstone and Glacier religiously. It works well on assaulting humans, too. A friend of mine was held up at knifepoint in Bozeman, Montana. He sprayed his attacker, who dropped his knife and fell to the floor until the police could take him away in cuffs.

The Bear Facts

❏ Bears have poor vision compared to their wonderful sense of smell and acute hearing. The average bear, however, sees about as well as a human does.

❏ Bears can run both up- and downhill very fast.

❏ Bears are most active at night, early morning, and evening.

❏ There are about 900,000 bears in North America. Black bears out-number grizzlies about forty-nine to one. There are, however, as many human-grizzly confrontations as there are those with black bears; grizzlies are more aggressive.

Here are a few commonly accepted ways to avoid bears when you hike. I must confess, I don't follow this advice, because I always hope to see bears. It's no wonder that of the forty-eight or so humans killed by bears in the past fifty years, most were probably photographers.

■ While hiking in bear country, think like a bear. Stay alert at all times. Remember that the land is the bear's real estate. See the bear on the bear's terms. Stay on established human trails, not bear trails.

■ Some experts recommend carrying a bell or metallic noise maker. The idea is bears will hear you coming and get out of the way. (Personally I'd rather be eaten than go *ding-ding* when I hike.)

■ Let bears hear you coming so they'll get out of the way. Make lots of noise, sing, talk loudly. Be careful when walking near running water, facing a heavy wind, or traveling in dense brush; a bear may not hear you approach. Take a few noisy friends along.

■ Be careful near berry patches. Eat your fill only after you've checked for bears. Stay in open areas.

■ Avoid bear caches (usually partially decomposed dead animals). They won't be difficult to know because they'll stink and often be partly covered. Running across a bear on its cache can be an explosive situation.

Counter Assault pepper spray is the only brand I'd recommend. You can buy it over the counter at most shops in Yellowstone National Park or from backpacking catalogs.

- Use a telephoto lens when photographing a bear. Cubs make cute pictures but stay back.

- Don't feed the bears. Don't take a bear to lunch. Bears can get too accustomed to our food. They are by nature lazy. It's much easier to rob a campground than to forage. Don't let them develop the habit.

- Don't stop at bear trails and in places where there are a lot of bear signs such as tracks, digging, and scat.

Camping in Bear Country

I'd bet that you're one hundred times safer in prime grizzly country than you are walking across Central Park next to a street cop. Follow common sense and you'll be fine.

Don't keep a dirty camp. Clean up dishes, food spills, and leftovers.

Don't camp on or near bear trails.

Avoid foods that smell. Food with a strong scent can float on the wind and attract every bear for 10 square miles. When backpacking in high-density bear country, use nearly odorless freeze-dried food.

Never, never eat in your tent. Never let the odor of your food collect in tent or sleeping bag fabrics. When in bear country cook and eat your food a hundred yards from where you sleep.

Never store food inside your tent. Hang it from a tree at least a hundred yards from where you sleep or lock it in a trunk.

Bear Encounters of the Close Kind

Enjoy meeting bears and enjoy it from a distance. Bears are a blast to watch. They are like big children. In the very unlikely event you run into a bear at close range, here are a few ideas.

- Back up slowly—while you softly talk or sing. You can't outrun a bear so don't try. A grizzly can outrun a race horse for a short distance.

- A bear will often rear to its hind legs and move its head from side to side. It may be trying to get your scent or focus its eyes. Don't be threatening and don't make eye contact with the animal.

Several overgrown "bear children" have a water fight.

- Big grizzlies can't climb trees, but small grizzlies can. Black bears are also excellent tree climbers. Climbing a tree may not be a good idea with a black bear. If you climb a tree to escape a grizzly, climb a large tree, which the bear can't push down, and get higher than 12 feet.

- When bears are threatened, especially grizzlies, they like to make noises. A bear will *woof* at you, not unlike a dog. A bear might also pop its teeth. Ignore it and continue to back up slowly.

- Grizzly bears often charge or false charge to determine dominance. This is frightening but normal grizzly behavior. It will frequently stop. *Back up in a nonthreatening manner*, lay your pack in the trail (the idea is that it might bat it around while you make your escape). Don't get aggressive or act threatening; this will make matters worse. Don't shoot a grizzly unless it's at very very close range (never kill a false-charging bear). If you have Counter Assault start spraying it.

- Black bears rarely false charge. When they do charge it's serious, and you are in trouble. Get aggressive yourself. Spray your Counter Assault. Use your weapon. If nothing else, throw your pack and try to punch the bear in the nose (a lot easier said than done).

- If you are charged by a grizzly, play dead and let the bear bat you around. (This may be easier said than done, too.) Cover your head. This would be an excellent time to pray. If a black bear charges you, kick, scream, and fight back.

- A grizzly is like a locker-room bully. It wants to dominate and will

It's a good idea to pay attention to bear-management signs.

do whatever it takes to prove it's king of the hill. If you act somewhat submissive and try to back up, it won't have to go through its adolescent, football-player posturing to establish superiority.

To put this all in perspective: About forty-eight people have been killed by bears since grim records such as these have been kept; however, 1,700 persons have been killed by dogs, 9,500 by lightning, 400 by spiders, 640 from snakes, and 4,900 by wasps and bees.

Bear attacks make great sensationalized headlines, but the threat is minor. If you want to talk threats, stay out of the way of lightning.

Poisonous Snakes

We share the outdoors with others. Some wear fur, some have feathers, and others slither on the ground. There are snakes out there, some that have venom. Only a few states, Alaska and Hawaii, for example, don't have some species of rattlesnake. Like most things the snake threat is blown out of proportion.

It's Rare to See a Poisonous Snake

You run a greater risk of getting in an accident on your way to your camping area than you do of even seeing a snake, let alone a venomous snake. You run a much greater chance of having a stroke or a heart attack. Most hikers and campers have never seen a poisonous snake, and they've camped, hiked, fished, and hunted in snake country. At times I've searched for snakes in the heart of snake country and I was lucky to see one or two.

It's estimated that maybe 6,000 people a year are bitten by poisonous snakes in the United States. Out of that number, between six and thirty die each year (most of whom are children). Unless you're one of the six to thirty, those are very good odds. Remember the number of people each year who die of bee stings. Be glad you don't live somewhere else. It's estimated that 45,000 people a year die of snake bites worldwide (most of these occur in Asia). Here are a few tidbits of information to keep in mind about snake bites in the United States.

- Some experts estimate *that more than half the poisonous snake bites occur when someone is trying to catch the snake.*

- A significant number of snake bites occur within city limits where most persons aren't watching.

- A significant number of the victims live in the Deep South and are children who are barefoot.

An Eastern diamondback rattlesnake is a tough customer and a snake to avoid.

What I'm saying is snakes are a pretty minor worry. If you learn a little bit about them, you can live in some sort of harmony if not a shaky truce. I've seen lots of rattlesnakes and copperheads, but mostly I've looked for them so I could photograph them. I can truly say they are more scared of us than we are of them. They will almost always get out of your way (with the exception of one or two subspecies). Most snakes will only get defensive if they feel backed into a corner. It pays to be cautious, but there's no reason to panic (you run a greater risk of being held up at gunpoint in the campground).

There are four species of poisonous snakes campers need to look out for in the United States: coral snake; water moccasin; copperhead; and rattlesnake. The water moccasin, copperhead, and rattlesnake are all second cousins and belong to the pit viper family (we'll discuss the pit in pit vipers later).

Identifying Snakes

The coral snake is a beautiful snake with venom very similar to a cobra's. While these snakes are deadly, they are very timid and will do everything they can to get out of your way. Coral snakes aren't just everywhere, either. They live in some locations in the South and in the southernmost parts of the Southwest. Coral snakes are small and rather delicate-looking; they aren't heavy-bodied like pit vipers. They look a lot like a king snake. You can tell the difference by looking at the bands. *Red and yellow kill a fellow!* A king snake is black and yellow.

They don't have needle-like fangs; you have to work to be bitten by a coral snake.

Rattlesnakes, copperheads, and water moccasins belong to the highly evolved family of snakes called pit vipers. Nature has provided a sensory pit between the eye and nostril to enable the snake to feel heat from warm-blooded prey. Pit vipers can

This prairie rattler was sunning itself not far from our camp in South Dakota. In all the years we've camped, this was the first rattler we'd seen by our actual camp. Because there were so many kids about, I shot the snake; otherwise I would have let it go.

sense changes of temperature up to ¼₀₀₀ of a degree up to 3 feet. Even a blind rattlesnake can strike accurately at an object in front of it whether it be a field mouse, a ground squirrel, or your foot.

When you look at a snake and see that pit, keep your distance. A pit is one way to identify a dangerous snake. Pit vipers are also heavy-bodied. (You'll rarely find a 5-foot-long snake the diameter of your thumb.) Another distinguishing feature of this group is the shape of the head. Rattlesnakes, water moccasins, and copperheads will *always* have a triangular-shaped head.

Water moccasins can be aggressive. They are fat-bodied and have a white mouth (which is why it is also called a cottonmouth). Found in the South and Northeast, they live near swamps, and in quiet water and low-lying areas. Often you'll find them near very good largemouth bass habitat. These snakes hang along the shores, or up in bushes, waiting for prey. They do not have a sense of humor. They aren't likely to get out of the way. Watch where you swim in moccasin country.

The copperhead is a beautiful snake that doesn't usually get longer than three feet. The top of the head is copper colored, but there are a lot of variations, and the body has brown patterns over a lighter backdrop. I've seen them as far west as central Texas (Arkansas and Missouri are loaded with them). For the most part, though, copperheads are frequently located east of the Mississippi River. It's the most common poisonous snake in the eastern part of the United States. With the exception of a breed of copperheads in central Florida, these snakes aren't overly aggressive. Most bites occur when a snake is accidently stepped on or is frightened by a rock climber.

In case you are interested, there are thirty-one species and seventy subspecies in this country. Each species has a different level of toxicity. The amount of danger in a bite depends upon the size of the snake (because of the volume of venom in the delivery) and that species's toxicity.

Most rattlers will get out of the way, but there are a few to avoid at all costs. They are temperamental. The Eastern diamondback, for one, can run almost 9 feet long; it lives mainly in the coastal regions of the South. This snake is somewhat aggressive, but the sheer mass of its body and the volume of poison it delivers makes it a fellow to avoid. Coming in a little smaller is the Western diamondback (Texas, Oklahoma, Kansas, New Mexico) and the red diamondback (Baja, Southern California). The Western diamondback is especially grumpy and may be the most aggressive rattler. The Massasauga (in the Midwest) and pygmy rattlers are also testy.

You can ensure your safety by never trying to tease or catch a poisonous snake. A guide friend of ours in Oregon was staying in the Greensprings. In the cool morning when snakes are sluggish, he caught a fat 30-inch-long rattler to show "the folks." (We never accused him of being all that bright where snakes were concerned.) That afternoon he was prodding the snake with his 12-inch Bowie knife. He wanted the reptile to move so it could be admired by his clients. He thought the snake would strike at his blade if it got mad, not his hand. He was wrong.

The coiled serpent never considered it. Those pits aren't there for show. The rattler reached up and nailed him in the thumb. His hand swelled up. Eventually he lost partial use of his hand.

I enjoy snakes even if I don't really like them on a warm personal level. I will not hold snakes, but I like to watch and appreciate them in action. While it's not very macho to admit, snakes have been know to scare me. I startle easily and a snake sliding 2 inches from my foot sends about twenty grams of adrenaline through me. While I shouldn't admit this—it's not politically correct—I've killed a poisonous snake or two in my time when I thought they were about to bite me or they were near where my children were playing. One was about ready to strike when I was fishing. I beat it to death with a $500 Sage fly rod. I gladly bought a new tip for my rod.

I'll admit I've never had even the slightest love for a water moccasin. As any Southern bass fisherperson will tell you, moccasins are something to be avoided.

I've never met an aggressive copperhead. I've never seen a coral snake

Rattlesnakes, water moccasins, and copperheads are pit vipers. Notice the pit or opening between the nose and eye. Vipers use this pit to sense prey. If you see a diamond-shape head or a "pit" you are dealing with a poisonous snake, and you should avoid it.

(except in the zoo). Rattlesnakes have to want to bite me to get up my dander.

Poisonous snakes have a place in the ecosystem. They do a lot of good. They should be left alone. Rarely will a snake need to be sent hastily to the next world. If you do find it necessary, remember a snake can still bite you with ill effect after it's dead. That mouth will snap for some time after you've killed it.

Most of the snakes you encounter will not be poisonous. My wife loves snakes. They seem to love her. She'll gently catch and love them. Snakes seem to hold still and tame instantly for her. She drapes them about her neck, shows the kids, then lovingly lets them go in a nice protected place after blessing them with good health and some sort of snake fertility charm. A couple of years ago we were camping near Moab, Utah, not far from Arches National Park. She caught a very colorful king snake that was about 4 feet long. Our little girl named him Weasel Lips.

We go back and camp there every spring, and we do an exhaustive search for Weasel Lips. We haven't found him yet, but we'll keep looking.

Chapter 21

If You Get Lost:
What to Do If Wanderlust Gets the Better of You

I was backpacking one day in the Yukon Territory about 20 miles from the nearest dirt road. I ran into an old miner skinning a poached moose by the side of a river. I asked him what happened if a guy became lost in that country. "The best advise I got, boy," he said as he spit a wad of tobacco, "is ya don't git ya sef lost." He gave me some moose steak, and I continued wandering. I thought about what he said.

Good advice. It's best not to get lost if you can help it.

You can prevent a lot of problems by watching your trail, observing landmarks, carrying a map, not pushing yourself beyond your experience, and staying on established trails.

If you do miscalculate and get twisted about, taking a few precautions may help you out of a jam.

- Let someone know where you're going.

- Let someone know when you'll be back and when to get worried.

- Always, always carry matches (butane lighter) and a pocket knife on your person. *Never be without them!*

There is little chance of getting lost on a well-groomed trail as long as you stay on the path.

- Carry a small emergency kit in your pocket, fanny pack, or day pack whenever you hike. Such a kit might include a whistle, compass, matches, fire starter, water, granola bars, jacket, and light poncho (disposable).

With a few emergency items, you'll be able to handle most situations until someone is sent to find you. But you have to keep your head.

So You're Lost

Getting lost. It happens more often than you think.

You take a shortcut going back to camp because it's getting dark. You take a wrong turn on a trailhead. You discover after an hour of hiking you've missed a turn and you

Pay close attention to the information at the trailhead. As you push farther into the wilderness, some trails and turns aren't always clearly marked.

don't have a clue where you are. Or you see a lovely butterfly in a meadow and start chasing it. For whatever reason you've strayed from the known and are into the unknown: *You are lost!*

Believe me, I know how you feel.

I've been lost at least 1,500 times myself. Now, what do you do? Let me give you some advice. I've spent more than one night alone in the woods without my gear. It's fun and scary at the same time. You wonder if all that survival stuff you've learned really works. The first bit of advice is hard to follow: *Don't panic!*

This is a lot easier said than done when night is closing in, it's getting cold, rain clouds are blowing in from the north, and you're hungry and worried about the people who are concerned about your not being back.

Stop and Think Before You Act

Sit down on a log and collect yourself. Swallow those feelings of panic. Eat a candy bar or take a drink of water. My old scoutmaster said to wait five or ten minutes before you do anything when you've discovered you're twisted about. My father always told me to *stop and take 500 deep breaths*. "The worst thing that can happen," he'd say, "is your running off thoughtlessly, panicked, without thinking. You'll just get yourself a lot more lost."

After you've collected and controlled your panic, tell yourself the situation isn't that bad. You're going to be fine if you stay cool. Start repeating all those cliches such as "all you have to fear is fear itself." The good news is you're probably not as lost as you think. It could be a lot worse, and it will be, if you start wandering without a game plan.

After your breathing is under control, think through your hike. Maybe the answer is in front of you. Many times the solution will come to you if you get yourself collected. Don't let a wave of panic cause temporary irrationality. Think! Do you recall where you took a wrong turn, where you stepped off the trail?

Look about you. Do you see a familiar mountain peak or landmark? Can you see a familiar lightning-struck snag, a clearing on the hillside, a burned or logged-over hillside? Can you identify a creek or river, a logging road, or trail? Can you find your tracks and backtrack your way to familiar ground (maybe it rained the night before)? Can you take a compass reading? Do you have a map tucked in your fanny pack?

If you get twisted around, stop and think things over. Don't overreact.

At least if you get lost in your vehicle and run out of gas, you've got your camping gear with you.

Think through all your options and don't strike out without serious consideration. Most people who simply "strike out" without thinking get more lost. Will climbing to the top of that peak or rise, the top of a tree, help you see where you are? If you're pretty sure you know your way out, carefully work your way back.

Will following a drainage or creek get you to a road?

If you have a compass use it. Look for peaks, a drainage, a canyon to keep your direction true. Line up on a landmark so you can walk in a straight direction. Walk toward a large tree in the distance, a notch in the mountains, a clearing on a distant hillside. This will help you keep your direction straight. If you are not careful, you'll walk in an endless series of circles.

If you miscalculate or need to return to where you found you were first lost, mark the trail you took so you can find your way back. Depending on the terrain, every 25, 50, or 100 yards use a bit of toilet paper to mark your path. If that isn't available, pile up three rocks, lean several large sticks against a tree, or use any other marker that will help you get back. Remember that unless you have a good plan for keeping your direction, you'll probably walk in circles (which is why landmarks or a compass are so important).

Another technique to use is a calculated "spoke" search. The purpose of this is to find something familiar. After you've marked your home point, walk 500 yards to the north, marking your path as you go. Return to your home point and, in turn, go west, south, east (like the spokes of a wheel). If you don't find something, next time go farther, perhaps 750 to 1,000 yards. Mark your path each time so you can return to your center point.

Follow a drainage and walk downhill if you get lost. Sooner or later you'll run into a camp, a trail, or a road.

Some Swiss Army knives come with emergency kits; this one includes a compass and flashlight.

As a last resort walking downhill or following a stream or river will often take you to a road.

When to Stay Put

If you're not sure where you are, or if night is coming on, your best bet is to stay put. Experts suggest that you'll have a better chance of getting found if you stay in one place. The old Boy Scout notion is to let them find you and not the other way round. There's a certain amount of logic to this, especially if you don't have a lot of backwoods experience.

As soon as you're missed, someone will come looking for you. The key in this situation is for someone to know you are missing. If you've been separated from a group of friends or family, someone will start the search soon. Position yourself in a clearing or on an open hill so that a searcher can see you. Don't stay in the thick stuff if it can be helped. Make three signal fires; write SOS with logs or rocks for overhead planes; shout; fire gunshots; or blow a whistle three times every five, ten, or fifteen minutes (listen carefully for a response). If you think you hear someone, make noise more often. Make sure you pause to listen. A whistle is a very practical tool to have at a time like this. The sound will carry farther than your voice, and you won't burn your lungs out.

Staying Comfortable through the Night

The last thing you want to do is wander about in the dark. If it looks like you aren't going to get rescued that night, or you won't have time to walk out, keep your head. Yes, they'll be worried about you, but you have to think of yourself for now; you have to prepare for a night in the woods, without all the comforts. If you have a few items, it will be a lot easier and more comfortable.

The first thing you need is a fire. Find a safe place, preferably one with a reflector, such as a big rock. If you can't find one, or if it looks like it's going to rain, make a simple lean-to. Start collecting wood before you make your fire. Remember, it takes

Emergency Shelter

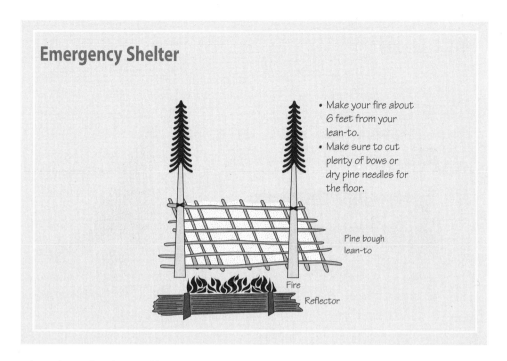

- Make your fire about 6 feet from your lean-to.
- Make sure to cut plenty of bows or dry pine needles for the floor.

Pine bough lean-to

Fire

Reflector

a lot of wood to keep a blaze going all night. You'll particularly want to build the fire up if it gets cold and that takes fuel. Collect all the wood you think you'll need to keep warm through the night. Now go out and collect that much again. Remember, once it's dark you're pinned to your camp. After you've collected enough wood—really collected enough wood—work on your shelter. If the weather is mild and it doesn't look like it's going to rain, you may not need much of a shelter.

If you have water, start drinking it. If you're near a lake or a stream, drink your fill and drink again minutes later. I know the water may not be pure and might have giardia or something else, but you can be treated for that later. Right now it's more important that you stay hydrated. You're about to face a night in the woods without a tent or sleeping bag. Having a belly full of water will help you stay warm. Remember dehydration increases the danger of hypothermia.

Fashion a crude lean-to and weave in pine boughs to keep off moisture and dew. It will also act as a firebreak. It's not environmentally sound to break or cut boughs when camping. In a survival situation, however, it's perfectly acceptable to take all the boughs you need. Next, look under pine trees and gather dry pine needles for the floor of your shelter. (Even if it's damp out, you can usually find dry needles under large pine trees.) Dry leaves will work nicely if there are no pine needles. You don't want to sit on bare ground.

Tree Lean-to

A quick lean-to can be made by stacking bows against a tree.

If you find yourself lost and can't make a fire, make a **deep** bed of leaves or pine needles between two fallen trees. Burrow under the leaves or needles for warmth.

Lean-to with a space saver blanket

This type of lean-to will reflect the heat nicely.

A bed of dry needles or leaves can be quite comfortable.

After your shelter is made, carefully collect dried wood and start your fire so you have a nice bed of coals. If you have time, collect more wood. Matches, obviously, are a must. A pocketknife is very handy for cutting branches and boughs to make a shelter. As a brief aside, the second I leave my house, I always have my Swiss Army knife (the Champ with all those fancy blades) riding comfortably on my belt. Several times in emergency situations, I've used the magnifying glass to get a fire started when something has happened to my matches or lighter. I use the blades and other tools all the time, too.

I have a standard emergency kit I carry with me (besides the matches and pocketknife in my pocket). It's a plastic case that holds waterproof matches. The top is a compass, the bottom a whistle. I have a ball of twine, fire starter, space blanket, disposable raincoat, plastic garbage sack, aluminum foil, a Powerbar or two, dried fruit, water, and water-purification tablets. The entire thing fits in my hand, weighs almost nothing, and tucks easily in my day pack or coat pocket. I've spent a few nights huddled about a fire wrapped in a space blanket.

If you find you are lost without matches and the evening will be chilly, you have several options. Your best bet, if you have dry leaves or pine needles, is to make a giant bed between two big logs. Lay boughs on the bottom and fill the bed up with needles or dry leaves. You'll want to make your bed at least 2 feet deep. You'll need a good bottom to keep you off the cold ground, as well as enough insulation to cover yourself. When night comes, bury yourself in the leaves, curl into a ball to keep warm, and try to get some sleep.

If there is no way to build a shelter for the night, try to pick out a path to walk before it gets dark—say a ¼-mile circle. Mark the path well so you can walk it in the dark. Walking will keep you warm. You'll never be without matches again.

Lost Children

Nothing is more frightening than losing a child while camping—something I know from experience.

This is my standard emergency kit when hiking. It's always in my day pack in a Ziploc. Besides the knife and lighter in my pocket, I carry an all-in-one "emergency tube" that contains a whistle, waterproof matches, compass, and small signal; a space blanket; a space emergency bag; 50 feet of string; a sheet of aluminum foil; a candle; tissue; dried fruit and a Powerbar.

Emergency Fire

- Spending a night outdoors means collecting a lot of firewood.
- Make a narrow fire about 5 feet long so you can lay down beside it.

While we occasionally hear dramatic stories about lost children, please keep in mind the outdoors is far more child-friendly and safe than any metropolitan area. Nearly all lost children stories have a happy ending. Besides, rarely do children wander very far.

To avoid aging ten years in an afternoon, you should consider a few simple points. There is no substitute for keeping a close eye on your kids. Picking camping spots where your kids can play without getting lost is important. When you first set up camp, walk them about the area and orient them to the land. Set up boundaries of where they can go and where they are to turn around. We require younger kids to check in with us either every half hour or every time they move to a new location.

Next we teach our children what to do if they're lost. First, we tell them not to panic. (We'll be doing enough of that.) Someone will miss them soon and come looking. We suggest that they have a seat and get comfortable. The worst thing, we teach, is to take off blindly.

We issue each child a whistle to carry about his or her neck. We insist they don't blow it unless they are lost or there's an emergency. If they are lost, they are to start blowing their whistle until they're found. Even a good whistle is rather inexpensive and will survive any amount of abuse.

If a child loses the whistle or it quits working, he or she is supposed to yell *help*! Count to ten, twenty-five, fifty, or sixty (depending on how well they can count), then yell *help*.

Our children know that if they're lost, they should stay put and blow a whistle or shout.

You'd be surprised how acute your parental sense of hearing becomes when a child is lost. A good whistle can be heard a long way. If a child is taught to hold to one place, it makes locating him or her much easier. For my own well-being, we hold getting-lost drills. I take a child to a spot in the forest and have him or her sit. I walk out of sight. Pretending to be lost, the child blows the whistle and I come to the rescue.

Like a fire drill, it's good practice.

Section Three

Different Ways to Camp

Chapter 22

Expanding Your Camping Horizons: Other Ways to Get There and Have Fun

Besides car camping and backpacking, there are other ways to camp or arrive at camping spots.

I guess I like about every form of outdoor camping. I can't think of any part of it I don't like. I discovered that I loved canoeing and canoe camping relatively recently. My only regret is I didn't start it earlier when I was bolder, stronger, and more reckless. Loading up a canoe with camping stuff and heading off into the wilderness is one of the great joys of outdoor adventuring. A lot of waters have yet to be discovered.

My wife enjoys packing in with horses and setting up a base camp in the middle of nowhere. She also has enjoyed trailer camping when the kids were young or it's really stormy. My son has a passion for bike camping.

In this section's chapters, I'll talk about other ways to enjoy the outdoors: canoe camping; mountain biking; and trailer camping.

There are more ways to get down the trail than hiking.

Chapter 23

Canoe Camping:
Paddling Your Way to Camping Freedom

I love canoes and canoe camping.

Canoe camping is a wonderful way to see a different face of Mother Nature. It will not only expand your outdoor enjoyment but it's also a way to get into the backcountry after your knees have given out. You neither have to be an expert paddler nor have a fancy canoe. All you need is a little skill and an appetite for beautiful country.

Canoe Camping Brings Back the Nostalgia of the North Woods

There's a certain nostalgia about canoe camping I can't escape.

I always feel a part of an outdoor brotherhood when I dip my paddle, when I hear wild Canada geese, or when I glide gracefully across the water. It reminds me of the great North Woods, the land of sky-blue waters and wide-open frontiers. Canoeing takes me back several hundred years to when this land was a new world, unspoiled and unpeopled; when all a person needed was a good rifle, a sturdy birchbark canoe, a dose of courage, and some big dreams.

Canoeing is a great pastime. It's a great way to fish, a great way to see new sights, and a great way to get to a new camping area.

I always feel a certain romance associated with a canoe (okay, I'm a hopeless romantic; I like Keats and Shelley, too). I'm paddling with the great voyagers, the Great Lakes Indians, the early trappers. When I paddle I try to see the land before it was tainted by white men. I love seeing a moose on a point, a beaver slap its tail, the turning of the leaves after the first frost, a she-bear and her cubs swimming between two shores. I like the pull of the water and the way my shoulder gets tight if I paddle too hard.

As I said I love my canoe.

When I canoe camp, I don't have to worry about packing as light as I do when I backpack. I take my forty-year-old cast-iron skillet because I like how it cooks. I like

Canoe Camping Tips

❏ Wear tie-on shoes that won't come off easily when you step in the mud.

❏ Use glasses straps or some other arrangement to attach all sunglasses and prescription glasses so they don't drop in the water.

❏ Don't overload the canoe.

❏ A rainsuit will keep you drier than a poncho.

❏ Keep a second pair of shoes and socks in Ziploc bags for hikes.

❏ Kids must always wear a personal flotation device (PFD).

❏ If your kids swim, they should still always wear a PFD and shoes to protect feet.

❏ Plan easy days.

❏ Bring toilet paper.

❏ Drink plenty of water.

❏ Bring Tylenol or aspirin for aches.

the feel of cooking with old iron, and I like how it makes my food taste. I also take a fire-burned enamel coffeepot that's brought me good luck. And while I ordinarily try to watch my fat grams, canoe cooking means fried bacon, ham, and eggs. It means Canadian bacon. It means buckwheat flour pancakes that will stick to your ribs for 10 miles. It means Roget's Cane Syrup and a tin of blueberry preserves.

When you canoe camp, you can take more weight than when you go backpacking. Four-star chef Alan is cooking up one of his masterpieces.

I love to sit at dusk—my fire crackling and popping, the coffee-pot steaming—and watch the water reflect the last rays of light. My canoe is tucked up on shore and the food stashed in a bear bag hanging from a distant tree. My green tent looks almost black in the failing light. Can anything be more lovely than looking into an infinity of treetops silhouetted against a slightly lighter sky? Soon the stars will slide across the sky and get brighter.

While I love everything about canoe camping, I have to admit, I'm not a brilliant canoeist. I'm not sure I'm good. In fact, I'm probably somewhat average. I've been canoeing for years and logged a lot of miles, but I've never arrived as a brilliant paddler. I'm not confident about shooting rapids, and I can't paddle all day without aching. I play at being a voyager, but in the back of my mind it's just a game and I know it. I'll always be a better fly fisherman.

The Canoe Itself

You can spend a lot of money on a canoe and get your money's worth. There are some expensive and well-built canoes on the market, and I've enjoyed paddling many

The Least You Should Know About Canoe Length

❏ A short 14- or 15-foot-long canoe will hold one person and his or her gear. It's a slower vessel but easy to control.

❏ A 16-foot-long canoe is a one- or two-person craft, plus gear. It's a good general-purpose canoe.

❏ A 17-foot-long canoe is a three-person craft, plus gear. This is a good-size canoe for longer trips. The longer the canoe, the faster it will go.

❏ An 18-foot-long canoe is a four-person craft, plus gear. This is an excellent canoe for longer trips

miles in them. Some are built for lakes, others for freight (carrying lots of gear), others for streams, others for white water, and others are all-purpose. The latter group isn't really great at any one thing in particular, but okay for use in a number of situations. While a specialized canoe is very good at what it's designed for, it doesn't always successfully cross to another use.

Your Type of Canoe

I use my canoe in a number of situations, so an all-purpose craft meets my needs nicely. Besides canoeing for pleasure and canoe camping, I do a lot of fishing and I need a craft that's stable. I use my trusty old Coleman on ponds and lakes and in streams and rivers. I don't have room in my garage to store a canoe for every occasion.

If you plan to do only lake or river canoeing, then you'd be wise to select a canoe designed for that type of water. For most of us, however, a general-purpose model does the trick. Once you've decided you're going to get a canoe, you need to decide how much you want to spend. There's a canoe to match every budget.

You can buy a Coleman canoe for about $300 (give or take a few bucks) that will last you for thirty years even if you neglect it. Or you can spend about $700 on a Mad River, $1,300 on a Dagger, around $1,800 on an excellent Old Town, or about $2,100 for a Sawyer. You can spend considerably more on a custom design. Any of these canoes will easily last a lifetime or two with proper care.

They're all good values for your dollar, and all the manufacturers I've mentioned make good products. Each will give you fine service. Certainly you can expect a more expensive canoe to be more responsive and to have features that you'll fully appreciate only as you grow into your craft. You can expect to feel a little dissatisfied with a lower-end canoe as your skills increase and you become a more discerning paddler.

It's a trade-off.

You won't feel reluctant to lend your Coleman to the local Boy Scout troop for a summer campout. You won't, however, want to loan your prized Old Town, Mad River, Sawyer, or Dagger unless you are there to supervise.

If you plan to take long canoe trips in which you'll be in your canoe for days upon paddling days, it will be worth it to invest in a higher-end

What do you want to use your canoe for? Before you take out your checkbook, have a pretty good idea about how you want to paddle. Few things are more fun than stopping to take a close look at lily pads.

My canoe fits on my car and goes where we go—it stays on our car top almost all summer. This Coleman is easy for one person to take on and off.

canoe that's more responsive and lighter. If you're taking shorter trips you may not notice the difference so readily.

I've done some serious paddling in several different Old Town and Mad River canoes, and I have nothing but good to say about them. For a long trip they are well worth the investment. The canoes I used were long and less affected by crosswinds. They cut the water splendidly. The difference is that of a Corvette versus a Taurus. They'll both get you there, but one does it more easily and with more style and grace.

I wouldn't want to take a really long trip in my current canoe. My Coleman, however, is a great workhorse, a super general-purpose beast. It's very good for fishing because it has a wide bottom, and it's stable. I stand up in it all the time. I've been abusing it since 1992. It's nearly indestructible and perfect for an outdoor writer. Once I put it on my Bronco and took off down a bumpy dirt road. A friend was supposed to have lashed it down. At about 40 miles per hour I saw a red blob drift off into space behind me and tumble nose-over-teakettle before going over the edge of a sharp bank. It bashed into several trees and came to rest in the midst of some Hereford cows.

We tied it back on and went to the next pond. I'm sure there were a few more scratches, but I couldn't tell you where. There was no major damage as far as I could see. I've not been gentle with that canoe. We've forgotten to strap it down at least three other times (we were too anxious to get to another fishing pond). Once we dragged it several hundred yards at 40 mph over rocks and such before stopping (I didn't know it had come off). In fact, I've been brutal.

The truth is: I use it a lot and don't have time to be gentle. Another thing I like about my Coleman is it's designed to carry cargo. For what it lacks in handling, it makes up in payload. If dollars are tight this canoe will give you a lot of value for your money. There's a reason so many Boy Scout troops and summer camps have Colemans. It's a good first craft.

If a new canoe isn't right for you, don't overlook the used market. Keep an eye on the papers or garage sales. I've seen some really good buys, canoes that have hardly been used. Be aware, too, that rental places and summer camps often sell off their used fleets of canoes. They might be a little banged up, but they are usable. I've seen a number of serviceable canoes sell for under $100.

Short of running over a Coleman canoe with a truck, it's almost impossible to hurt it. When new, my canoe looked like this; now it's battle scarred and scratched, but ready for another twenty years.

Old Town makes the excellent Penobscot.

Canoe Skills

Unless you are going with a friend who is knowledgeable, practice before you go on your first official camping trip.

When the canoe is loaded, even on calm water, we wear personal flotation devices. It looks like this canoe is overloaded; all the heavy gear is on the bottom, however, only light gear is on top.

There are several reasons for this: Most important is that your life is valuable. Let's keep canoeing a safe sport. Don't take off with a payload until you know how to maneuver the craft. It doesn't take very long, but it does take practice.

Safety

Camping and canoeing are wonderful sports alone and combined they are double the fun.

Keep it safe. Buy good life jackets or personal flotation devices (PFDs). Buy even better ones for your kids. Don't consider those stupid little orange things. They're only a little better than nothing! Get a good PFD!

Size: Get a PFD that fits you. Remember you're going to be paddling in it so don't buy the first thing you see (even if the color is trendy or it's on sale). You need to be comfortable when you'll be paddling in it all day. Different life vests are made for different reasons so get one that fits you and your use.

Set up rules about wearing a PFD: My rules are simple. If you're under 18 years of age, you always wear a PFD in my craft (I don't care how hot it is). If you can't swim, you always wear a PFD in my craft. If you are an average swimmer, you always wear a PFD:

I confess: If I'm within a couple hundred yards of shore on a calm lake or small pond (usually I'm fishing), I don't always wear my PFD. I like having it right by my feet, though. If there's more than a ripple on the water, I put it on; if I cross any large body of water, I put it on; and if I'm on *any* flowing water—no matter what—I wear a PFD.

Practice

Learn what it's like to face a wind without a payload. Don't be too proud. Know when you need to head for shore. Swamp your canoe in shallow water and try getting back in. Try some basic techniques. See how much it takes to capsize your craft. Learn your limits. You should know the different canoe strokes and a little bit about reading water. Get an expert friend to teach you, or select a book on the subject (consider Globe Pequot's *The Complete Book of Canoeing*).

Review first aid and know what to do if someone has inhaled or swallowed water. Wear your PFD.

A Few Ideas to Consider

A good rope: I always tie about 15 feet of rope to both stem and stern. Use a good grade of rope that is thick and supple so you can grab it bare-handed without it cutting your skin. You'll use this rope to tie up the craft, to tie your canoe to your car, to pull the craft from shore, and to tie it to another canoe. I also lash in another 20 or 30 feet of rope to the center beam in case I need it for something.

An extra paddle: Up the creek without a paddle is an old cliché worth remembering. Use a couple of bungee cords to lash in a spare paddle that stays with your boat. This is especially critical on a long trip around white water. Each craft should have an extra paddle.

Loading Your Canoe

If you're not going to make any portages (or only a small one), you can pack like you would for a normal camp. A canoe will hold a lot of gear. Most of us, however, have found that cutting back on the weight in the long run is probably a good thing (especially if you have to portage often or over long distances).

I've come to think of packing for canoe camping as packing somewhere between backpacking and car camping. If you have to err, err on the side of lighter. Before you leave home, lay out your gear, and load it in your canoe. Now is the time—not on the beachhead before you leave—to catch any problems.

Waterproof Your Gear

Always assume you're going to get wet.

It makes sense that if you get wet, your stuff is going to get wet, too, unless you take precautions. When you canoe, you must make sure everything is waterproofed. All sorts of fancy white-water bags are available to keep your belongings dry. If you keep canoe camping, no doubt you'll want to invest in such gear. In the meantime you can cut corners the way we do.

I go to my favorite grocery store and buy a box of heavy-duty garbage bags. I also buy an assortment of heavy-duty Ziploc bags (especially the gallon size). Unless I'm using a compression sack, I line my stuff sack with a garbage sack and put in my sleep-

On a gentle paddle, or when fishing, canoe chairs are a comfortable addition. Make sure you pull your canoe out of the water enough so it doesn't drift off.

A last-minute shakedown before paddling across Green River Lake in Wyoming's Wind River Range. This lake is the headwater of Green River. This is famous mountain-man country.

ing bag. Then I wrap it again with another garbage sack. I do the same with my clothes. If I can stuff them in a Ziploc, I will. If not, I put them in a garbage bag, squeeze out the air, and seal it.

Next I line my backpack with a garbage sack and put in my gear. I obviously can't get as much in as I could normally, but what I have will stay dry. With foodstuffs, I put as much as I can in Ziplocs. Then I take a plastic box, line it with a plastic sack, and load the Ziploc bags inside. Later, I run a strip of duct tape around the seams for added measure.

I like my creature comforts, so I usually take an ice chest filled with frozen foods. I line the bottom with a good supply of dry ice topped with a layer of newspaper. Next I put in frozen foods and cover them with another layer of newspaper. Then I duct tape it shut, so it's waterproof and won't open if it's dropped.

I wrap the stove in a plastic bag, and, along with the cooking ware, secure it in another plastic box, then, of course, duct tape the seams.

Now my gear is waterproof if the canoe takes a roll. (And if you do much canoeing, eventually it will.) I've never dumped a boat in the middle of a lake, but I haven't been as lucky in rivers and streams. Once we were "pull-portaging" our canoes upstream via a handy path. There was a stretch of strange currents and my boat got crossed and flipped upside down. The current was so strong it was all I could do to hold it. After pulling I tied the rope off to a tree and jumped in to drag the boat shoreward. The canoe was upside down for about ten minutes before I righted it. Everything we'd wrapped was dry.

Distributing the Weight

There is a postulate that never varies when loading a canoe: *Keep your gear, and especially the heaviest stuff, close to the center line and keep it low!*

To say that canoes are load-sensitive would be an understatement. They draw very little water because of their inherent design, so they are at the mercy of breezes, waves, and how the weight is distributed. Unless your craft is properly trimmed, it will be tough to control and possibly dangerous to you and your passenger.

A canoe's hull (remember there are different types) determines much of the craft's stability. The rule of thumb, however, is to keep the weight as centered and as low in the canoe as possible. If you get too much weight to one side or another, you'll not be trimmed and the craft will list.

Don't load to the point where you are sitting low in the water. You want plenty of freeboard, which is the distance between the water and the gunwale.

Securing Gear in the Canoe

There's an art to packing a canoe. I'm not sure I have it completely mastered, but there are a couple of things to keep in mind. If you load your canoe and it doesn't feel right when you go on a test run, immediately return to shore and repack. Don't take a chance.

Pack the gear so it is balanced: Your craft shouldn't be lopsided. After your canoe is loaded, it must float evenly. If it lists to one side, it will throw off the balance in tight turns and will make you work harder than necessary. If it lists too much, you will be a rollover waiting to happen.

Secure your gear: If your canoe tips over, having

Lee is about to arrange the gear and make the canoe stable in the water. He loaded his equipment to get an idea about how to arrange it. In addition to being a great camping friend, Lee is one of the best dry fly casters I've ever fished with.

your stuff waterproofed won't do any good if it floats away. Lash it in carefully so it stays put even if the canoe is upside down. When in doubt, secure your gear again.

I once saw a canoe flip. The gear stayed together but was strung out behind the boat—partly floating, partly sinking—precariously secured by a common rope. It was a struggle to get it to shore because the gear acted like an anchor.

You want the gear to stay put snugly tucked.

You must remain comfortable: Don't pack your gear so it cramps you or your partner. You need to be comfortable. Don't straddle stuff. If you're overpacked, leave something in the car.

Every canoe manufacturer lists how much total weight (cargo and people) its canoe will hold. In a pinch I've loaded to the limit, even beyond during an emergency, but I always try to stay below the prescribed total weight. The canoe is a lot easier to control. The first few times you load your canoe, you'll be a little clumsy, but after a while you'll be doing it like a champ.

Your First Canoe Trip

Before you plan a long trip, take a few short adventures (maybe even a trip without portages). Get the hang of it before you head off for a three-week sojourn into the North Woods. Get all the hitches worked out. Make your mistakes when you aren't too far from home. Go on a short trip!

How Far You Want to Travel

Paddling a canoe can be fun and almost lazy, like Huck and Jim on the Big Muddy. Or it can be an endeavor in physical endurance, an Olympic trial. If you've taken a few trips near home, you'll know how long you want to paddle in one day. You may find you like the thrill of paddling from first light until late afternoon; you like to get a lot of water miles under your belt (you're cut from the same bolt of cloth as the packer who likes to see how many miles he or she can do a day).

You may find you like to stop and smell the lily pads every few minutes. You enjoy "the going." Rushing to make the itinerary isn't part of the fun. You love the journey itself and don't want to miss one bit of it.

A small lake such as this is a good place to practice your canoeing skills.

Planning Distances

Water and conditions vary from place to place. These estimates will give you a rough idea, but no more. I've assumed that the beginning paddler has some experience and this trip isn't a first-time adventure. I've been on some very easy 10- to 15-mile-long paddles and some very difficult 5-mile trips. I've seen times where we stopped after 6 miles because the wind was so taxing. Build a lot of slack into your plans. Most campers don't want to feel they're in boot camp. They'd rather have a little more time in camp to romp about.

	Lakes and Ponds (flat water)	Lakes and Ponds (some wind)	Current 1–3 mph (several portages)	Current 4–8 mph (several portages)
Beginner	5–10 miles	6–13 miles	7–15 miles	12-plus miles
Average	9–15 miles	10–17 miles	10–17 miles	18-plus miles
Advanced	12–18 miles	13–22 miles	15–22 miles	25-plus miles

Deciding what sort of a paddler you are takes time. This is why you need to take a few practice trips. Depending on the water, I'm comfortable doing 5 to 14 miles a day. I like to cover some water, you can be sure, but I like to see the sights along the way. I enjoy having enough time to stop and watch a moose. I also like to stop and set up camp early. I want time to take a few hikes, to paddle around areas of interest, to cast a few lines at big fish. I like to lay over a day or two if I find a wonderful spot.

This is how I like to do my trips, so I find people who feel the same way I do. If you want to do 10 miles a day and your buddy wants to do 26, there might be a conflict. I have several friends with whom I enjoy backpacking, but I know better than to canoe with them. Their canoe-camping goals are different from mine. Our differences would cause a big argument. Canoe with those who have the same goals. Remember, if you go with a group, you are never faster than your slowest paddler.

Planning Your Trip

There are a number of water trails about. Get maps and plan your trip before you hit the water. It makes good sense, and it's fun. Make sure you leave some downtime in the schedule to account for different water levels or for an extra-long difficult portage.

Note take-out points and portages (and their lengths) on your map. Make a rough determination of how many miles you want to do in one day. On one waterway we

Make sure you have your canoe strapped down tightly when you transport it. Stop a few miles after you've tied it on to make certain your canoe is still secure.

worked all day but covered only 4 or 5 miles because there were so many rough portages. We were beat and that was all we could do. Take into account how much your gear weighs and how many trips it will take to pack it. (This is one reason why I load a lot of my belongings in backpacks. It makes portages easier.)

Beware: Not all water maps are made by careful people. Some are made by folks who've gotten into the cooking sherry and are tipsy. Maps covering older, more established water trails are somewhat more dependable; they've been adjusted and tweaked until most of the information is right. Some water trails are thoughtlessly chronicled so you must take your chances and figure a certain amount of map "slop" into the equation.

Some water trails have established camping areas along the route. This often makes it easy to plan your trip because the sites are usually an easy day apart. I've found most of these camps wonderfully kept and delightful places to stay. If there aren't established camps, look at a topographic map to get ideas of where you might like to stop or lay over. On most waterways there's a good chance that someone has preceded you, so you should be able to find a good spot that others have used. This will help reduce the impact on the area.

If you are in an area that is somewhat untouched, be careful to have as marginal an impact on the land as you can.

Camping with Little Impact

Just a reminder. In the nineteenth century Paul Bunyan's job was cutting down endless forests. Today your job is to save some forests for your children and grandchildren. Use only dead wood for fires. Don't cut down live trees (they burn poorly anyway). And be careful with fires.

Go potty a good distance from the water's edge.

Pack out all your garbage.

If there are more than four canoes in your party, you might want to consider different camping areas to help reduce the impact.

Canoe Emergency and Fix-It Kit

I keep a small bag strapped inside my canoe. Jon-Michael calls it the emergency/fix-it kit. I've never been able to come up with a better name. It's there "just in case." In the bag there are:

- ❏ several Powerbars
- ❏ water-purification tablets
- ❏ a water bottle
- ❏ a butane lighter, fire starter, candle
- ❏ a coil of wire
- ❏ a four-in-one Phillips-head screwdriver
- ❏ a space blanket
- ❏ several nails
- ❏ a small amount of duct tape

I've never been stranded overnight in my canoe, but cold afternoon winds and high waves have sent me shoreward several times before I could reach camp or my truck. To weather the layovers I built a cozy fire and used my space blanket as a windbreaker. I was glad I had my kit. On another occasion I came across a kayaker who had ripped a hole in her craft. I gave her my duct tape to patch the hole and get the kayak seaworthy.

Canoe Lean-to

- • Use your canoe with a tarp for shelter
- • Use extra tarp for a ground cloth

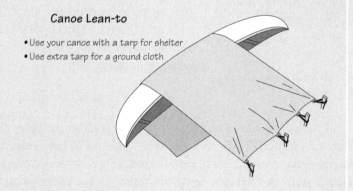

Chapter 24

Mountain Biking:
A New Twist to Camping

In the mid-1970s a few outdoor daredevils (who grew up terrorizing the neighborhood on Schwinn Stingray bikes) brought the sport of mountain biking to the twentieth century.

Mountain Biking Catches on Fast

Using a balloon-tire bicycle frame, homemade parts, and some old-fashioned Yankee ingenuity, these backyard diehards started experimenting with off-road "motocross" bikes that could climb a steep hill, jump a ditch, travel gracefully over mountain or desert trails, handle rough terrain, or carry enough gear to take you bike camping. Something beyond their wildest imagination happened. Mountain biking caught on.

Many campgrounds have special camping areas just for bike campers.

At first, mountain biking attracted only the super athlete with calves and thighs the size of The Terminator. Before long, however, regular folks realized that these fancy bikes would handle trail conditions. It dawned on them that a mountain bike would also be a great tool for simply getting off the beaten path.

Before long, people of every age and physical-fitness level were mountain biking. It opened up a whole new vista for enjoying Mother Nature. There are few places you can't mountain bike (as long as it's legal to do it). It's become a favorite camper's pastime. It's not far behind hiking and fishing.

You Too Can Ride Like a Pro

If you've never been on a mountain bike, don't worry. Yeah, there are a lot of gears and you can nearly ride up a telephone pole on it, but remember biking is only as intense as you make it. Like many sports, it appears more complex and complicated than it really is. Certainly mountain biking is not as complicated as the bike shops make it. You don't have to take your bike to all those rough-looking places the bike-shop posters seem to glorify.

The truth is almost anyone can enjoy biking. *If you ride a bike, you can mountain bike.* You can pedal on the logging roads of the Pacific Northwest or the Southeast, you can pump the mountain trails of Colorado, you can ride through the Appalachians, you can wander among the wonders of Yellowstone, or you can travel the slickrock desert country of southern Utah.

You can make mountain biking as gentle or as extreme as you wish.

If you already have a mountain bike, you're halfway to enjoying this new twist on camping. Maybe, though, you haven't succumbed to that little voice in your head telling you how much fun mountain biking or bike camping looks.

A little biking is also a great way to beat that middle-age spread. It's fun to bike with your kids, too. Besides, biking is low-impact exercise. Visit your doctor, see what he or she says. Start slow and easy; try biking to a picnic.

Maybe you decided last year to get into shape so you went out and bought yourself a brand new Specialized Hard Rock mountain bike to help you in your worthy pursuit. Now, though, it's collecting dust in some distant dark corner of your garage. Maybe your spouse is still upset that you spent so much money on that bike, and you haven't even used it (except that first time when you rode it down your street).

It's time to start pedaling. There are a lot of possibilities. Take your bike(s) and ride about the campground. Your kids will love it. Take your bike and explore the outdoors in a new way. Take your bike and get off the road to ride some trails. Or take your bike and do some camping.

Picking the Right Bike

If you don't have a bike and you're thinking about getting one, this section will help you make a proper choice.

If you've been into your local sporting-goods store or bike shop lately, you've probably noticed a great number of "mountain" bikes taking up the majority of the floor space. There are indeed many bikes and many models from which to choose.

Before you spend your precious money on some hybrid frame with fancy space-age aluminum alloys, decide what kind of biking you plan to do. Are you the adven-

This camping family is also a biking family. They enjoy setting up a base camp and riding the many roads and trails in the area.

A lot of trails are open for mountain biking. Check the regulations in your area and have fun.

turesome type who would like to go on a five-day quest through the red rocks of southern Utah? Are you the more conservative type who would like to take a relaxing ride through Yellowstone Park, camping as you go? Or are you the sort who wants to use your camp as a base for bike riding?

By deciding now how the bike will be used, you'll be able to buy the bike best suited to your purpose. To help you make this important decision, let's talk about which bikes are best suited to particular terrains.

Tires: 26-inch versus 28-inch

There are two types of bikes suited to camping adventures. The first is the 28-inch-tire bicycle or mountain-touring bike. As you've probably already figured out, it has 28-inch wheels that are geared for riding on paved or smooth dirt roads or campground trails. They will smooth out some of the rough stuff. The other major player is the 26-inch wheel. This is the traditional wheel for a "hard-rock" mountain bike. It is more adapted to riding in rough terrain. The tires give you a little better traction and control in the rougher stuff.

Let's look at these bikes in more detail.

Mountain-touring bikes, 28-inch wheel: Think of touring as low-impact mountain biking. You ride around on roads in popular national forests and parks, gentle trails, and dirt roads. There are fewer hard bumps and no technical trails along steep mountain crevices requiring insanely precise steering ability.

Touring can be enjoyed by people of all ages. If you'd like to bike and camp but you're not up to hard and bumpy terrain, touring is the way to go. If you've decided that touring is your style, consider a mountain-touring bike. Touring bikes are also known as hybrids (a mishmash of the traditional ten-speed road bike and the more modern mountain bike). The wheels are slightly bigger in diameter than those on a mountain bike but slightly smaller than those on a ten-speed.

Make sure you buy the bike with tires that will be suited to your type of riding. Hybrids can usually be purchased with smooth tires strictly for riding on roads or "bumpy" tires more suited to lightly bumpy dirt roads. If you plan on doing both types of riding and you have a few extra dollars, buy an extra set of tires and change them as necessary.

One feature of the touring bike that I dare not forget is the larger seat. Although some touring bikes try to appeal to the svelte crowd by putting on a puny, light-as-a-feather-titanium rail seat, most companies still use bigger seats with a lot of padding and/or gel. If you want ultra comfort or you've got a big bottom, order your bike with a bigger seat (preferably with springs).

Mountain bikes, 26 inch-wheel: Maybe you're the hardcore bumpin' jumpin' type who is always looking for the greatest thrill. Perhaps you prefer riding through forests on isolated deer trails or riding on bumpy red-rock surfaces. If you intend to ride on a lot of dirt roads, consider a mountain bike.

Mountain bikes are smaller than touring bikes and more suited to harsh terrain. The wheels are smaller and the fork is straighter to provide a better steering response. Mountain bikes are usually sold with some sort of suspension and suspension can be great for ironing out all those bumps. You get what you pay for: You'll save yourself a lot of headache and repair time by making the proper investment.

Don't expect a big seat with a mountain bike. There are some mountain bike seats that are comfortable, however, even though they are light. If you want a spring-loaded seat, and you really want a mountain bike, consider buying a more comfortable replacement seat. Or ask the clerk if you can trade for something else. If he or she won't trade, see if another dealer will and take your business there.

Test Ride Before You Buy

You'd never go to a car lot and buy a car without driving it around the block a few times. The same goes for bikes.

After you've narrowed your choices, ask the clerk if you can take the bike out and ride it. Is the seat too hard, too narrow, or just right? How does the bike steer? Does it seem to turn too fast, too slow? Do you feel well-balanced as you ride? It better feel darn good in the parking lot.

Ask if you can take the bike on a longer ride, maybe thirty minutes to an hour. Leave your keys and a credit card as collateral. You might think that all bikes ride the same, but every bike has its own feel. After you've spent some time riding several different bikes, buy the bike that feels the most natural to you. Color and paint jobs look nice, but bikes that get used get scratched up. Go for feel, not cosmetics.

This family camped in the foothills and biked the many old mining roads. They saw a half dozen other people in a week.

Racks and Panniers

After you get a the bike, you're halfway to bike camping if that's part of your plan.

Day Activities: For bikers who want to go on day adventures, a day pack is made to order. Put the stuff you need such as your lunch, a book, a jacket, a water bottle (unless you have one attached to your bike frame, which is a good idea) in the pack and you're on your way.

Bike Camping: If you want to camp you have to carry your gear in something. You can strap on a backpack and hop on your bike. If you're not sure you want to bike camp this might be a good way to go for your first few trips as long as you're not going too far. A backpack can throw off your balance. It makes your butt sore, too.

There's a better way to outfit your bike. It costs a little more, but it's a great convenience. Install some racks and panniers (the technical term for bike bags).

A rack is simply a piece of metal you put over the wheels. The rack hooks onto the wheel hub and the bike frame so you have a platform on which to load your gear. The rack is the support skeleton for the panniers. The pannier is a bag that folds over the rack. It is no different than any other bag except that is was designed to conform to the shape of your bike.

The next step is to determine how many racks and panniers you need. If you plan on doing multi-day adventures in the Colorado Rockies where space is critical, you probably need a front and back pannier. This will allow you to carry all your gear and supplies. If you plan on doing short day trips or overnighters, you may only need one pannier for your back wheel.

What really matters is performance on the trail. How does the bike feel? A fancy paint job isn't as important as a comfortable ride.

There are many bags you could buy for your bike, including seat, frame, and handlebar bags. I use a small seat bag to carry all my tools. It's nice to have them apart from the rest of the equipment. Many people use a handlebar bag. These can be very handy. Many nicer models have a plastic sleeve on the top so you can view your map as you ride. They are also handy for storing quick snacks, water, tools, toilet paper, and other items.

Buying the Necessary Equipment

There is no reason to spend a fortune on racks. Racks are racks; a titanium alloy rack isn't any better than an aluminum or even a steel rack. Don't be fooled by crafty salespeople who are paid on commission. Do avoid, however, very cheap, soldered bike racks. They will break apart and cause unneeded problems along the trail. Plan on spending at least thirty dollars for a good sturdy rack.

Panniers come in all shapes, sizes, and prices! They aren't cheap either. Be wary of any pannier that is cheaper than forty dollars. Look

I can mountain bike far enough away from the crowd to get to the best fishing. I load my waders and vest into my backpack and go.

at all the different bags your bike shop has to offer. Is the bag roomy enough? Is it made out of high-quality material? Is the stitching reinforced? Is the bag waterproof (a real necessity on wet days)? Some panniers can be mounted only on certain bikes. Other models can fold out into backpacks, which is a real two-for-one deal!

Attaching Your New Equipment

Most places mount the racks on your bike for free if you buy them there. Ask the sales clerk if they do (if they don't, find a new shop). Putting on a rack is not difficult, and the mechanics in the shop can do it in less than five minutes. Make sure you bring your bike when you make the final purchase.

Pannier installation is fairly straightforward. The bag usually just clips on at various places along the rack. There should be instructions on how to mount the pannier. If not, have the clerk show you how to do it. It's easy. After you've seen it done, you should have no problem doing it yourself back at home (and on the trail).

Packing Panniers

Just as there is an art to packing a backpack, there is an art to packing panniers. The first tip is to put all heavy items on the bottom closest

Yurts, round tents with hard sides, are popular with bikers on the Oregon coast, but you have to reserve them well in advance.

to the wheel. If you load your bike with the heavy items on top, your center of gravity will be thrown off and you won't be able to control your bike. The heavier you pack, the harder the bike will be to balance, especially if the weight is unevenly distributed.

Before you head off, pack the bike and ride around your neighborhood. Is it properly balanced? Is your center of gravity okay? Is it hard to steer? The first few times might involve a little trial and error. Before long, though, you'll be a bike-packing pro and you'll know exactly where to place everything in the panniers for maximum performance.

Getting Your Bike from Here to There

Unless you plan on camping near home, you're going to need a rack on your car so you can get your bike from here to there. Just as with any other piece of gear, there are plenty of choices. There are top-mount, back-mount, and front-mount racks. Many Suburbans, Blazers, Explorers, Expeditions, and other vehicles already have factory-installed racks. Just call your car dealer to find out if there is a bike bracket you can buy for the vehicle's existing rack (this will save you from having to buy a complete rack).

If you don't have a rack on your car, plan on buying one. Where do you want your rack: on top, in the front (good for RVs), on the back? The back-mounted rack is probably the best choice if you are worried your bike will be chipped and scratched by flying debris.

Brain Buckets, Tools, Camping Tips

There are a few other things you need to have to ensure the success of your biking adventures.

Helmet

You should wear a helmet. If you fall and hit your head and die, you'll ruin your family's vacation. I've made it a rule that my kids aren't to get on their bikes without brain protection. In some states, it's a law. It took a while to get them used to it, but now it's second nature.

While I preach this, I need to follow my own advice. My wife makes me pay her ten dollars every time she sees me without my helmet. I'm getting better. I always wear a helmet on trails and off-road, but I'm a little sloppy about keeping my head buttoned up when I ride on pavement. She's made $400 this year.

Tools

Ask the clerk what tools you need when you buy your bike. Buy a small bag and attach it to the back of your seat. Put your tools in it. Get a patch kit and a tire tool and include them, too. If you already own a bike, check with your bike shop for the best tools for your bike. It's likely you can get an all-in-one tool. It's also a good idea to have a spare tube or two with you and maybe even a spare tire.

Don't leave home without the tools to do a simple repair.

These are some of the essential tools you should carry with you. Trail-side repairs are not uncommon. Wear a helmet.

Camping Gear

You need to keep things light if you bike camp. Review the chapter on backpacking. Over the years I have learned a few lessons that I'd like to share. When I ride I like to go lighter than I do when I pack because I generally ride longer than I hike and after several miles I can really feel the weight.

Food: I carry commercial freeze-dried food, so all I have to do is add water. I like Mountain House and Backpacker's Pantry foods. They're tasty, and there is very little cooking. All I take is a small stove to boil water. I also take extra food because I get really hungry after all that pedaling.

Sleeping Bag: It is critical that you have a light, very compressible bag.

I take one of two sleeping bags. I often pack a Cascade Design Quantum 20, which will fit in an 8-by-18-inch stuff sack and weighs about 2.4 pounds. I love this bag. The Quantum has a trapezoidal design that lets my feet assume their natural position and maximizes bag loft, so not only is it comfortable, it's warm.

If I take a down bag, I take The North Face Kazoo. As far as I'm concerned The North Face is the first and last name in down bags. This bag com-

A small tool kit fits nicely behind the seat.

My wife Shari uses a North Face Kazoo down bag. Packed to almost nothing and is an excellent choice for bike camping.

Set up biking rules for your kids in the campground. Tell them how far they can go. Remind them of cars and to be courteous to campers taking a stroll.

presses down to about nothing and weighs two pounds something. You want a bag that can get really small because space is at a premium when you're camping.

In addition, I use bags rated to twenty degrees Fahrenheit because I do so much riding in the mountains. If the weather is really warm, I stick my legs out. It's easier to get cool than warm.

Sleeping Pad: If I can swing the weight, I take my Therm-a-Rest LE, which weighs more than my bag. I sleep very well on it, so I try to give up weight some place else. Even with this pad my sleeping bag and pad are coming in at a little over five pounds. If weight becomes critical, I take my Ultra Light Long (full size) pad, which weighs a little more than a pound.

Tent: Go as light as you can. I often pack my Peak 1 Orion.

Miscellaneous Stuff: There are a few other things to consider. An outfit named Platypus makes a collapsible water bottle, which stands on a stable base. As you use the Platypus, it can be flattened. It can be boiled, frozen, or used as a pillow. There is

Trail mix is a good food for biking. Include lots of nuts and dried fruit.

also a shower head that you can attach to it so you can get the road grime off.

After a shower, how do you dry off? I take a couple of Packtowls (by Cascade Designs). They are super-absorbent and made from 100 percent viscose. You can wring out 90 percent of the water and use them again. These little jewels weigh nothing. Hang the towels up high, however. If there are any mice around, they'll chew them up if they can reach them.

It's probably a good idea to lock up your bikes at night.

Chapter 25

Camping in Trailers:
The Great Outdoor Cabin on Wheels

"Ah, wilderness," as my favorite playwright penned.

Whether you're sleeping out looking up at God's stars; smelling the spicy, pine-scented breeze as it wafts across the canyon; listening to the flutter of a flapping rain fly as it flops in the wind or the plopping sound of raindrops on canvas; or camping in the Garden of Eden or in a slightly more substantial arrangement like a trailer; there's nothing like being there.

When I was younger, I thought only wimps camped in trailers. I assume that if you couldn't feel the hard earth you weren't really camping. I've had a shift in thinking, however, in the past few years—especially on days when the rain keeps coming down, there's no letup in sight, the mud is 9 inches deep, and you're sopped from head to tail.

I'll never give up sleeping on the ground. There's no better way of celebrating the outdoors, but every now and then trailer camping is okay.

An advantage to camping in a trailer is you have all the luxuries of home. A trailer is a portable cabin. On an autumn camping/fishing trip to Fish Lake, Utah, where the temperature went down into the single digits, a heater was a comfortable bonus. We've enjoyed our Salem trailer, especially in cold weather.

A Portable Wilderness Cabin

While I may be sacrificing a lot, I have to admit that a trailer can be darned nice, too. I no longer think of trailering as wimping out. I like to think of it as an alternative way of camping. My wife suggests that trailer camping should be likened to having your own personal wilderness cabin; the difference is that you can move it about whenever you want. You're not locked into one place.

When I was writing *Fly Fishing Made Easy*, I needed to get away from telephones, cell phones, fax machines, doorbells, and interruptions. I wanted to write, fish, and take photographs in the immediacy of nature.

I wanted to be in "wilderness," but I had neither the time to do many traditional camp chores nor could I be subject to the whims of nature without protection. I also needed power to run my computer. I needed a dry place to work and a place I could set out books and notes where wind and water wouldn't disturb them. Most importantly, I wanted to be able to move about as the fishing demanded.

Many trailer campers find a folding trailer a handy way to camp. This Coleman trailer is much easier to tow than my full-size Salem.

Several times I "hooked up" at recreational vehicle (RV) camps if the fishing was good. Mostly, though, I wandered off into forgotten canyons and forests and camped in the midst of water, pines, big trout, and no people.

I enjoyed having a trailer and becoming spoiled.

I got a lot of work done and managed to keep my sanity. I also decided that there were times when it's really nice camping with a few luxuries. I liked having a good heater when it was 3:00 A.M. and thirty degrees Fahrenheit with a strong west breeze. I liked having a microwave when my generator was running.

Our wheeled cabin also has these extras: air conditioning for hot days (especially nice in the South), closets, microwave, four-burner stove, oven, toilet, shower, hot water, and lots of windows. Our 19-foot-long trailer would sleep six persons without problems and even more if you stacked a few folks on the floor.

You can still have a campfire and do many fun camping things. The difference is you retreat to a little more upscale shelter to sleep, although you're more limited to where you can camp.

Getting Ready

There are a few things you need when you're pulling your cabin. No matter how humble, there are a few items that you must keep in your trailer. In addition to your regular tool kit, you should have the following essential items. (I won't go into detail on the specific food and bedding items you need. This information is

Here we camped within 100 yards of the Pacific on a rainy Oregon salmon fishing trip. When we want to spend our time fishing and not doing traditional camp chores, a trailer is a nice choice.

A tent trailer has a lot more room than you'd expect. Our kids like the change of pace. You don't get on each other's nerves on a rainy day when you're trailer bound.

Small trailers can be wheeled into tight spots.

covered in other chapters.) If you've been trailer camping, you'll know and appreciate this list. If you haven't, and you plan to rent, borrow, or buy a trailer, you'll be forewarned for any emergency.

- Large crescent wrench: For taking off and tightening gas fittings when you change the propane tank.

- Leather gloves: For connecting and disconnecting the ball hitch.

- Various Phillips and slotted-head screwdrivers: For tightening all those things that always come loose each time you pull out of the driveway and drive down the road.

- Assorted screws, nuts, bolts: You always need one of these items. I started collecting these odds and ends and have a can with an assortment.

- Electrician's and duct tapes: You always need tape to repair a wire, fix or reinforce a drawer, work on a taillight.

- Fuses: From time to time trailers blow fuses (usually a heater fuse in the middle of the night when it's below freezing). Find out what fuses your trailer uses and stock up.

- Blue stuff for the toilet: Toilets, especially in hot weather, can get a little ripe. Pour the blue stuff down the toilet. It not only helps with the smell, but also breaks down the matter and helps it decompose quickly.

- Five-gallon water jug and funnel: If you want to fill your water tank, but don't want to move your trailer, you can fill the water jug at the campground tap and pour it in your tank. A funnel really helps.

- Plug adapter: This way you can run your 220 plug off a 120 outlet.

- Hose: You need a 20- to 30-foot-long hose so you can hook up to water.

- Electric extension cord: An extension cord will expand the length of the cord that comes with your trailer and give you more flexibility.

- Box of latex gloves: These are nice to have when you drain your sewer and water tanks.

In addition to this list of equipment, you need to have your wheel bearings repacked and your tires balanced every year or two. Check the pressure in your tires before each trip and check again every day or so. Irregular tire pressure will wear your tires and could be hazardous (let alone vacation-delaying).

Every spring, check the condition of your spare tire. See to it that it's in working order.

I've always felt that trailer brakes were an essential safety item. Some smaller, hard-sided trailers don't have them, but most do. Many tent trailers also have them. They are worth having, especially if you are going down a hill. The first time your trailer starts to fishtail and you tap the trailer brakes and it corrects, you'll never go without them. Check the brakes on your vehicle, too, because they take quite a lot of abuse when you pull a trailer. Your brakes need to be in good condition. If they aren't, have them repaired.

If you are buying a new vehicle, get one with a towing package. It will be prewired

Always check the trailer's spare tire before you go on an adventure. If you're taking a trailer on a maiden voyage, make sure your lug wrench fits the lugs on your trailer wheels.

After each trip I fill the propane tank so it will always be ready. Before you leave on a trip, check the condition of your battery and always buy a top-grade battery.

A good camp starts at home. Make sure you are prepared. At the campsite is not the place to find out you've got a problem.

for a trailer. It might also have a little larger radiator, a stiffer suspension, and a better battery.

A larger radiator is a good idea. I also have had a transmission cooler installed. It cost about $120 but was worth it.

Trailering Down the Road

If you haven't pulled a trailer before, you'll have to adjust your time schedule. You probably won't be able to travel as far in a day as you would in your car. Factors such as afternoon winds and hills affect your time and your driving. The higher your trailer's profile, the more winds will affect it. This is one reason why small tent trailers are becoming so popular; they have far less wind resistance.

Another particular to keep in mind is your engine versus the weight of the trailer. A little more engine is always a better thing. Don't push the limits. Look in the owner's manual and find out how much your vehicle can tow. Look at towing weight and tongue weight.

Remember that you're adding more weight when you load the trailer with gear, add water, and fill the propane tank. Don't push the weight limits.

I have spent time in almost every trailer model on the market during the past twenty years as an outdoor writer. My favorite trailer is one that's paid for. We've owned several. We now have a Cub with pop-out sides that gives us a lot of room.

We especially like trailer camping when we are going someplace to see the sights and we want to be outdoors; we're not there to camp in the traditional fashion.

Camping Spots

You don't have to camp in RV parks. They have hookups and such, but they are expensive and often you're cramped in with others. We like to use traditional campgrounds or to find a deserted place somewhere.

We pull into RV parks when there's no other choice or when we need to recharge or dump tanks. We use such a park when we want to visit some place nearby and the location is central. Otherwise, RV parks are too crowded and have all the aesthetics of an amusement park.

As a rule, RV parks aren't what we think camping is all about.

Hard-Sided Trailers

Full-size trailers have their moments. You have four hard sides that are accessible on demand. We've owned four small, full-size trailers. We've enjoyed them all.

We've always favored smaller trailers because they are easier to park in campgrounds and are more maneuverable than larger models. When we bought our Nomad several years ago, we got a model with a heavier spring so it would ride higher and not be a problem on rutted dirt roads. (The trailer sat higher, so we didn't lose the plumbing on hidden rocks). The only drawback was the increased wind resistance.

If you're driving down the road in a trailer and you want to stop and make lunch for your family, all you have to do is pull over and open the door. Within minutes you'll be serving lunch to your starving crew. The fridge and stove are right there and the table is always handy. You don't have to rearrange things. Even if it's raining out, there's no problem. If you want to sleep or use the potty, all you have to do is stop, open the door, and walk in. This is a great advantage. If you can't find a nice camping spot and you're tired, you can pull into a rest area or off the road and sleep safely and securely. You have your ready-to-use portable home.

There are some drawbacks. A full-size trailer

One of the advantages of a folding trailer is you can take it on rougher roads than a hard-sided model. Here we're camping in the middle of nowhere yet we have all the luxuries. We don't feel restricted to campgrounds and expensive packed-in-like-sardines RV parks.

Camper shells are made to fit on all sizes and shapes of pickups, and they are a great way to get "out there."

comes with a price tag. You also need to have a large enough vehicle to pull it. It is critical that you have enough engine. Another factor is fuel expense. The mileage on my vehicle is reduced dramatically when I tow the trailer. On a good towing day I *might* get 9 or 10 miles to a gallon. I get only 6 or 7 if there's any sort of wind or hills. Physical exertion is another thing to consider. On a short trip I don't feel the extra tow weight; on a longer trip, especially with a strong crosswind, I'm beat to death.

We recently took a three-week-long trip to Canada, and by the time I was done, I was exhausted. I vowed this was my last long trailer trip.

Tent/Folding Trailers

An increasing number of hard-sided trailer owners are changing to tent trailers. They are doing so with good reason: You get most of the conveniences of a full-size trailer without the bulk.

I was a little skeptical myself. When I was a kid we rented a folding trailer for a camping trip to Starr Valley, Wyoming. It took forever to set up, and it had none of the extras. I resented that it cut into my fishing time. Things have changed radically in the past few decades.

We can set up our Coleman Westlake (made by Fleetwood) in a matter of minutes. And it has most of the things we've come to expect from hard-sided trailer living.

The biggest advantage is that you can tow a tent trailer with a lot less horsepower. With the exception of the largest folding-trailer boxes, you can easily tow most folding trailers with a vehicle with a V–6 engine. Instead of a larger vehicle with a gas-guzzling V–8, most minivans, sport-utility vehicles, or other passenger cars can be used to pull a tent trailer. There's a trailer size to match every car.

We can pull the Westlake (which is large and heavy by folding-trailer standards) with my wife's Trooper, but you can feel it. When I pull the Coleman with my V–8, I have to look back to see if it's there. A folding trailer is certainly a lot lighter than a traditional hard-sided trailer, and there's little wind resistance.

I've always felt it's better to have too much engine than not enough. Take a look at your vehicle and get a trailer you can pull easily. *Don't tax your vehicle's limits!* Stay under your vehicle's towing maximum.

In the old days setting up a tent trailer took about twenty minutes. It now takes five minutes—if that—and it's so easy a child can do it. As a matter of fact, my child does. My nine-year-old son can pretty much set up camp by himself.

Before we got our tent trailer, we worried that we'd be giving up a lot of living space. We were pleasantly surprised. There's a lot of room. Most units have at least a heater and a fridge. Ours has a toilet and shower, too.

On smaller models you can wheel the box

There is nothing austere about a folding trailer these days: Our Coleman has an indoor shower, an outdoor shower, and a toilet. It doesn't have a stove or a microwave like our Salem, but you can't have everything.

To set up our Westwood, all you do is plug the wrench into a socket in the bumper and crank. Jon-Michael, my nine-year-old son, gets a charge out of doing it; it's that easy.

The roof is lifted by a crank. After that all you do is pull out the sides, support them, and hook on the canvas. One person can set up camp in about five easy minutes.

Shari cooks breakfast during an autumn snowstorm. The trailer's heater was blasting, so we were very comfortable.

These charming children of mine are getting ready to help Shari fish for brown trout during the spawn. Note the spacious sleeping area.

about by hand and set up your camp in places you could never fit a hard-sided model. You can also take a folding trailer down primitive roads you could never take a hard-sided model. You won't catch branches overhead or hang up the plumbing either.

It's also much easier to turn around with a tent trailer. With a smaller Coleman trailer, we took off down an old logging road until we came to a big wash that was 4 feet deep. The road was too narrow to turn around in with the trailer hitched.

My wife disconnected the hitch and I inched the vehicle around. We took the trailer by the tongue, rolled it off the road, and turned it about so I had enough space to drive around it. We hitched up again and went back the way we came. The trailer was light enough so we could easily roll it off the road. We discovered some wonderful wilderness camps, yet we had the luxury of a trailer.

One of our favorite steelhead spots is just such a place. It's often raining and muddy, and a folding trailer is a real luxury when you're back in the bush for a week. We fish all day and come into a nice warm, dry, up-off-the-ground home. All we have to do is concentrate on fishing.

Section Four

Having Fun Outdoors

Chapter 26

Favorite Activities Among Campers: Some of the Finest Things in Life Are Done Outdoors

There is great joy in camping. There are other adventures, however, to be savored along with the camping experience. There are literally thousands of miles of trails waiting to be explored. It doesn't matter whether you strap on a backpack and head across the Wind River Range to enjoy a ten-day packing trip, slip on a day pack and leave your comfortable camp for a day's hike in the Sierras, or saunter down a nature trail near the campground in the Adirondacks.

It's a lot of fun to simply camp. My daughter, Abbey, wants a tent of her own for her fourth birthday.

Although hiking is probably a camper's favorite pastime, it's followed closely by my own favorite enterprise, the sublime quest for water-borne, finned creatures: fishing. There's nothing I enjoy more than casting a line. Although I'm a born-again trout fisherman (cutthroat being my favorite), I'm also partial to fishing for largemouth bass and pike. I've walked miles for smallmouth bass, perch, and blue gill. I've driven thousands of miles to throw flies at salmon, and I consider steelhead fishing with a fly rod almost a religion if not an art form.

After casting—with luck—to hungry fish, viewing (and photographing) wildlife is the noble camper's third most popular pursuit. Viewing animals is a serious avocation, if not practically a vocation for some folks. It's worth getting up early or staying up late; it's worth hiking a few miles; it's worth sitting in one place for a long time. Few things are more rewarding than seeing a wild creature in its natural environment, especially if it doesn't see you in the process, so that it can act naturally.

In the following chapters, we're going to take a look at these three virtuous outdoor activities and talk about a few ways for you to enjoy them more. We'll look at: how to enjoy and get more out of your hike; how to improve and more fully enjoy fishing; and how to see more wildlife and enjoy the natural world.

Chapter 27

Enjoying Your Hike:
The Journey Is the Adventure

I'm glad to see a renewed interest in the sport of walking. It's an excellent, healthy way to exercise. Low-impact, it burns up as many calories as jogging. The nice thing about walking is it can be done just about anywhere. Walking, or hiking, as we outdoor sorts like to call it, is the most popular activity among campers.

There's nothing more peaceful and relaxing than a nice walk in the fresh air. Some of the great joys of a camping trip are hiking to areas of interest, walking established trails, and simply striking off across country in any direction that looks interesting.

Many of our greatest natural wonders require you to make the effort to reach them. You can't drive, so you have to use your feet. You've never really seen the outdoors until you've seen it by trail.

Most Everyone Can Hike

Walking, or hiking, is a continual process of discovery. The path or trail is always different because nothing in nature stays the same for more than an instant.

Walking keeps you in touch with the earth; you become one with it. You smell the smells, taste the breeze, and see the rocks, flowers, and animals. The experience of walking in nature is not ruined by noises from an internal combustion engine, smells of exhaust, or speeds that make the scenery nothing more than a blur. Walking keeps you honest.

Hiking is the number-one pastime of campers. There are thousands of miles of trails waiting to be hiked. All you have to do is put one foot in front of the other. There are trails for every kind of hiker.

Two nice things about hiking are you get better with practice and you don't have to be an expert to start. All you do is put one foot in front of the other. It's great to get out of your steel-lined automotive coffin and hike into the heart of nature.

You're in complete control. You can go for gentle hikes, climb steep trails, or strap on a backpack. You can go as fast or as slow as you feel. You can go as far as you dare,

To hike into a set of mountains like these, you need to be in pretty good shape. Before long the trail gets very steep. It's a good idea to see your doctor before you undertake a long, strenuous hiking adventure.

stop and smell the flowers, or look at bugs without guilt. You can wander aimlessly in a large field or hug trees in a virgin forest. Put a flower in your hair and chew on some tender blades of grass. You can even run about in your underwear.

Hiking is simply moving your feet. There are trails now for everyone. There are even sections of terrain that are wheelchair-accessible (although I'd like to see a lot more of them).

For an easy hike, just point your body down a gentle forest path, put your watch in your pocket, lift one foot at a time, and breathe that sweet country air. It's not a race. You're out to have fun. My son, a friend, and I were climbing a fairly steep trail last week. We saw a couple—I'd guess in their eighties—coming up the path on our descent. We stopped and talked. I mentioned something about its being a steep grade. The white-haired lady said, "Yes, son, but it's not bad if you pace yourself. We take a few steps and stop for breath. We see an awful lot that way." They were an inspiration.

In this chapter let's take a closer look at the joy of hiking.

Your Physical Shape and Hiking

Almost anybody, in any sort of shape, can do some hiking. It might be 7 miles or 70 yards. Your good judgment and the trail will determine the distance. There's a fine line between pushing yourself within healthy limits and overdoing it.

Visit Your Doctor

If you plan to do some hiking and you're not in the best shape, a good place to start is with your doctor for a checkup. For that matter, no matter what shape you're in, if you haven't had your physical this year, get in to see your doctor. Your physician will help you assess your physical condition and how far you can go safely.

You don't want a heart attack. It'll ruin your vacation.

Tell your doctor where you plan to camp and hike. Be specific about the altitude. Remember: Air thins in high mountains. You'll know you're in poor condition if after about twenty steep steps you need to catch your breath.

Gear You'll Need

You don't need much to start hiking: a trail, two feet, and a desire to see what's around the bend. Here are a few ideas to consider.

Footwear

Good footwear is important to a hiker. (You may want to review the section on boots.) If you're hiking gentle trails and the path is smooth, about any footwear will work as long as you aren't hiking a long way.

If you're going to hike for more than half an hour or step over roots, rocks, and other obstructions, you want a shoe that offers some support. I've done a lot of walking in New Balance running and walking shoes. They have good support (and they're made for people like me with wide feet).

You never know what you'll see when you go around the next bend. We saw this elk bugling to his would-be lovers, who were taken later by a stronger bull.

If you're going to walk more than an hour or so and/or the terrain is rough, you'd be better off in a boot. A boot will give you better support and protect your ankles. Even though a boot is heavier than a running shoe, you'll actually be less fatigued.

Incidental Stuff

I usually carry a day pack with a few things in it even on short hikes. You don't need much. If I go on an early hike, I can stow away my jacket or heavy shirt. I can also keep a canteen, snacks, and a camera. Sometimes I take a book or a writing pad. I always have a small emergency kit with matches, a fire starter, a whistle, a space blanket, an extra pair of socks, and a first-aid kit (including moleskin).

If you're going very far, or if the weather is warm, take plenty of water. If I'm in an area with a lot of streams or I'm hiking with my kids and will have to pack their water, I'll carry my PUR water purifier. That way I need to take only a bottle and can pump water as we need it.

You'll often find wonderful hiking trails on the edge of your camp.

If you see horses, move out of the way until they've passed. Don't do anything to spook them. Most horses are people- and trailwise, but a few spook easily.

Some like to use a hiking staff. You can make one out of wood—willow works very well—or buy a telescoping staff that fits into your pack. I've never needed a staff, but I have friends who swear by them.

Far from the Madding Crowd

When you're on the trail, you need to use good sense and polite manners.

If a loaded packer is coming toward you on a narrow trail, let him or her take the easier path. Tradition says the person with the heaviest load gets the easiest part of the path. If a faster hiker is coming up behind you, gracefully let him or her pass.

If horses are coming either behind or in front of you, step well off the trail so the animals can pass. That's a good idea for several reasons. It keeps those sharp hooves on the trail so they don't tear up the surrounding ground. It keeps the horses from getting spooked, and it keeps your toes from getting flattened. If you have a dog, hang onto Rover's collar so he won't spook them. Some dogs get excited by horses and run out to investigate. Such actions could have drastic consequences on a mountain trail.

I saw a woman break her arm after being thrown from a dog-spooked horse.

Don't sit down in the middle of the trail when you take a break. Step off to the side so you won't impede others. And if nature calls, make sure you answer her no closer than 200 feet from a trail. Dig a small hole and cat-box the evidence.

Don't litter! Put wrappers and such in your pocket or backpack. Show your children you respect the outdoors and teach them to do likewise. Your fine example will be a great teaching tool. Go one step further: *If you see garbage on the trail, pick it up.* If every kid saw his or her folks pick up stray bits of garbage, we'd have a cleaner world. I'd propose lining up all litterbugs before a firing squad, but such a notion isn't politically correct.

Be an example: *Leave the trail cleaner than you found it.*

Going Downhill

A good way to tell whether your boots fit well is to walk a long downhill stretch. You'll get blisters if your boot is too loose and your foot slops about. Your foot should be comfortable but snug. If you feel a blister coming on, put some moleskin or a bandage on it right away. You might want to slip on an extra sock, too. Take the friction off that part of your foot.

Unless you like to live on the edge, don't run or jog down steep trails. It's a good way to get yourself injured. Come down the trail at a steady pace, but avoid the temptation to come too fast. About 70 percent of hiker falls are downhill. Make sure you're in control. You'll be glad you have the support of a good pair of boots, too.

Going Uphill

This is where you'll learn what kind of shape you're in. Remember to tell yourself you're having fun as you sweat your guts out and wheeze for air. Don't overdo it. Stop and rest as often as you want. It's your vacation. There's no shame in taking a breather. If the rest of your party is moving ahead and you can't keep up, don't try. God made us all in different sizes and shapes and with different endurances.

Tell those mountain goat–like friends of yours you're stopping to smell the flowers. Don't let yourself get pushed on the trail if it makes you uncomfortable.

We carry a water filter instead of a large canteen in areas with a lot of water. It's a lot lighter than a canteen, and you can drink all you want.

Avoid the temptation to start too fast. Slow and steady is what wins the uphill race. If you feel a burst of energy, don't pick up the pace and break out in front of the pack. Keep a little energy in reserve.

If you're feeling winded, stop and catch your breath. If you're not in the best shape, now is not the time to start that exercise program and push yourself to your limit (especially if you're a little overweight and heart-attack prone). It serves no purpose to get really sore either. You'll need a day to recover, and vacation days are too precious to waste hanging around camp popping Motrins as if they were M&Ms.

Take a step and breathe. Take a step and breathe. If the goal you've set for yourself is not realistic, then reassess. It's easy to say you're going to a certain point when you look at the sign on the trailhead. After you make it halfway there, you can decide whether your goal is unrealistic. A good way to check your progress is to talk or sing. If you can do it easily without gasping for breath, your pace is just fine. You can't get into or out of shape overnight.

Reward yourself. Pick a point and walk toward it: a big tree, a bend in the road, or a creek. When you get there, pamper yourself, take a drink, eat a piece of dried fruit, smell a flower.

If you're in fair shape, you might want to do 500 to 700 feet of vertical rise per hour. If you're in better shape, maybe 1,000 feet of vertical rise is your speed. If you're not used to hiking, don't worry about how many feet. Take a step and breathe.

Remember, slow and steady.

Rests

I love to hike, but I like to enjoy the trip. I don't put my mind and body on hold to enjoy it when I get to the end of the trail. I enjoy the trail as I go.

The journey itself is as much an adventure as the outcome. Depending on terrain, you should have at least a five-minute rest every thirty to sixty minutes.

Sit down on a rock or a log, take your pack off, and look at the clouds (see what sorts of animals they form when you stare at them). Unlace your boots and soak your feet in a cold stream.

Eating and Drinking

You need three to four quarts of water a day to keep from getting dehydrated. You may need a little more water if you're hiking on the desert. I get thirsty and tend to go through a lot of water; If I'm hiking hard, I drink four or five quarts a day (six or seven quarts while desert hiking.)

You should take a drink at least every hour.

Don't eat a heavy breakfast or lunch before you walk. It's better if you snack all day. This will keep you fueled up and your energy level flowing. I like to eat Powerbars, nuts, and fruit. Foods such as peanut butter are also excellent for lunch.

If you're sweating a lot, you'll lose some important chemicals (some persons' metabolisms are more prone to this than others). Drink Gatorade or dump Gatorade powder into your water. This recharges your body with electrolytes and salts.

Let's get hiking.

Hiking with Children

Children love to hike.

Very young children can still hike: You have to hold their hands from time to time, but you can do it. When my daughter was young, I walked with her, and encouraged my wife and son to romp on ahead. They were getting a little eager to pick up the pace. When Abbey got tired, I put her on my shoulders and we caught up with the others.

If you have a toddler, a good child backpack will be very helpful. You can pop your child into the pack and hike at your leisure. REI and Kelty make good baby packs. Before you purchase one, take your child into the store, place him or her into it, and try it on. Mess with the adjustments and see how the pack feels. Walk about the store with your child in it.

If they're allowed, many of the newer jogging strollers work well on gentle trails as long as the path is wide and not too steep. Jogging strollers have big wheels and can take the abuse a trail might dish out. Make sure you have a safety strap that attaches to your wrist in case your stroller gets away from you. Make sure, of course, that the baby is strapped in before you start.

Just as children's eyes are bigger than their stomachs at dinnertime, their enthusiasm for a long walk can be greater than their ability to pull it off. Many times I ended up carrying a kid or two back to the car. After a few broken backs, we've learned that the time to turn around and head back is long before the kids run out of gas. There's no formula about how much is too much because every kid is different.

Abbey is taking a rest on a stump in Redwood National Park in northern California. Frequent rests are important for kids and adults. Not only do you need to catch your breath, you need to stop and smell the wildflowers.

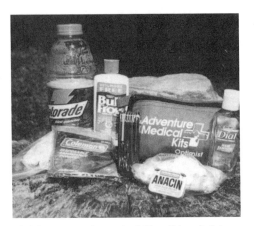

A hiking parent's survival kit. Although I have each child carry his or her own pack, I always pack a few essentials for the trail to cover any "incident": baby wipes for pit stops and spills; antibacterial hand cleaner; sun screen; plastic disposable rain ponchos; a Victorinox Champ Swiss Army knife; hard candy; a first-aid kit; and Anacin (for me, since kids, God love 'em, can be a real headache).

Stop often for snack and water breaks. We give our kids nuts and dried fruit to munch on. This plan seems to give us more energy. We've learned not to be too itinerary-oriented. If we're hiking to an old abandoned cabin, it's okay if we don't make it. The journey is the fun. If the kids want to stop and throw rocks into a beaver pond, that's just fine. We're out to have fun and build family unity.

If you're hiking with your children, have them tell you when something is getting sore. I have my kids tell me the second they feel a blister coming on so I can slap a bandage on that tender spot. Having your children wear two pairs of socks helps a lot, too.

Give your children something to look for when you hike. You might tell them you're going to walk past the beaver ponds where there might be an old moose standing in the water. Tell them to look for beavers, for three different-colored leaves, for leaves with different shapes, for three round rocks, or for six pointed rocks. Point out things of natural interest.

It's best to let your kids set the pace at their level. The exception is if you have teenage boys with more energy than good sense. In that case let them go ahead, and tell them to wait at the top.

Drink lots of water to stay hydrated while you're hiking.

We like to stop and look about. We also like to tell stories. Abbey, age 6, is telling a story about a princess who got lost in the mountains until her father found her.

Chapter 28

Catching Lots of Fish Means Knowing How to Read the Water: A Camper's Favorite Pastime

There's nothing like camping near water!

There's something about the bubbling of a gin-clear brook, the hypnotic flow of a river, or the crashing of surf. But in addition to its own natural beauty, water suggests another beautiful thing: fish. It's no wonder so many campgrounds are near tempting bodies of water. Whether you cast flies, throw spinners, bump jigs, or throw bait, fishing is a wonderful outdoor religion. Besides hiking, angling is probably the most popular camping pastime. It's certainly my favorite.

It doesn't matter if you're a dry-fly snob or a wet-fly specialist; if you throw spinners, troll from a canoe, drift worms in the current, or wad gobs of disgusting PowerBait on a cheese hook. The basic principle of fishing is the same: You have to fish where there are fish. Experts call this reading the water; this means you can look at the water and have a pretty good idea where the fish are holding or feeding. Fly-fishing folk usually have a slight edge in this regard because *reading* is a critical element in presenting a fly.

In this chapter, we'll take a crash course in reading water. Knowing how to look at the water will have everything to do with your success as an angler.

Catching a fish like this one is rarely an accident. A fisherperson has to know what he or she is doing.

Have you ever wondered why the same few people catch all the fish day in and day out? Is it that they cast a fly or a spinner better than the rest? Do they have a deeper tackle box? Do they have better equipment? No. The truth is they know where to fish. They don't waste time casting where there are no fish. They understand many of the important tactics you need to know to catch fish consistently. They have learned:

- What fish eat.
- What feeding patterns fish have.
- What a fish's comfort and safety needs are.
- Where fish hold in a stream or lake.

If you know how to read the water, you'll spend your time casting in water where there are fish. Many would-be anglers spend most of their time fishing in water where there's little chance of catching a fish.

This was our base camp. Every day we fished a new lake or stream.

They understand how fish act and react. They understand what our finned prey need to survive. These successful casters know how fish react to their environment. Let's take a look at what makes a fish tick so you can join the few who do catch consistently.

A Fish Is Feeding or Dormant

Before you cast your line, you need to decide if the fish are active or dormant. An active fish is a fish that's feeding or looking for food; a dormant fish is one that's resting or is not feeding or looking for food.

Feeding fish are easier to catch because they're aggressively looking for food. They go where the food is—even into uncomfortable or unsafe water. A dormant fish can still be caught because it's often opportunistic, but it won't go out of its way to investigate, and it will only stay in water that is safe and comfortable. The fishing term *lie* refers to where a fish holds or stays, where the fish rests when it's dormant, or where a feeding fish waits in the stream for the current to bring it food.

Understanding How a Fish Searches for Food

A key to reading water is to learn how a fish feeds. If you randomly cast into a lake or wade into a stream, you aren't going to catch a whole lot of fish. On the other hand, if you make a concerted effort to judge the water and then throw your line accordingly, you'll be reeling them in. When you stare at the surface of fishing water, look to see where the active fish are feeding or where the dormant fish are holding. If you can't actually see the fish, try to identify the likely places they might go to feed or to hold.

Take a look at how the fish are getting their food. The food comes via the current or drift in a stream or a river. When a fish is hungry it goes to the most likely spot in the stream and waits for the current to bring its dinner. As a result a stream fish often has to make snap decisions about its food. A lake or pond fish must go more directly to the food. It will cruise to fulfill its food needs. Thus a fish has a chance to study its food more carefully. This means you have to fish a stream differently from a lake or pond. The basic needs of each kind of fish are the same, but how they meet those needs is different. Once you understand these concepts, you will catch more fish.

Fish the Most Likely Places First

Where would you go to eat if you were a hungry fish? During feeding a fish will lie or cruise where it can get the most food with the least amount of effort. Fish don't want to work any harder than necessary. The more food a fish can consume with the least amount of energy expended the better. Big fish are those that learn how to make every movement count. A fish in a stream, for example, learns to position itself in a current and move just a few inches to eat bugs floating on the water. A fish must gain more calories feeding than it loses looking for food.

Catching a brown trout means you've presented your lure in a realistic fashion.

Fish Can Be Greedy or Finicky Feeders

Fish feed a lot like humans. Sometimes everything looks good to us, and we don't seem to get full. We aren't very discriminating because it all looks tasty. Other times we are interested only in one or two things. That's all. We want lots of pizza and nothing else will do. Then there are times when we aren't hungry and the sight of food, even prime rib, is disgusting and repugnant. We might take a little nibble of

Respect the fish and game laws and teach your children to do likewise. It's important that our children understand the heritage we're passing down to them.

You need to ask yourself where you'd hold if you were a fish when you get to a new stretch of water.

something to be polite, but food is the last thing on our minds. Our finned friends act the same way.

Fish can be very opportunistic. They'll eat anything in sight and will take anything you throw at them. Any attractor pattern, anything that looks like fish food—even a dry fly fished wet—will hammer a fish. Almost any fly, lure, or bait will work. The fish have a mighty hunger and they're out to gorge themselves like a famished football player at the $7.99 Chuck-a-rama Buffet.

Then there are times when fish are hungry but precise eaters. They are focused on an insect and if you want any fishing action, you'd better match it exactly. If you throw out a fly, it had better be a fly that looks exactly like what they are eating—the same size and color—and that acts the way its natural counterpart does. Even a small hatch is worth feeding on if a fish can eat in volume and do it without expending too much energy. If fish are focused on one particular hatch, and you can't match it, it sometimes works to try something completely different. They might gobble up a spoon or a spinner on impulse. Keep fishing. Their mood could change as quickly as it began. If necessary, try other fish in the same water—they may be less picky.

At other times fish don't seem to be interested in feeding at all. They're dormant for one reason or another. You can still catch fish by tempting them with something that looks tasty and is presented perfectly—something that is dragged right by their lazy noses. Fish may take such a lure more out of a conditioned response than hunger. The good news is you can catch them; it just takes more work. On the bright side, such a dormant mood rarely lasts too long and you can outwait moody fish. Hunger will grow or other conditions will change. Sometimes moving to a new section of water is all it takes to catch fish.

Where to Find Fish in a Stream

Some sections of a stream are better than others as far as a fish is concerned. Remember they want it easy and they want it often. It takes a lot of energy to hold in the drift. Fish naturally seek out structure that breaks up the flow. This is the first element of a good lie. Look at the stream and try to determine where the current is broken or slowed down. Fish lie there because a break in the current slows the drift so they can get their food with less energy. A good angler always looks over the water before he or she starts to fish in order to detect both food sources and structure in the water that breaks current flow.

Look for what many fly casters call seams in the flow of the stream. Look for any break or disruption—a seam—in the flow of the stream. Look for places where the current is altered or modified by rocks, boulders, logs, islands, bends, sand bars, dropoffs, cars, tires, bridges, and piers. Notice whirlpools, current changes, and color changes on the surface that might indicate large rocks on the bottom that could break up the course, look for currents or shallow and deep water that abruptly meet, and look for a place where there is a moss line or a feeder creek.

Seams are good places for fish to find food without fighting the current. A productive seam is where fast and slow currents meet. Here a fish can rest in the slow current and observe the food going by in the fast lane. If a fish is positioned correctly, all it needs to do is move its head to feast on items in the tasty stream buffet.

I love to cast near a moss line or a shelf. Such a spot is an excellent place to start the fishing day. A lot of organisms that fish call food live in this watery, weedy jungle. Bugs and small fish live and hide in such a place and the fish know it. Sandy bottoms make swell swimming holes, but they usually don't produce much food. Casting over a sandy bottom, unless you have reason to believe otherwise, wouldn't be a good way to spend your time.

Notice how the wind and waves have stirred up the water by the bank? A good place to fish would be the "seam" where the cloudy and clear water meet. Fish patrol such areas for food.

Where would you start fishing this river? A good place might be near the large boulder. This is a likely place for fish to hold.

Reading Moving Water

Moving water can be divided into four groups: pools, runs, riffles, and flats. It's important to know how each of these function and how to fish them.

Pools. A pool is a slow deep hole that generally holds the biggest fish. Fish can easily feed at the head or the tail of the pool and can lie dormant in the middle water where it's safe. Pools are ideal lies because they meet so many of the fish's needs. It's no surprise that the largest fish, fish which have played king of the hill, have claimed this water.

Tips: Watch your shadow and don't spook the fish. If you do spook them, they will swim upstream and, in turn, spook others. Pool water is usually smooth, so fish can see you.

This water is a lot deeper than it looks. In what section of this water would you start fishing first? Start at the bottom and carefully work upstream.

Wading is by far the best way to fish. Stand well below the tail of the pool and cast your fly, lure, or bait carefully. Many good fish hold on the tail. After you've worked the water, move up a few feet. Pick out sections of the pool and cast, working each section of water carefully. Don't fish the head of the pool until you've carefully worked the tail and the middle.

If you are fishing a wet fly, put on enough weight to get your pattern to the bottom. If you are working a lure, start on the top, then count it down, working at various depths until you find the depth with the most fish. If a fish isn't taking a lure or a fly off the top water, you will need to get it down closer to the bottom.

Runs: The top of a run is generally smooth with occasional swirls, because the bottom is often broken up by rocks and other structure. From the surface the water looks flat, but the bottom offers plenty of hiding places even though the water isn't deep. A run will meet many of the fish's needs. The structure breaks up the current, and there's a place to hide while resting or feeding. The water also has plenty of oxygen.

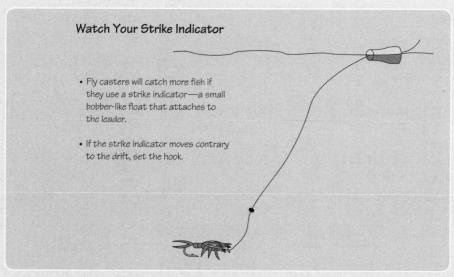

Watch Your Strike Indicator

- Fly casters will catch more fish if they use a strike indicator—a small bobber-like float that attaches to the leader.

- If the strike indicator moves contrary to the drift, set the hook.

Tips: Because the water is more broken up, you can usually get a little closer to where the fish are holding. The water won't be as deep as a pool, and the fish will probably be a little more active. The trick is to drag your fly or lure across a likely pocket to tempt a response. Continue to work the pocket until you are sure you've exhausted it. Then try the next likely spot.

If this isn't working, try shotgunning. This is really effective when you know there is structure, but there's so much it's tough to isolate, or when you simply can't identify the best water. Start working the water systematically, moving upstream to quickly cover all sections. When you see fish activity, or get strikes, slow down and work that area.

A spinner works well because the water is deeper, so you won't get hung up as easily.

A fly caster will appreciate this water during a hatch, but can successfully use a nymph here, too. A bait caster will do well on the surface or by weighting the offering—especially a worm—and bumping the bottom.

Watch where your shadow falls; the fish will see you and take off if you're not careful.

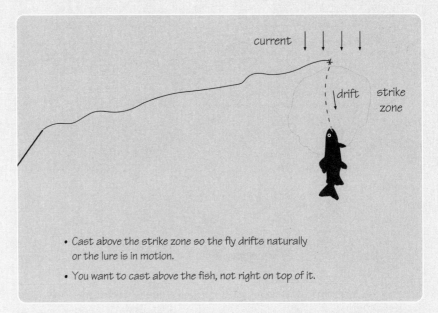

- Cast above the strike zone so the fly drifts naturally or the lure is in motion.
- You want to cast above the fish, not right on top of it.

Riffle: A riffle is an endless food dole. The water is 1 to 3 feet deep; the top is broken and choppy. There is a lot of aquatic life. Feeding fish can often be found in the riffles. Surprisingly, a lot of anglers overlook this part of the stream. Fishing here can be quite exciting. Fish have to react quickly because the water is moving fast. A fly caster in this water gets a lot of fast action. While the water isn't deep, the broken surface gives fish a sense of confidence so they aren't skittish. Fish come to the surface quickly and have a very splashy rise because they must act so quickly.

Tip: This is wonderful water for fly fishing. I love casting a terrestrial on riffles. This water can be a little tougher on spin casters because it's often shallow. A spinner will do well, though, and I've caught some mighty cutthroat trout this way, but I've hung up badly, too. This water is great for a natural-bait angler because fish are aggressive and willing to take a tasty mouthful.

Flat: A flat is shallow smooth water. There is little protection for the fish, so when they come into the flats to feed they will be very uneasy. Fish come into a flat and feed heavily during a hatch. The angler who fishes here has to be very careful not to startle the prey. Even the wakes from wading, let alone you or your shadow, will send fish to the far reaches of the pool.

A Double Clinch Knot

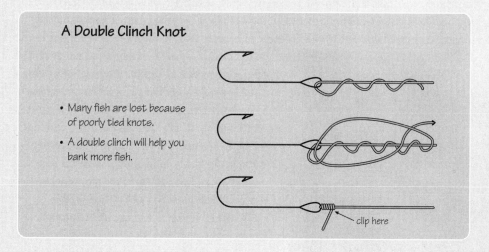

- Many fish are lost because of poorly tied knots.
- A double clinch will help you bank more fish.

clip here

Tip: I'd fish this a lot like a pool, work up, fishing the likely water carefully. Wading is the best way to fish such water because you get a better presentation. Be very careful not to spook the fish.

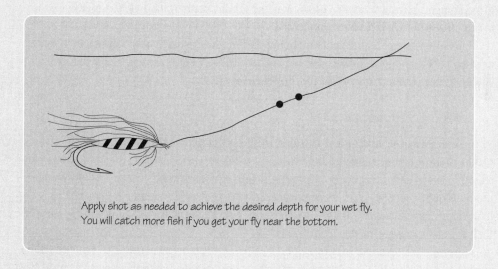

Apply shot as needed to achieve the desired depth for your wet fly. You will catch more fish if you get your fly near the bottom.

A Fish Has to Feel Secure

Finding food is a fish's first priority; shelter and safety are close seconds. Even the largest fish in the river aren't high on the food chain. Fish always act somewhat frightened, and they have good reason: For most of their lives something or someone is out

to get them. If a fish is going to make it past guppy stage, it had better be scared of its shadow. Birds and mammals (including man) chase fish with a vengeance. Perhaps the biggest predators of all, though, are big brother and big sister. A fish must always look over its respective fin. Fish get bold if they survive and feel like it's their right to try and eat any other fish that are within a few inches of their size.

The life of a fish is a game of dodge ball, a game of final elimination. If the fish lives, it moves up to the next best place, knocking the other fish out of the way. Being the biggest fish gives it the right to hold in the best lies so it gets even fatter until that one time it forgets to look over its fin. A big fish is hardest to catch because it has seen more, lived longer, and is understandably more paranoid. As a result of making it up the ladder, it doesn't have to be so aggressive a feeder because it gets to hold in the best lies. Once a fish gets big, its life is somewhat less complicated.

This brown trout was an aggressive feeder. It swam halfway across the pool to take a fly.

This is why we all catch so many baby- and medium-size fish. Small fish by nature have to be more aggressive to survive and are thus easier to catch. Such fish live in less desirable water and work harder for their meals.

Look for Shadows

Fish are most visible and vulnerable in direct light, which—not coincidentally—makes them uncomfortable and nervous. As the water gets deeper, they get less panicky. Always look for a more comfortable fish in the shadows. Is there a shadowy side of a boulder or a rock? Is there an undercut bank that offers shade? Is there an overhanging tree or shadow from a steep bank? Look closely. Can you spot a movement? Fish love to hang out in the shadows.

Certainly you can fish in direct light, but you must be very careful. You must make sure you don't throw a shadow or that fish see your movement. Remember, all that

In small streams fish the shadows because they often hold fish.

A fine bamboo fly rod. There is no better cane pole.

light makes you quite noticeable. It's critical that you don't cast your shadow anywhere the fish will see it! Get down and crawl if necessary or approach from another direction. Once a fish sees your shadow it's all over. On the bright side (pun intended), sun is known to make bugs active and to kick off hatches. This is good news for fly-fishing folk. If it's worth the food effort, a fish will venture out into the light and eat. The feeding, however, will be fast, furious, and nervous. After the last bite a fish will swiftly dart back to a comfort zone.

There is relative safety for a fish in deep water. The depths mask the effects of direct light and provide a buffer from surface predators. Depth means safety. When a fish gets spooked it goes deep. If there is no structure, the depth of the water is a "structure" of sorts because it offers some semblance of sanctuary.

Temperature Comfort Zones

Fish have a great desire to be in water that is comfortable. For ideal conditions to exist, the water needs to be in a fish's temperature range and have the proper amount of oxygen.

To understand what makes for an ideal lie, consider what we've talked about thus far and add temperature. Although they're cold-blooded, different fish have different temperature ranges in which they feel comfortable. Dormant fish seek a part of the stream or lake that offers shelter and the right temperature. A feeding fish travels outside its comfort zone but returns when it's finished feeding. As the seasons and water temperatures change and the water levels fluctuate, a fish's ideal lie changes to meet the conditions. This means you'll need to move as the conditions shift if you want to

After you teach children the fundamentals of fishing, they do very well on their own.

Fishing from a canoe is a good way to reach under the banks of a lake or a pond.

Ideal Temperature Ranges

Brown trout	52–68 degrees F
Brook trout	48–65 degrees F
Rainbow trout	52–65 degrees F
Cutthroat trout	52–65 degrees F
Largemouth bass	69–80 degrees F
Pike	39–64 degrees F
Smallmouth bass	65–75 degrees F

cast your line to the highest concentration of fish. A stretch of water that provides an ideal lie in the summer might not be as wonderful during the winter or fall.

A successful angler seeks water as close to a fish's ideal comfort zone as he or she can. This is especially important when fish are dormant and there don't seem to be any active feeders.

It's not a bad idea to pack a pocket-size thermometer to check the water temperatures. Fish feed heavily in the middle of their temperature range. When a fish is comfortable, it is more aggressive and has longer feeding periods. As you fish the fringes of the comfort ranges, fish become more sluggish and less likely to look at a fly unless it is dragged or floated right past their nose.

A Look at Oxygenation

Water processed through the gills produces oxygen (which is why you have to be careful about touching the gills when you release a fish). If water is oxygen-poor, it's uncomfortable for the fish and they slow down accordingly. Perhaps the best analogy for us would be mountain climbing. There is a comfort zone for humans. As we start to push our comfort zone and climb higher into thinner air, we have to move increasingly more slowly. A gulp of air at 18,000 feet is certainly not as satisfying as a gulp of air at sea level. We'd have to take seven or eight breaths to get the same effect. Cooler water holds oxygen better than warmer water. The ideal temperature range for a given species is determined largely by how effectively the fish takes oxygen.

Ponds and Lakes

■ When fishing in ponds and lakes look for edges or seams. Fish can be anywhere, but the successful angler doesn't fish at random. There is protection in the depths, and there is food in the shallows. Look for places where deep and shallow water come together. It's easier for large fish to come into the shallows from deeper water.

Tip: Whether you're fishing with a bubble or a fly rod, cast a fly and let it sit. If you know what the fish are taking, present that pattern in the appropriate size. If nothing happens after a dozen casts, try a bigger fly in the same pattern. If that doesn't work, try other flies. Try an attractor or a terrestrial. If there's a breeze on the lake, let the fly drift. If the water is still, leave it alone. Then try retrieving it very slowly.

Just because the bank is lined with casters doesn't mean they're in the right place. The point extending into the lake would be a much better place to fish.

Work the edges with your spinner. After you've retrieved several casts on or near the surface, let the lure sink for ten counts and bring it in. Then try thirty counts; sixty counts. Vary the retrieve. Try a different spinner.

If you are in a boat or a canoe, troll the edges or seams. If the seam is long, try plowing through the center. Work your lure at various depths. If you don't have a downrigger, try countdown lures or heavier spoons. You can also attach weight to your line to get it down.

If you're not sure where to fish, start along the bank until you start getting action.

■ Moss lines, especially if you cast flies with a fly rod or a bubble, are excellent places to fish because they provide homes to insects and smaller fish.

Retrieve for Jig or Wet Fly Casters

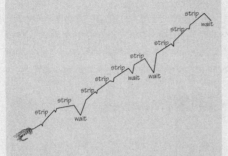

- Make your lure look like a wounded or frightened minnow.
- Make the jig or fly look alive. Strip or pull in line, pause, then strip some more. Make up different variations.

Lee is working a section of water near this fallen log and beaver dam. Such structured areas often attract and hold fish.

Tip: You can fish moss lines the same way you'd fish seams. Moss lines are also excellent places to vertical jig if you are in a boat or a float tube. The best times to jig are when the lake is calm.

Drop the jig to the bottom and reel up two turns. Most people yank the jig too radically. You'll be more successful if you barely dance the tip of your rod, varying the motion. A very aggressive feeding fish will be stimulated by aggressive motion, but a dormant, neutral, or a semi-aggressive feeding fish will be turned off. A subtle dance, however, will stimulate an aggressive fish and tantalize a dormant one.

Every eight to ten seconds, stop your rod tip, then drop it, letting the jig drop 8 inches to 1 foot. A fish will usually hit the jig when it drops.

A moss line is the trophy angler's paradise because large fish swim up and down it looking for prey.

■ Look for fallen trees and snags. Bugs and small fish thrive in such areas. Large fish like these places, not just because there is prey, but because they can ambush smaller fish. In reservoirs the old streambed is a good place to start.

Tip: Any type of structure will hold large and small fish. Small fish take refuge and eat the bugs in it; large fish patrol it for smaller fish. Depending on the structure and how you approach it, there is no really wrong way to fish. Basically you need to work the water in the hopes of luring a patrolling fish.

The key is not to get your bait, lure, or fly hung up. If you do, make a note where your lure is, break your line, tie on a new lure or fly, and fish the water thoroughly.

Bring enough flies and lures to meet the demands of finicky fish.

Then, when you are done you can disturb the water to get back your lure.

If your favorite lake or reservoir ever gets very low in late summer or during a drought, look to locate the old streambed and take careful notes so you can later cast over it or sit on top of it in a float tube or a boat. This channel will hold very good fish (especially near the edges where it enters the water).

■ Look for streams and creeks, even very small ones, that feed into the lake. Besides bringing in fresh food, they often are an excellent source of oxygen.

Tip: These are deadly any time of the year because they're a conveyer belt of food for the waiting fish.

These places are especially good in the spring and fall when fish might spawn. There is a constant flow of fish coming and going to reproduce, and other fish coming and going to eat the eggs.

In the late summer when oxygen levels fall as the water warms, fish often are stacked like cordwood near the stream's mouth.

Rocky and bouldered shorelines often provide good fishing.

Chapter 29

Tips for Hooking More Fish:
A Few Fishing Strategies for Your Fishing Toolbox

While I worked as a fishing guide, I picked up a few pointers I'd like to pass on. Add these ideas to your fishing bag of tricks for those days when fish don't seem to be cooperating. After all, your license isn't a guarantee of a limit (which is why they call it fishing).

Other than at the local pay-by-the-ounce trout pond, you shouldn't depend totally on any one lure, fly, or bait, or on any one single technique. If you are, you're limiting yourself. You'll still catch a few fish, just not as many or as frequently as you'd like.

A float tube is an excellent way to work the moss lines on ponds and lakes.

If the fish aren't cooperating, you'll need to switch tactics. The lure or presentation that worked like a charm yesterday might be cold today. Remember that fish like to pout; and this usually happens about the time you think you have them figured out. In such cases you need to try a number of things until you hit on the right combination. Sometimes that means a radical change. Sometimes it means just a slight change in size or color.

My son and I were camping on the Bear River in Wyoming not long ago. The first day he used a white Rooster-tail, my favorite spinner for stream cutthroats. We caught and released so many fish it was almost criminal. We took one fish in that small stream that weighed almost four pounds. We were getting a strike on every other cast. We walked up the middle of the stream, casting to every pool as we went. We knew we were about the best fishermen in Wyoming, if not the world.

The next day, confident we were going to set a new world record for the number of cutthroats caught and released in one day, we hit the water. The same rods, the same lures, the same presentation, the same us. For half a morning we worked those sterile pockets of water. Nothing.

We changed our strategy. We tried different lures and picked up a few fish. Then we went to weighted jigs and started doing better. My son switched to black and bingo. We were on our way to becoming the best fishermen in Wyoming again. We caught half a million or so before dark shut us out.

The point is that fishing only in a traditional way or using a favorite method is a luxury you can afford if the fish are biting. Otherwise switch tactics.

Flies with a Spinning Rod

Even if you aren't an official fly caster, that doesn't mean you can't fish flies on your spinning rod. You can successfully fish dry flies or emergers on lakes, ponds, and on some rivers. You can also seriously fish a wet fly on your favorite river or stream.

Nymphs on a Spinning Rod

If the fish in a river or stream are feeding heavily on nymphs or aquatics, you can use a spinning rod. It helps if you have a sensitive rod because you can feel a pickup sooner and, thus, set the hook faster.

You need four- to eight-pound test line (I'm fond of six- to ten-pound MagnaThin because the line diameter is rather skinny). Fishing line this size is very effective on any type of trout.

You want to *dead drift* the nymph in the water just above the bottom. It should float naturally with the current. You want just enough weight to get it down and drift, but don't weigh it down too much. The key is to bump the bottom. You'll usually be fishing in water that's 2 to 6 feet deep.

You should be able to feel the lead bumping across the bottom. As you shift water, you need to adjust the weight. Cast upstream and reel in enough line to keep it taut. If you feel any sort of change in the drift, or any pressure, lift the rod to set the hook.

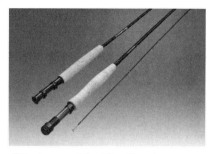

Whether you fish with a fly rod or a spinning rod, rod selection is important. Get the best rod you can afford. Fly rods don't come cheap; try a number of models so you get one with which you're happy. I personally like Sage for high-end fly rods and Reddington for the entry- and intermediate-level caster.

Lay all your gear out at home so you don't forget anything. Be sure to pack a camera to record your fish.

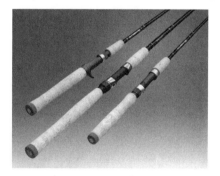

Get a spinning rod that feels good in your hand. There's no reason why a good spinning rod can't last a lifetime.

Nymphing Setup

Take off or add shot as needed to keep the flies on the bottom. Shot works well. If it gets hung up, it slides off.

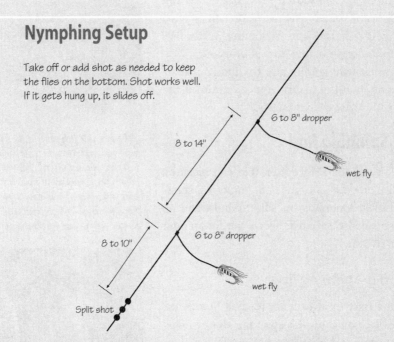

6 to 8" dropper

wet fly

8 to 14"

8 to 10"

6 to 8" dropper

wet fly

Split shot

Nymphing with a Spinning Rod

- Get your shot to bump on the bottom. If you're not bumping the bottom, you'll catch fewer fish.
- Keep your line taut.
- Most fish hold on the bottom where your flies need to be floating.

current

Streamers

When you use a fly line, the line itself helps either to hold up a streamer or to keep it at the depth you want it if you're using a sinking line. A streamer will imitate a minnow or something like it in the water. This setup is deadly on bass, and it works nicely on trout.

You won't be able to cast as far, but you can tie on a streamer or a wet fly and fish it with your spinning rod. I like to use four- to six-pound test line for this. I tie on the streamer and see how it casts. If the streamer is weighted, you might be able to get enough distance. If it isn't weighted, I like to twist on a section of lead about a foot above the fly. (Split shot will also do nicely.)

Cast the fly into likely-looking water and let it sink. Make the fly dance slightly with the tip of your rod as you retrieve it. Experiment with the depth and the retrieve.

Dry Flies on a Float

A dry-fly line is the best way to present a dry pattern to a trout in a river or a stream. It is also arguably the best way to present a fly on a lake. When you cast a fly, the fly line itself does all the work, projecting the fly to the target. With a spinning rod, the weight of the line is hardly noticeable: It's the weight of the lure that does the work.

If you're casting a wet fly or a nymph, you can add weight the way I suggested earlier. A piece of lead would help you cast a dry fly but it could drown your fly, too.

You can get around this by using a bubble or a float that will give you enough weight to cast but won't sink your fly. You can also cover a lot of water with a float, because you can cast farther than you can normally. This is particularly true when it's windy.

My son Jon-Michael uses a Reddington Red Start, which is a very good entry-level rod. Don't forget to take polarized sunglasses; you'll catch a lot more fish if you do.

Kirby's fly casting Wooly Buggers for trout.

This is my nephew Andrew's first fish. He used a float to get his lure over a likely spot. We decided to eat it that afternoon.

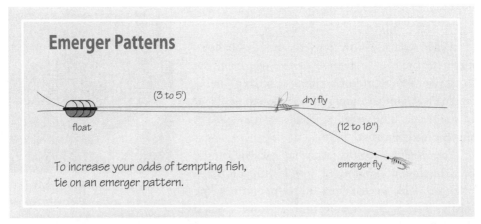

Emerger Patterns

(3 to 5')

float

dry fly

(12 to 18")

emerger fly

To increase your odds of tempting fish,
tie on an emerger pattern.

Take a good selection of flies (or lures). You never know what will entice a fish.

We release most of our fish but keep a few now and then for dinner. Fish that are going to be released need to be handled carefully.

A bubble or float is a fancy word for a bobber. The other advantage to a bobber is seeing the float itself, especially in choppy water. It lets you identify where your fly is so you can watch it. Watch your bubble: When it moves, set the hook.

Once you have cast your rig, reel a few times to put some tension on your fly. Let it sit. Then, ever so slowly, start retrieving. It's usually best if you reel in slowly enough so there isn't a wake. The advantage of doing this is there's tension on the line so it's easier to set the hook.

Different Ways to Use Spinners and Spoons

There's a real science to spinner fishing. Most spin casters just fling their lures. If you want to catch more fish, you have to be a dynamic not a static angler. You have to read the water carefully and fish accordingly.

Float Tips

❏ Cast over rising fish so the retrieve brings your offering to the general areas where the fish are feeding.

❏ Use leader that's a pound or two lighter than your regular line to tie an emerging pattern fly (Brassie, Serendipity, WD-40, and so on) on the bend of your dry fly. This trailing fly should be about 12 to 18 inches behind the dry pattern.

❏ Even if fish aren't feeding on the surface, they often feed on emerging flies making their way from the bottom to the surface of the lake. You may want to use a micro shot 3 or 4 inches above the emerger to ensure it submerges.

❏ If fish seem finicky and aren't going for your pattern, try using a fly that's a size or two smaller. As most fly casters know, size is usually more important than shape.

❏ Sometimes fish are line sensitive, so always carry light leader. Use a swivel with the float above. Tie the leader to the bottom. On several occasions, I couldn't get a strike on four-, five-, or six-pound test line so I tied on a two- or three-pound test leader and start to get a lot more hits.

❏ Always carry a spool of light leader. Use a swivel below the float.

❏ If the fish are finicky or your float is spooking them, try switching to a 6- or 7-foot-long leader.

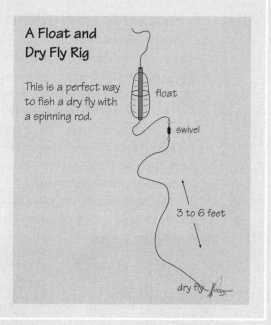

A Float and Dry Fly Rig

This is a perfect way to fish a dry fly with a spinning rod.

float

swivel

3 to 6 feet

dry fly

Stainless Steel Swivels

Before getting into specifics, let me give you a tip that has helped me fight fish and spend less time reeling. *Consider upgrading your swivels to stainless steel*. I learned this from my good friend Kirby Cochran when we camped at Strawberry Reservoir for a little spring fishing.

We were on the water at the "crack" of 9:55 A.M. after a large breakfast and a gallon of hot chocolate. It was very cold, a few snow flurries were threatening, and I desperately needed to catch a few fish to warm up. We were both chucking spinners frantically. We were both using the same Jake's Spinner, the same rod and reel. Yet Kirby was catching more fish. I started a bonfire so I could warm up while he stripped off his jacket; he was bringing in a fish almost every cast.

I finally asked. Kirb told me it was my swivel. His lure was getting a lot more spin and action. By comparison, my brass swivel was lethargic. I bummed one of his fancy stainless steel swivels and started to get fish almost immediately.

I've been using stainless steel swivels ever since. Instead of buying cheaper brass swivels, pick up a package of stainless steel swivels; bet you'll see a difference right away.

Getting Deeper

You have to get your lure to the fish. Most anglers stay too close to the surface. They would improve their odds dramatically if they'd get their spinners down to where the fish are swimming. A downrigger is nice but not always practical. If you have your own boat, it's easy to install it and let it go. If you're traveling and space is a premium, a downrigger is a luxury in which you can't indulge.

One low-tech method, though, is counting down. The easiest way is to cast and count before retrieving. The depth of the water and the weight of the lure have to be considered, but you want to get that lure nearly to the bottom, if not hitting the bottom. Sure you'll lose some tackle and get a handful of moss every now and then, but you'll catch more fish overall.

An added benefit to this technique is that the angle of the lure on the retrieve is more vertical because it comes from the bottom to the top. This excites fish. I can't

This brown trout took a Jakes Spin-a-Lure. It was a wonderful fighter and we sent him back to his pool. In a small stream where Kirby caught him, it was quite a monster.

A Super Duper # 503 spinner is one of the best lures you can have in your tackle box. It may be the best all-around lure ever made.

count the number of big fish I've caught doing this. As a bank and a boat fisherman, I have doubled or tripled my take. One afternoon at Fish Lake in Central Utah, I caught a twenty-five-pound lake trout on four-pound test line. I let the Super Duper # 503 hit the bottom, then I brought it up in a ragged, crippled-fish action. It took fifty-nine minutes to land the fish. My long-time fishing and camping friend Gary was there with his camera. This fish is one of my finest trophies. We still talk about it.

Another way to get deeper is to weight the lure. Sometimes counting down isn't practical. You might fish in fast water, want the lure to dive or dip, or need the weight to cast effectively. You want to weigh the line down, but you don't want to impede the action.

If you need just a little weight to get your spinner to where you want it, a split shot or two or a twist of lead will work nicely. If you need to weigh it down more, try using an egg sinker. This oblong or egg-shaped sinker also has a hole running down its center through which you thread your line.

The sinker is streamlined so it slices through the water with little resistance and the line free-floats, so there isn't so much drag on the lure. It's important to feel the action of the lure, and you can't do this if the lead is firmly affixed to the line.

The best way to use an egg sinker is with a swivel. Put the sinker above the swivel. Tie leader to the bottom of the swivel and attach the lure.

You'd not want to handle a fish like this if you are going to release it. Andrew was so excited by his fish he carried it for twenty minutes. There's no doubt in my mind that he's going to be an excellent fisherman.

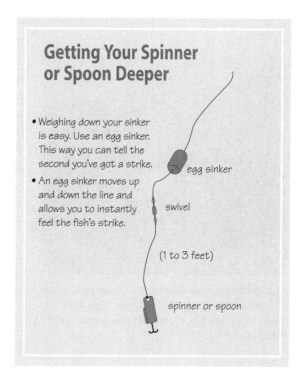

Getting Your Spinner or Spoon Deeper

- Weighing down your sinker is easy. Use an egg sinker. This way you can tell the second you've got a strike.

- An egg sinker moves up and down the line and allows you to instantly feel the fish's strike.

egg sinker

swivel

(1 to 3 feet)

spinner or spoon

Tip: Using an egg sinker is also an excellent way to fish streamers and jigs. A jig is weighted but sometimes they're not heavy enough to cast it as far as you want, or

This is a good way to get about.

Don't just jump in and start casting. Look at a stretch of water and come up with a plan for how to fish it. Those who catch a lot of fish, don't fish haphazardly; they fish with a purpose.

to sink it in the current, or to go deep enough. Using an egg sinker and a swivel is a great way to combat these problems.

Keep Your Spinner Up

Sometimes you want to keep your spinner near the surface of the water. This is called floating the spinner because you want the lure to practically "float" on the surface when you work it. If you are fishing a moss line, casting over structure, or working pockets of water in a river or a stream, this can be a handy technique. It works very well for bass and panfish, but trout and pike also die for this combination.

There's usually no weight problem if you are fishing a small spinner because the spinner isn't that heavy. Your normal retrieve will keep the lure near the top. It's when you fish a heavier spinner or spoon that you have problems, especially if you want to use a slow retrieve.

This is a good time to use a float. Your leader's length depends on the weight of the lure, how far you want the lure to sink, and your retrieve. Depending on how fast you're reeling, there is a certain amount of water displacement from the float. This can work to your advantage if you're fishing for bass, pike, or aggressive trout. The wake will actually act as an attractor.

If fish are nervous, however, the wake can be a problem. If there's a little chop on the surface, then it probably won't matter. If the surface is calm, you might need to increase the length of the leader.

Bait

Except when fishing for salmon, I rarely use bait. From my bait fishing days of yore, though, I can suggest that you'll catch more fish if you get the bait off the bottom just a little. You can do this by injecting the worm's bladder with air so it floats or you can put your sinker at the bottom and run the bait off a dropper.

Except when you fish a drift, you'll want your bait to be stationary. If it moves about, your chances of getting a strike are reduced considerably.

If you are going to fish with cheese or PowerBait, you want to use a cheese hook. It has a coil that holds the bait on. What you save in lost bait will more than pay for the hooks. Also avoid the temptation of using too big a wad of bait. A smaller ball will catch more fish.

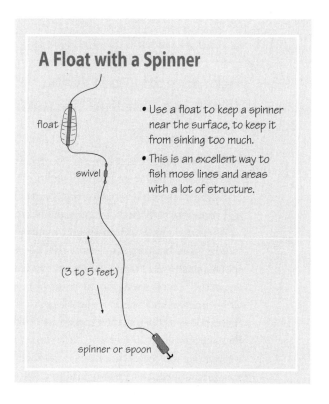

A Float with a Spinner

float

swivel

(3 to 5 feet)

spinner or spoon

• Use a float to keep a spinner near the surface, to keep it from sinking too much.

• This is an excellent way to fish moss lines and areas with a lot of structure.

Chapter 30

Fishing with Your Kids: The Mind-Set You Should Have Before You Go

Fishing with your kids is one of the great adventures of parenthood. Watching a boy catch his first fish at age five or seeing a little girl brag to her friends about catching her limit doesn't have a price tag. Neither do the other memories that are created. I still remember my first fish; you probably remember yours.

Fishing with children should be a time of building and bonding. It's a time to teach good sportsmanship and train a youngster in fishing etiquette: Teach them not to disturb a pool when another fisherman is working it; teach them not to litter (and that means old fishing line and jars of PowerBait, not just candy wrappers); and teach them how to respect our natural resources and how to release fish.

Kids learn fast. My daughter Abbey couldn't wait to fish.

By following your good example, they'll surely grow into good sportsmen and sportswomen. They are the future. Teach them there's more to being outdoors than catching fish and keeping score.

Taking kids fishing involves a lot of work. Why do we go through all this when we could be quietly fishing alone or with other adults who can take care of themselves? Maybe someone did the same thing for you and you feel obligated to pass on the skill. Or maybe someone didn't and you feel it would be a good thing. The rewards that come from taking kids fishing can outweigh the headaches.

Make sure you take a camera so you can catch that Fuji or Kodak moment. I have my kids' first fish on film.

Let's look at a few things that will help ensure your success.

Don't Let Yourself Get Frustrated

I won't lie. Fishing with kids requires a great deal of patience and effort.

You have to have the right mind-set before you leave. Everyone is going to have fun, and you're going to see to it. You have to assume that you're going to be the children's fishing guide. You're taking your kids fishing so they will learn how to catch fish. If you actually end up catching anything, that's just frosting on the cake.

Maybe later on, if things settle down, you can join them, but your being able to fish isn't the purpose of this adventure. If this makes you feel a little ambivalent, as it does me, make sure you schedule in some very generous blocks of fishing for yourself. Set aside some time when you can really pound the water on your own. Besides the fact that you need it, it's good strategy, as I'll explain in just a moment.

I drove up to find my son Jon-Michael waiting on the front porch. He was afraid I'd leave and go fishing by myself. Mostly patience and their seeing you having fun on the water is all it takes to excite the fishing bug in kids.

Your enjoyment will be in their fishing. It will pay off and before long you'll have a great fishing partner(s). Right now, though, you're a lovingly committed servant. If you go with the mind-set that you won't do much fishing, you'll be a lot happier.

My good friend Casey wanted his son to love fly fishing. He took him to the Provo River not far from where I live to introduce him to the noble sport of fly casting. Casey (because you don't know him) is one of our best friends. He's also one of the most intense in-the-fish's-face fly casters in the Rocky Mountains. When he's on the stream, rod in hand, he's so focused on trout that a thermonuclear explosion wouldn't distract him.

Bret releases a fine fish.

One night we were out to dinner and he told this story as we ate salmon.

"I looked up after thoroughly fishing a

Kids can become great anglers. Jon-Michael at age 13 is my best fishing partner. He's a fun companion and a good friend. When you teach your kids to fish, also teach them to catch and release. Don't keep more fish than you can eat.

Kids go through a lot of tackle so bring enough.

pool below The Rock and saw my kid throwing rocks, rod against a tree. It dawned on me that I needed to do more than just hand Brett a rod and take off fishing. I needed to sacrifice a few days away from my precious trout. I realized giving my kid a Sage rod, waders, reel, and boots wasn't enough. I needed to give more of myself, my time. I needed to patiently take all the time necessary and show him how it was done.

"I broke down my rod and put it away in my Blazer. Then, I walked over to Brett, put my arm around his shoulder and said, 'I want to show you how to fish with flies.' I took him below The Rock and taught my number one son how to cast and fish a nymph."

Under his care, Casey showed his son how to cast, giving him gentle pointers. Casey said he knew if he had his own rod with him, he wouldn't be able to give his kid the help he needed. It might be too much temptation. After a few days on the water, they were fishing side by side. They've been fishing together now for a couple of years. There's a bond that might not have been formed.

You are a fishing guide, not a line coach barking out orders. Be gentle and prepare yourself not to be flustered if things go wrong. You must hold your temper and not swear when all the dumb things that can happen do. You have to be willing to let your kids catch and lose fish while you stand watching. You have to be able to comfort a child when he or she has lost a nice trout and starts to cry.

Prepare Before You Go

Before going, it is important to tell your kids that fisherpersons don't always catch fish.

Being skunked is a part of the game that every angler has to experience and accept. Remind them that being on the water is more than half the fun. Tell them about animals they might see if they are observant and how to appreciate nature. Tell your kids that the real fun is getting out in the fresh air.

Occasionally you'll get so frustrated you'll feel tempted to fling a certain rod (if not the kid connected to it) into the deepest part of the water. Fishing with kids isn't always easy. There never seems to be a middle ground. Your kids will either be catching fish left and right or there won't be a bite all afternoon, three reels have crow's nests all at once, a kid has fallen out of the boat, and you have a hook snagged to your seat.

One of the secrets to making a fishing outing with children a success instead of a disaster is to prepare before the trip. Your goal is to give your kids as positive an experience as you can; you want to pleasantly introduce your wonderful family to the sport and make them want to go again.

Getting Geared Up

The time to check fishing tackle is at home. It's disappointing to get on the lake or stream and find a reel doesn't work or you're out of flies, spinners, worms. You want your kids to love fishing. Help them have a positive experience. Test all the equipment before you go.

New line: The line on every reel should be changed once a year. Buy line in a large spool and do it yourself. New line doesn't have memory problems, will cast easier, and won't be as prone to tangle. You'll save money doing it yourself.

The right pound test: Don't slap on any old line. Get the right-pound test for the reel and rod. Look on the reel and see what the manufacturer suggests. There will be several options. (Six- to eight-pound test is my favorite line weight for most children because it's tough but light enough to cast easily.) Remember, too, that heavy line won't cast well. When you buy line, buy a "softer line." Staff at your favorite tackle store will advise you. This line will have less memory and be less likely to crow's nest.

Check the reel: Take all the reels you'll be using to the nearest lawn and cast with them. Does the bail work smoothly, does it retrieve properly? You might want to dab on a little oil, according to the manufacturer's specs, and give

I'm holding Abbey's first bass.

Andrew learned how to cast effectively in less than half an hour.

It was a cold day but the fishing was hot. My son Jon-Michael brings in a nice trout.

it a cleaning. Repair a broken reel or buy a new one.

A basic reel is not too expensive. It's sometimes cheaper to buy a new reel than to pay to have it fixed. If you shop for a new reel, take your intended purchase out of the box and work the action. It should work very smoothly. I went into Wal-Mart last month to buy my wife a new spinning reel. I went through five identical reels of the same brand before I found one that worked properly.

Middle-of-the-road reels are less expensive and may be the best deal when a child is learning. You won't cringe when he or she forgets it, lays it on the bumper just before you drive away, or drops it in the lake. The drawback is such reels don't always last that long. If you fish much and your kid won't lose it, higher-end reels are much better value in the long run.

Shorter rods: If you have a choice, have your smaller kids use shorter rods. They'll handle a shorter rod more easily and cast more accurately. If you have only longer rods about the house, that will be fine. But if you're buying new tackle or have a choice, go with a shorter rod.

I like 5- and 6-foot-long rods for kids under the age of eight.

Zebco makes a cute little Mickey and Minnie Mouse rod. These rods are sold by the handful to parents taking their kids fishing for the first time. This is not a serious fishing instrument.

They are cute and kids love them, but such rods have no lasting value beyond a photo opportunity. A closed-face reel where all you have to do is push the button and cast is handy. Such a rod, with its heavy line, works for casting a big, heavy spoon, but it's not a good rig for casting smaller lures. My son had one when he was three or four. I rebuilt the reel four times before I became so frustrated I threw it out. He caught a 20-inch cutthroat at Yellowstone Lake, and the reel acted up so much it took us forever to get the fish in. Also the rod is too short. It provides little shock value. I bought him a real outfit and he still has it five years later. I'll soon pass it on to my daughter.

Tackle: Show your kids how to tie on hooks and spinners before you leave. The young ones will need help, but it will speed up the learning curve. I use snap swivels for connecting and taking off spinners. It keeps the line from getting tangled, and it speeds up changing lures. Be prepared for your kids to snag and get hung up. Even if it is $3.25 a lure, it's part of the game. Buy enough tackle at home before you leave. You can expect to pay almost double if you have to buy it in a small-town store or at the resort.

Whatever you think you'll need, get some extras. If you keep most of your spinners in the package they came in, they'll last longer and be in better shape (they'll stay shinier and more attractive to the fish). Save whatever you have left for next year.

Do Your Fishing Homework

You can't guarantee success, but you can do your best to ensure it. You need to do your fishing homework. Get information about where you are going fishing. Find out all there is to know so you can be successful. Get your information from as many different sources as possible. Get tips from dock hands, bait-shop owners, other anglers, magazine and newspaper articles, and even the Internet. Don't take everything you discover as gospel truth, but what you learn will give you a place to start so you are partly up to speed. Nothing will replace getting out on the water and experimenting. But at least you won't have to waste a few days doing trial and error. Consider the whats, wheres, and hows.

What are fish biting on (specifically): You want to get as much detail as you can. What are the preferred flies, spinners, or baits? What hatches are coming off when you'll be on that water?

Don't settle for a fish biting on a Super Duper spinner. You want to know that a Super Duper # 503, silver with a red band, is great when the sun is out, while a Super-Duper # 503, bronze with red band, is great when it's overcast.

How to fish (specifically): Knowing what to use isn't enough. Now that you know what to use, ask how you use it. If a Super Duper # 503 has been hot, how has it been fished? Was it trolled behind the boat, was

Teach kids to be patient. Their lures are going to get hung up and catch a lot of moss between fish.

I think it's a good idea to let kids pretend to fish.

Don't insist that a child stay on the water if he or she gets a little cold. It's okay to come in and get warmed up.

it put on a downrigger? Was the lure jigged, was it spin cast? If it was spin cast, how? Did they let it sink before reeling it up?

Where are the fish: On your home water you naturally learn more easily where fish are at at different times of the year. Try to get a general idea where the action has been taking place. This is especially important on a large lake. Fish move to different locations as water temperatures change. The discussion on reading the water will help you home in on your quarry.

You won't always get accurate information, but if you get enough information, you'll be able to choose a good place to start.

Once you've done your homework, it might be a good idea to go fishing. Fine-tune what you've discovered.

What I've suggested won't ensure fish, but it certainly increases your odds of getting your kids into action. So often I've seen the dad or mom take the kids out fishing and know it will come to nothing. They're lined up on the bank casting; I know they've got a snowball's chance of catching a fish. They're in the wrong place. A ¼-mile shift, or even moving a few hundred yards, would make all the difference in the world.

Chapter 31

Viewing Wildlife Naturally:
Where to Look and Choosing Optics and Lenses

If hiking is the favorite pastime of the camper, viewing wildlife is the favorite pastime of the hiker.

It sounds too simple, but this maxim is as essential to wildlife watching as keeping your eye on the ball is to golf: *To see animals you have to be out when the animals are out.*

About 20 percent of the wildlife enthusiasts see about 75 percent of the animals. Once in a while you can sit about camp until noon and see a moose walk by the garbage can near the pit toilets, but the odds aren't in your favor. You have to put forth a little effort to see game.

The Cochrans and the Rutters were spending a week camping at Bridge Bay Campground at Yellowstone. We were having a grand time fishing, watching and photographing wildlife, seeing the sights, and enjoying each others' company. Kirby and I were at the community water tap one evening filling up five-gallon water jugs.

While we were waiting, talking about grizzly bears and Yellowstone's bear-management policy, we ran into a fellow camper, a frustrated would-be wildlife watcher.

Elk are beautiful animals. The best time to see them is in the fall during the rut. We were able to get close to this bull because he was more worried about his cows than he was about us.

This baby bighorn sheep was on a steep cliff, but it let us get within camera range. It stood there so we could capture the moment on film.

Bears are always fun, and my favorite animal, but you want to see them on your terms, which is from a safe distance. Bears can be frightening close up.

A trail is a good place to see wildlife but you'll have better luck early in the morning or later in the evening. Rarely do you see game in the middle of the day, which is nap time.

He asked if we'd had any luck seeing animals. Kirby said we had. Evidently all this poor fellow had seen were buffalo, a dead cottontail rabbit, a grouse, and one scraggly cow elk.

He pushed Kirby for information, because he wanted to know what we'd seen and what magical powers we employed. He must have been eavesdropping. As the man's jaw plummeted lower and lower, Kirby catalogued what major animals we'd seen during the previous five days: grizzly and black bears, moose, bull elk, mule deer bucks and does, coyote, wolf, antelope, swans, and geese.

This fellow had gone out every day after brunch with his kids but had seen precious little. Kirby told him he needed to follow the ten *To Be*s. Then he listed them off. The man took notes as Kirby spoke. What he said wasn't that profound. It's common sense, but it works.

Ten Wildlife To Be's

1. You have to be out very early in the morning.
2. You have to be out very late in the evening.
3. You have to be off main roads (go on dirt roads and trails) as much as you can; if you are on main roads, drive very slowly so you can look carefully.
4. You have to be willing to get out of your car and walk.
5. You have to be quiet when you walk.
6. You have to be willing to walk slowly.
7. You have to be where you think the animals are feeding.
8. You have to be where the animals are resting.
9. You have to be carrying some optical help (binoculars, spotting scope, and so on).
10. You have to be willing to learn about the animals and their habits.

Learning about Game

One of the first things you need to remember is animals are out in the morning and evening. By mid-morning critters are holed up until very late afternoon. This doesn't mean you won't occasionally see something at noon. From time to time, you will. What this does mean is you have a better chance of spotting game if you are out and about when the animals are at their most active.

Besides being out when the animals are out, you can't know enough about an animal you want to see. Get a guidebook and learn about an animal's characteristics. Know what foods a species likes and when it feeds.

If you're looking for black bears, for example, you want to know that when the bear comes out of hibernation in early spring, it grazes a lot on fresh spring grasses. After a long winter of sleeping, it's not ready to eat solid foods. Glass open slopes that have a southern exposure, where the snow has melted, and the freshest shoots are budding. Bears graze in these areas so this is a good place to start your search. Later on in the year, when it's warmer, you'll be hard-pressed to find a bear on such a slope (unless berries are ripening there).

It helps to know that moose become very scarce by midsummer, so you're not likely to see them except in the deep forest. It's good to know that coyotes catch a lot of mice, and that big fields with large mice populations draw coyotes. It helps to know that cow elk favor certain slopes when they are calving, and that sow grizzlies follow the large calving herds. Know your beasts.

It helps to know what an animal eats and when, so you can narrow your search. A good field guide will be a lot of help. If the information is too generic, call your state wildlife office or talk to a biologist that

This may be closed to vehicles, but not to foot travel. Old roads such as this one are excellent places to look for animals. They're also good places to take a hike because few other hikers travel down these old roads.

This young elk was thirsty and so were we. We let her go first.

My kids like to see wildlife. It must be hereditary.

This is a chukar, a Western game bird that's pretty spooky.

manages or studies the animal you want to see. Most field workers are eager to talk to you about "their" animals.

Walk Slow, Stop, Look, and Look Again

If you love to hike for the sake of hiking and putting miles under your belt is your fun, so be it. If you see an animal, as you will from time to time, that's great. It's frosting on the cake.

If seeing animals is your fun, you'll have to do a few things differently from the hike-for-it's-own-sake hiker. Distance isn't the critical factor, seeing animals is.

Slow Down

People who walk fast and furious are people who miss a lot of wildlife. There's nothing wrong with fast walking, but it's not the way to see critters.

You must remember that those big ears, the pretty round brown eyes, and those black, cold noses aren't there for show. They're an animal's early warning system. Most creatures will hear, see, or smell you and be long gone before you come on the scene. The fast, noisy, or talking walker is a hiker who won't see many animals.

Go slow. Even if the animal doesn't flee, there's a good chance the speedy hiker will walk past it without seeing anything. If you want to see creatures of the desert, forest, or plains, you have to slow down and walk quietly. Don't advertise your presence any more than necessary.

Stop and Look

Besides walking slowly you need to stop and look every few steps. It would be a mistake to watch only in front of you. Keep a close eye on both sides of the trail. Many times I've spotted animals who were as interested in watching me as I was in them or animals shuffling quietly out of the way. It also pays to watch your back trail. Animals, especially bigger hooved animals such as deer, elk, and moose, often cross the trail after you pass it. Maybe it's some sort of game, a hooved hide-and-seek.

Stop, Look, and Glass

Stop and look about you. If there's anything that looks animal-like, glass it. Is that an ear, or a leaf? Is that white splotch a deer or a birch trunk? Is that black patch a bear or a dark rock?

If you have suspicions, glass it. A lot of the time you'll see a leaf, a birch trunk, or a dark rock that only looked like an animal. Every now and then, however, enough times to make it worth the effort, that thing is an animal. It's worth giving every suspicion a double take.

After a while you'll start to get the feel for where an animal might hold. These are also good areas to glass. I've found, though, that it's a good idea simply to glass an entire, all-about-you area every so often. I've been amazed at the number of animals I've found this way. I once discovered a family of angry badgers several hundred yards off the trail. I saw a gray-brown flash and took a closer look through my optics.

I moved in a little closer and what I observed amazed me. A young, somewhat stupid coyote was trying to dig out some baby badgers for its dinner. It saw the young ones and thought they'd make a good meal. This wasn't the smartest coyote in Colorado by any stretch because the parents were in plain view, too. The coyote started digging at the den hole until daddy badger came out another hole and glared. As soon as the badger went underground, the coyote was back flinging dirt.

This went on for about a half hour when, finally,

Many of our natural parks are good places to look for bison.

Pronghorn are beautiful animals, but you have to approach them carefully. They have eyes like 10x field glasses.

A buck antelope takes a snooze.

Teach your kids to point if they see something. If they call out the noise might scare the animal away.

the badger family had enough. Mom and Dad came out and charged. Like a slapstick movie, the coyote jumped up the in the air as they passed beneath it. They went back in their holes and it went back to digging. Mom slipped out and latched onto its nose with her teeth and wouldn't give up. There was a giant tug-of-war for about three minutes until the coyote ripped his nose back. It learned some lesson: Don't mess with badgers, and don't stick your nose in their den.

I captured the entire event on film. I would have missed it, though, if I hadn't stopped to glass the sides of the trail. I was carrying a small set of Discoverer binoculars by Bausch & Lomb that my wife gave me after we got out of college. I've had them for years, and they've been all over this continent with me. They fit snugly in my front pocket. They go where I go.

Last year in northern Canada, I was hiking down a deserted logging road with my informally-adopted son, Kasey Kox. The road was somewhat overgrown. We saw what might have been a black movement several hundred yards ahead of us. We both brought our binoculars up, just as we had two or three dozen times earlier that day (to find only rocks or dark tree trunks).

This time the movement was fuzzy and waddling. It looked like a beanbag chair with four legs and a tiny head. We never would have known the bear was there if we'd not glassed it from a distance. It would have spotted us before we'd gone much farther. Don't let anyone tell you bears have bad eyesight. Compared to their nose and ears, their eyes aren't marvelous, but they see every bit as well as a human who doesn't need glasses.

The wind was in our faces, so the bear couldn't smell us. It was ambling down the road, as bears are prone to do (they'll always take the easy way if they can). It didn't have a care in the world. We melted into the edge of the thicket and watched for nearly eight minutes as it came in our direction, checking this and that. The bear came to within 20 feet of us, caught our smell, and then melted into the thicket on the other side of the track.

We never would have had this close encounter of the furry kind without moving slowly, quietly, and glassing. There's nothing like a bear at 20 feet to make you feel alive. It's the high point of animal watching.

Optical Equipment

A moose near our campground.

There are several things you need to remember about optical gear: One, almost any optical equipment is better than nothing (but not by much); two, you always get what you pay for.

Everyone agrees that you should buy the most expensive optics you can afford. With that out of the way, many of us have tastes that certainly outstrip our bank accounts. Nevertheless, after a quick look, and then a long stare through the eyepiece, cheaper optics become unsatisfactory. You wish an uncle had left you big dollars in his will.

If you like to watch animals, you'll be looking through a lot of glass. If you're trying to see bears during the spring and you're searching greening slopes, you'll literally spend hours glassing likely clearings and hillsides. A comfortable optic arrangement will make your life a lot easier and reduce eye strain. You'll be able to look longer and see more animals.

Eyestrain is the big drawback on less expensive glass. The clearer the glass, the easier it is to look for longer than a few seconds. Cheaper optics are more likely to distort the image, have wavy lines on the edges, and make you as sick as a dog.

Bears are like children. This one is finished with its bath.

There are different types of binoculars for various uses. Larger and heavier optics are generally a little easier on your eyes if you're doing a lot of glassing. Smaller optics are lighter and easier to carry, but aren't as comfortable to use.

This wolf is sleeping.

If you want to pay more, you can push the envelope: A smaller, but more expensive, binoculars are less fatiguing than their cheaper counterparts. The more you pay, the better optics you get. If you're only going to hold the glasses up to your eyes and stare for a few seconds, you won't need the same quality as someone who is glassing for a longer length of time.

As much as good optics can cost, the good news is you can expect a lot of life from a pair of binoculars. It might be comforting to note that you can expect years of use from your optic equipment even if you use it roughly. As a rule of thumb any optic under $100 can be considered marginal for the serious wildlife observer and will be eye-fatiguing before long. If that is your budget, though, consider the Bushnell Powerview Series or the Bushnell Instavision (I personally don't like instant focus optics but some do).

I like binoculars and I have several pairs for my various outdoor needs. It might seem a little extreme, but I'm a pushover for stuff like this (and they are tax deductible for outdoor writers). Some people collect shoes or baseball cards, I gather binoculars. You should also be aware that I don't own a business suit (which has saved me a lot of money over the years). You can buy a good pair of optics for the price of a suit these days; the optics will last longer and give you infinitely more satisfaction.

Here are several choices that I think provide excellent optics for the money. Some are Bushnell, the others are Bausch & Lomb. Each optic is a good buy in its price range and you can stare into it for quite some time without feeling sick.

Bushnell Natureview 8 x 30: This sub-compact-size optic was specifically designed for bird-watching and naturalist pursuits. It is endorsed by the National Audubon Society. It has a long-eye relief for maximum field of view. These binoculars have the performance characteristics required by bird-watchers.

These Bausch & Lomb Legacy Compact binoculars fit in your pocket nicely. They weigh about eight ounces and are very clear yet reasonably priced. These are great for hikers and packers who don't want to carry a lot of weight.

The binoculars weigh 16.5 ounces; their field of view at 1,000 yards is 340 feet, and they cost about $135.

Observation: While this optic was designed for bird-watching, it will work on big game. These glasses can be used for medium-term spotting. They would be a little fatiguing for long-term use but will certainly work. They are well made and will last a long time.

Bausch & Lomb Legacy Compact 8 x 24: This compact-size set of optics are the right binoculars for the outdoor person on the go. They are light and will easily fit into a pocket or pack. The O-rings are sealed and nitrogen-purged to be waterproof and fogproof. The top section is black-rubber armored.

The Legacy weighs 8.3 ounces; its field of view at 1,000 yards is 335 feet, and it costs about $145.

Observations: These optics are very light and a great choice for backpackers, hikers, and others who want binoculars but aren't sure when they'll use them. If you spend a lot of time glassing, you might want another optic. These glasses weren't designed for long-term use, but they would be good for spot-and-stalk or short-term big game and bird watching. If you want a small optic, this is the route to go.

Bushnell Trophy 8 x 32: These are an excellent choice for anyone who spends a lot of time in rugged conditions. These compact-size glasses will take any weather and more punishment than most. They are waterproof, fogproof, and rubber-armored. They are also ribbed so you can hold them when wet or while wearing a glove. The glass is amber coated to provide high contrast in low light.

The Trophy is waterproof and, short of a 100-foot drop, they'd be hard to hurt.

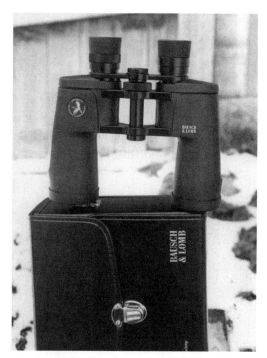

The Custom is one of the best optics I've ever used. They are very clear. When you're going out specifically to look at wildlife or birds, this is the optic I'd use.

If you want really outstanding wildlife shots, you need to use a tripod. Gary photographs some waterfowl.

The glasses weigh 16 ounces; their field of view at 1,000 yards is 385 feet; and they cost about $250.

Observation: This optic is designed for watching big-game in rugged conditions, hunting, and hiking. It will work on birds. These glasses can be used for medium-term spotting; they could be a little fatiguing for long-term use. The nice thing about these optics is they are nearly indestructible.

Bausch & Lomb Custom Armored Binocular 10 x 40: These are excellent optics with superior light transmission and high resolution of image details. They also have an extreme close-focus capability. They have a long-eye relief for maximum field of view even if you are wearing glasses. These regular-size binoculars are endorsed by the National Audubon Society.

The Custom weighs 29.3 ounces and has a field of view of 273 feet at 1,000 yards. It costs about $550.

Observation: Some of the best optics I've ever used! These binoculars have all the features and eye comfort of optics costing twice as much. I can spend an hour or two looking through the Custom without eye fatigue. These optics would get a little heavy on a long hike, but the weight might be worth it if I was going to spend much time glassing.

Photographing Wildlife

Hunting with a camera is one of my favorite sports.

While holding a 35-millimeter camera, I've metaphorically chased grizzly bears, black bears, and all sorts of hooved creatures with big racks. I suppose I can also admit that I've been chased, or treed as the case may be, by several large furry sorts with claws, teeth, or horns.

Don't Get Too Close

A good way to avoid trouble is to not get too close. Even park animals, which aren't completely

If you're shooting near water, use a polarizing filter so your camera won't be deceived by the reflection of the water.

wild, like you to keep your distance. This is more than a good idea if the critters in question have teeth.

I was in Yellowstone National Park a few years ago and saw a black bear sow with three cubs. She was up a tree a scant 10 feet with her babies, apparently unconcerned. The serious photographers, and those who had respect for claws and teeth, kept about 50 yards between them and the sow. A number of photographers who wanted that great shot no matter what, inched up on the sow in question and tried to shoot her with 50-millimeter lenses or less.

After a few minutes she'd had enough and, I assume, felt threatened by the crowd. She vented her bodily functions all over several tourists and came down from that tree roaring with her jaws popping. The crowd dispersed and luckily no one was hurt although several photographers had their pride ruffled. (They wouldn't smell good until they hit a long shower, either.)

A bull elk with his cows.

You need at least a 200-millimeter lens as a minimum so you can fill the frame. You don't want to get too close.

Any animal with babies to protect will get very defensive and needs to be respected. I had a friend charged by a doe when he got between the fawn and mom. Bret Hicken and I once spent nearly an hour and a half in a tree. We stumbled onto a cow elk who wasn't going to move. She charged us, and we barely got up the tree before she hooved us. Our tripods with cameras were left on the trail as she watched us in the tree. When we tried to get down, she charged again.

Enjoy those animals!

Chapter 32

Twenty-Five Camping Tips

1. *Sleeping cold:* If you're cold during the night, put on a stocking cap. Much of the heat loss in a sleeping bag occurs via your head. You can also put on a pair of socks.

2. *Tent zippers:* Make sure the zippers are closed before you pitch your tent. You might have a hard time getting the zippers closed otherwise.

3. *Start out short:* If you haven't camped much, take a short trip before you take a long one. A short run will teach you what you've done right and what you haven't.

4. *Campground hint:* It might seem convenient to camp next to the restroom area in a campground; however, restroom lights could be disturbing at night when you are trying to sleep. There may also be a lot of traffic that disturbs your beauty rest.

5. *Propane is safer:* Propane is a little more expensive than liquid fuel but it's safer and easier to use.

6. *Set your lantern out early:* Set out your lantern while it's still light so you won't have to search for it after dark.

7. *Drying your boots:* If your boots or shoes get wet, heat some sand over the stove and pour it into your footwear. Doing this several times will help dry out your boots rapidly.

8. *Plastic garbage sacks:* Take along extra garbage sacks and various size Ziploc bags. They have a thousand uses in camp. Go on a trash-collecting campaign.

9. *Keep your tent clean:* If you have the space when you car camp, bring along an old piece of carpet to put in front of the door of your tent. You'll be surprised how clean this keeps your tent. Bring along a whisk broom and a small dustpan for tent-cleaning chores.

10. *Electrical storms:* If there's a thunderstorm, don't take shelter under a large tree. Head into the middle of the forest.

11. *Sleeping warmer:* If it's cold and your bag isn't that warm, don't sleep in any of the clothes (even underwear) you've worn during the day. They will have retained moisture, so they will cool you down. Slip into a pair of long johns you use only for sleeping.

12. *Cleaning a dirty pot or pan:* If you make a mess in your pot or fry pan, pour in some vinegar water. Warm it up on the stove and let it soak for a couple of hours. It will be easier to clean.

13. *Lighter tents are cooler:* If you are camping primarily in warm weather, buy a light-colored tent. If you camp in cold or wet weather, then consider a darker-colored tent because it will be warmer.

14. *Weighing your pack:* Weigh your pack on the bathroom scale before you leave the house. The basic rule of thumb when backpacking is to carry a pack one-fourth of your body weight. I've noticed, however, that a lighter load increases my trail pleasure. I figure on packing no more than one-fifth of my body weight. I weigh just under 200 pounds and feel very comfortable with a thirty-to-thirty-five pound pack. I guess I'm a wimp.

15. *Exploding rocks:* Be careful when you ring your fire with rocks. Some rocks explode when they get hot. Use a shallow pit to keep your fire contained. Keep rocks away from the hottest coals.

16. *Increase the life of your tent:* Dry your tent and sleeping bags out in the garage when you get home. Putting away wet gear is a good way to rot the fabric and make it smell.

17. *Stuck zipper on tent or sleeping bag:* Rub a bar of soap generously into the zipper. It will help get things moving.

18. *Fix broken tent pole:* To fix a broken tent pole, carry a 4-inch piece of copper or PVC tubing with a diameter slightly larger than the pole. Tape the broken pole with electrical or duct tape. This will build up the diameter on the broken piece so it will fit snugly in the sleeve.

19. *Use gloves for more than keeping warm:* Carry a pair of leather gloves to protect hands and pick up hot pots and pans or firewood.

20. *Cooking pots and open-flame cooking:* A blackened pot will heat much faster than a silver pot. If blackened pots bother you, however, rub liquid detergent about the outside or wrap it in foil to facilitate cleaning.

21. *Cleaning dirty dishes, pots, or pans:* Use sand or steel wool to clean a blackened

pot. Use a wad of grass to scrape pots and pans, plates, and utensils clean.

22. *Slippery sleeping pad:* Applying drops of glue or seam seal to the surface of your sleeping pad will give it more friction.

23. *Dental-floss thread:* Dental floss, besides being good for your teeth, is a great thread for camp use. It's strong and durable: You can fix a tear in your tent, mend a sleeping bag, or sew a rip in your pants.

24. *Opening canned goods:* It's best if you remember your can opener! Many campers have found that carrying a GI can opener on a keychain is good insurance. Don't forget that many pocketknives have can openers on them. In a pinch use your hatchet. Turn the hatchet at an angle and use a rock to pound the head. If you're really hungry, you can use a sturdy knife or pocketknife. Be careful so you don't cut yourself.

25. *Heating up cans on the campfire:* Take off the paper wrapper. Open the can but don't take off the lid (to keep ashes from getting in your food). Place the canned goods over the coals. Watch carefully and stir.

Index

A

Adrenaline kit, 174
Adventure Medical, 116
A-frame tent, 32, 39
Air mattress, 26
Allergic reactions, to bee and wasp bites, 174
Aluminum cookware, 66–67
Avon's Skin So Soft, as insect repellent, 175
Axes, 73

B

Baby packs, 235
Backpacker Magazine, 26, 67, 103
Backpacker's Pantry freeze-dried food, 215
Backpacking
    checklist, 120–21
    flashlight, 75–77
    food storage, 175
    getting lost in, 185–92
    meals, 141, 142, 146
    tent, 38
    weight rule, 281
    See also Backpacks; Hiking boots
Backpacks, 48–55
    external-frame, 50–53
    fitting, 53–54
    internal-frame, 52
    loading, 54
Bacteria, in drinking water, 156
Bait fishing, 261
Balaclava, 92
Bandages, in first-aid kit, 116–17
Bathroom habits, 131

Batteries, 77
Bausch & Lomb binoculars, 277, 278
Bears
    avoiding, 178–79
    encounters with, 171–72, 179–80
    facts about, 177
    food storage and, 175
    photographing, 178, 287
    precautions, 177
    spray against, 176
Beaver dams, water contamination at, 157
Beaver fever, 131, 154, 156
Bee stings, 174
Biking. *See* Mountain biking
Binoculars, 275–78
Blankets, as sleeping pad, 23
Boiling, as water treatment, 158
Breakfast menu, 145, 148, 149, 160, 161
Bureau of Land Management, 134
Bushnell binoculars, 276, 277–78
Butane lighter, 136

C

Calories, in backpacking meals, 143
Camp craft, 112–13
children, camping with, 162–70
    cooking, 140–53
    drinking water, 154–61
    fire, 134–39
    in getting lost, 185–92

for low-impact on land, 128–33, 163–64, 206
planning and packing, 114–22
site selection, 123–27
wildlife, 171–84
Campgrounds, site selection at, 125–27, 280
Camping equipment, 5–7
    axes, 73
    backpacking gear, 37, 75, 121
    backpacks, 48–55
    checklist, 120–21
    children's, 164–65
    cooking gear, 55–68, 120–21
    day packs, 48–52
    emergency kits, 185, 191, 207, 231
    first-aid kit, 116–18
    hatchets, 72–73
    hiking, 231–32
    knives, 69–72
    lighting, 75–81, 120
    for mountain biking, 215–17
    optical, for wildlife viewing, 273–78
    optional, 121
    personal items, 121
    planning and packing, 114–15, 166
    saws, 74
    shovels, 75
    sleeping bags, 8–22
    sleeping pads, 21–27
    storing, 115
    tents, 28–47, 120
    See also Clothing;

233–24
at recreation vehicle (RV) camps, 222
in tent/folding trailers, 224–25
time schedule, 221
Training pants, 86
Trenching, 44
Trout almondine (recipe), 152
T-shirts, 89, 91
Typhoid, 156

U

Underwear, 86
children's, 86–87
polypropylene long johns, 9, 84–85, 88

V

Vasque
Kids Klimber boot, 106
Sundowner boot, 103, 104
Vestibule, 42
Victorinox Swiss Army Knife, 71
Viruses, in drinking water, 156

W

Walking. *See* Hiking
Wall tent, 36
Wasp stings, 174
Water
in campgrounds, 125
campsite near, 124
for freeze-dried meals, 144
See also Drinking water; Fishing
Water bottle, 216
Water jug, 220–21
Water maps, 205
Water moccasin, 182, 183
Water pollution, 154–56
Waterproof canoe gear, 201–03
Waterproof tent, 35, 41–42
Water treatment
boiling, 158
chlorine, 156–57
filtration, 158–59, 240
iodine, 158–60
Whistle, in emergency situations, 188, 192
Wildlife, 171–84, 270–79
bears, 171–72, 175–80
photography, 178, 278–79

snakes, 169, 180–84
See also Insects
Wildlife observation, 270–79
animal habits and, 272–73
optical equipment for, 275–78
stopping, 273–75
ten to be's, 270
walking slowly, 272
Windbreakers, 90, 93, 95
Women, sleeping bag for, 12
Wool hats, 93
Wool shirts, 89–90
Wrench, 220

Y

Yellowstone National Park, 10–21, 125, 163, 177, 279
Yosemite National Park, 119, 122

Z

Zippers
sleeping bag, 19, 281
tent, 42, 289, 290